ANCIENT ETHIOPIA
AKSUM: ITS ANTECEDENTS AND SUCCESSORS

ANCIENT ETHIOPIA

AKSUM: ITS ANTECEDENTS AND SUCCESSORS

David W. Phillipson
M.A., Ph.D., F.S.A.

BRITISH MUSEUM PRESS

Published in 1998 by British Museum Press
A division of The British Museum Company
46 Bloomsbury Street, London WC1B 3QQ

A catalogue record for this book is available from the British Library

ISBN 0 7141 2539 3

Designed and typeset by John Hawkins
Printed in Great Britain by Butler & Tanner Ltd,
Frome and London

CONTENTS

ACKNOWLEDGEMENTS

Much of the research which forms the basis for this book has been carried out under the auspices of the British Institute in Eastern Africa. Numerous colleagues and collaborators from Ethiopia and other countries have contributed to this work and their contributions are gratefully acknowledged. Drs Laurel Phillipson and Jackie Phillips have read the manuscript and made many useful suggestions. It has been a pleasure to work with Ms Carolyn Jones and Mrs Emma Way of British Museum Press.

For permission to reproduce illustrations, the author and publishers are grateful to Dr Chris Scarre (fig. 13) and to Dr David Buxton and Mr Derek Matthews (fig. 41). The Institute of Ethiopian Studies in Addis Ababa University, through its Director Dr Abdussamad H. Ahmad, has given permission to reproduce fig. 58, and Dr Francis Anfray has approved the use of fig. 52 (below). Fig. 8 (right) is © Trustees of the National Museums of Scotland 1998. Figs 16 (right) and 57 (left) are © Comstock Inc. Figs 19, 28 and 51 (above) are © British Museum Photographic Service, reproduced by courtesy of the Trustees of the British Museum. The photographs reproduced in plates 1 and 4, figs 4 (below), 5 (below), 6, 35 (below), 43 (left below) and 51 (above) are by Dr Laurel Phillipson; those in plate 3 are by Mr Michael Harlow; while those in plates 2 and 5–12, figs 3, 4 (above), 5 (above and centre), 7, 11, 15, 16 (left), 17, 20–25, 30, 35 (above and centre), 36, 38, 40, 42, 43 (above and right below), 45–6, 48–50, 53–6, 57 (right) and 59–60 are my own.

The maps (figs 1, 2, 14 and 27) were drawn by Mr Eric Robson. The line drawings in figs 29 and 31–3 are by Mr Gavin Rees, Mr Eric Robson and Ms Sarah Semple. The surveys in figs 18, 44 and 47 were undertaken by Mr Douglas Hobbs, Mr Alistair Jackson and Mr Tom Pollard.

David W. Phillipson
9 September 1997

INTRODUCTION

E thiopia fits few categories, prejudices or preconceptions. It maintains an ill-defined separateness from the rest of Africa, yet has links with Arabia and the Middle East of which it is not a true part. It is the home of one of the world's oldest Christian civilisations,[1] but remained virtually unknown to outsiders for over a thousand years until the late nineteenth century, and attracted very few foreign travellers before the second quarter of the twentieth. This book sets out to summarise current understanding of ancient Ethiopia in the light of the most recent research. It will concentrate almost exclusively on the predominantly Christian civilisation of the highlands, now shared with the new nation of Eritrea,[2] and on its immediate precursors and successors. This is not to belittle the importance of other Ethiopian peoples, past or present, but rather to provide the present narrative with a clearer focus and to emphasise that other books can and should be written about the Muslim and other societies of the southern and eastern regions.

The past of Christian Ethiopia is best illustrated at the modern city called Aksum, which forms the principal focus of this book. For most of the first seven hundred years AD Aksum was metropolis of what one researcher has described as 'the last of the great civilisations of Antiquity to be revealed to modern knowledge'.[3] It was heir both to a cultural tradition of South Arabian origin that had been established for several centuries previously on the African side of the Red Sea, and also to much older local traditions whose economies were based on indigenous cultivation practices. In its heyday Aksum displayed great prosperity, organisational power and technological sophistication. Sections of its population were literate in Ethiopic and/or in Greek. From the third to the seventh centuries it issued a tri-metallic coinage which is without parallel in sub-Saharan Africa. Wide-ranging trade contacts were maintained through the Red Sea port of Adulis with the Mediterranean lands and, in the opposite direction, as far as India and possibly China. On occasion its rule extended over part of what is now Yemen, on the Asian side of the Red Sea. The kings of Aksum adopted Christianity during the second quarter of the fourth century, probably within a decade of that religion being formally tolerated in the Roman Empire. Although Aksum had declined in prosperity by the seventh to eighth centuries, it has remained a major religious centre, dominated by the Cathedral of Saint Mary of Zion. Here, according to the traditions of the Ethiopian Orthodox Church, is kept the Ark of the Covenant, brought to Ethiopia by Menelik I, the son of Solomon and the Queen of Sheba.[4]

Varied sources are available for the study of ancient Ethiopia.[5] Archaeology has prime place and can provide much of the raw material on which specialist studies such as numismatics and epigraphy are based. Much valuable information is preserved in historical traditions, many of which were long ago committed to writing. The history of the past eight or nine centuries may be based at least in part on contemporary documents. Study of recent phenomena, such as the genetic diversity of cultivated plants, or spoken languages, can reveal valuable historical information. Lastly, but of no less importance, there are the buildings, monuments and artworks that continue in use from earlier times. A comprehensive view of the Ethiopian past, such as that attempted here, requires use of all these sources. Numerous aspects of these studies are only just beginning, with the result that several topics are poorly understood. Many Ethiopians have a profound knowledge and respect for their past; they play a leading part in current studies. Such enthusiasm is by no means restricted to academics: popular interest and involvement is characteristically widespread.

It is striking how much continuity may be discerned between ancient Aksum and more recent Ethiopian civilisation. Such links as well as the antecedents of Aksum are discussed in this book, in an attempt to dispel the current popular view of Ethiopia and Eritrea as countries memorable only for civil war and famine. These elements, happily no longer current, have inevitably added to the outside world's dearth of information and scholarly interest. Many other factors have contributed to this state of affairs, including the two countries' physical isolation and rugged terrain, their separation from other Christian centres, the difficulty of their languages and the complexity of the scripts employed, and the fact that Ethiopia was virtually the only part of Africa that escaped systematic European colonisation.[6] Despite their proudly guarded independence, Ethiopia and Eritrea are today among the poorest countries in the world in terms of per capita cash income. Such material poverty, in western eyes, contrasts both with the region's cultural richness and with its ancient greatness. This book seeks to aid understanding of these apparent contradictions.

The present writer has directed research at Aksum since 1993 on behalf of the British Institute in Eastern Africa.[7] This has involved annual seasons of large-scale archaeological excavation conducted in close collaboration with the relevant Ethiopian authorities. The research, some of the results of which are here discussed and set in context, has been far more than a foreign academic exercise. It has sought at all stages to involve and contribute to the training of Ethiopian personnel at all levels, to succour local understanding of the nation's heritage and to contribute directly and indirectly to the local economy through employment, provision of equipment, aiding monument conservation and its dependent tourist development.

The unique status of Ethiopian civilisation should be stressed. It is set in sub-Saharan Africa but is in very many ways distinct from its neighbours in that continent. Certain scholars have regarded it as essentially a South Arabian transplant on to African soil - a view shared by some Ethiopians - but this is now seen as a fallacy. Links with the Nile Valley, both in Sudan and Egypt, although present, have never been dominant.[8] Visitors to Aksum often wonder what connection there may be between the spectacular monuments there and those of ancient Egypt: the answer is that, other than common cultural elements widespread in north-eastern Africa, the two traditions were virtually independent. Not that Aksum was isolated - its international trade links were highly developed and contrast markedly with those of later times. Although Ethiopia has often been receptive to cultural influences from beyond its borders, the local element has prevailed and its identity has been retained. It is this autonomy that must explain why the Ethiopian past has featured so slightly in most accounts either of African civilisations or of the ancient world more generally.[9]

This lack of scholarly attention is all the more remarkable when the region's overall contribution to human history is considered. Leaving aside the strong probability that it was in this part of Africa that human beings first evolved and, later, that our present species, *Homo sapiens*, developed,[10] it is abundantly clear that the Ethiopian highlands have seen major innovations in plant-cultivation which have formed the basis of traditional subsistence in the region over thousands of years. Later, urban civilisation arose and developed contacts with contemporary centres in the eastern Mediterranean, South Arabia and the Indian sub-continent. At this time, the early centuries AD, the area that now comprises parts of northern Ethiopia and Eritrea occupied a pivotal position in the development of international commerce. In the third century, a Persian writer classed Aksum among the world's four greatest kingdoms.[11] Its culture represented a blending of indigenous African elements with those common to a wider part of the ancient world. It is this mingling of diverse components that has given Ethiopian civilisation its uniqueness and which makes its study such a rewarding exercise not only for Ethiopians and Eritreans but also for international scholarship.

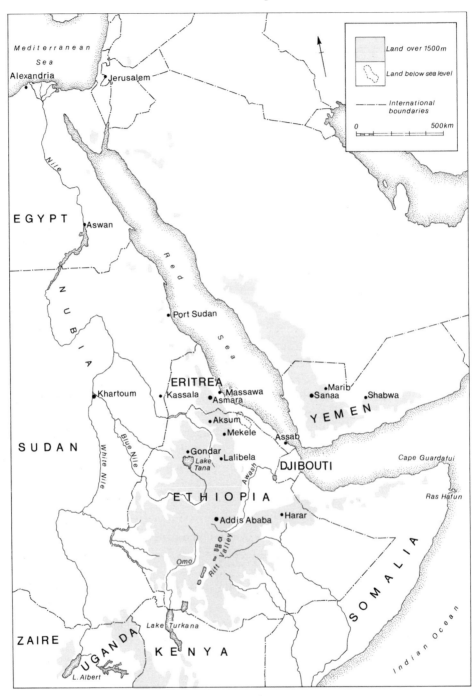

Fig. 1 Ethiopia, Eritrea and neighbouring areas.

Chapter 1

BACKGROUND

The physical setting

In the easternmost part of the African continent, adjacent to the southern section of the Red Sea which separates it from the Arabian peninsula, lies an extensive region of mountainous terrain which is physiographically separate from adjacent areas of Africa (fig. 1). This region, now divided between the nations of Ethiopia and Eritrea, has for long provided the setting for unique developments of human culture which form the primary focus of this book. Conventionally known as the Ethiopian highlands, the region includes one of the continent's largest mountain massifs, reaching a maximum altitude of over 4600 m (15,000 ft), and extensive high plateaux between 2000 and 3000 m (6500 -10,000 ft) above sea level.[1] The highlands are bisected by the Rift Valley and also by the huge and precipitous gorges of the Blue Nile and the Takkezze, up to 600 m (2000 ft) deep, through which much of the highlands drain and by which great quantities of silt from soil erosion are transported annually to the Sudanese plains.

The rugged relief results in lands of diverse climate and agricultural potential being encountered within remarkably short distances. This diversity has long been recognised and is reflected in vernacular terminology.[2]

In the north-east, the highlands face the Red Sea from which they are separated by the steep and rugged escarpment, 2000 m (6500 ft) high, behind the Eritrean port of Massawa. A southward continuation of this escarpment separates the highlands from the arid Danakil lowlands stretching southwards to Djibouti and northern Somalia. To the south-east and south the highlands fall more gently and with increasing aridity to the plains of Somalia and northern Kenya, while to the south-west the land is increasingly forested as it drops to the Sudanese lowlands. Further north, especially beyond the Blue Nile, the western edge of the Ethiopian highlands becomes more precipitous again until, in their northernmost part (in what is now Eritrea) they merge imperceptibly with the Red Sea Hills.

The close proximity of the highlands to the Red Sea has for millennia provided their main line of external communication. When the Red Sea has been under Ethiopian control, external links have grown strong; when such access has been denied, the highlanders have retreated into isolation.

Demarcation from the rest of Africa is emphasised by the region's physical geography (fig. 2). The Ethiopian highlands have more in common with similar regions in the

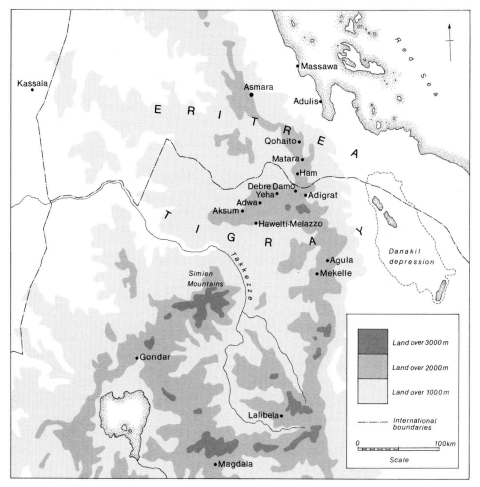

Fig. 2 The highlands of northern Ethiopia and Eritrea, showing the
principal sites, places and features mentioned in the text.

southern and south-western parts of the Arabian peninsula than they do with contiguous
parts of Africa. It is, however, separated from Arabia not only by the waters of the Red
Sea but also by the great escarpments on either side (that behind Massawa being a
particular barrier) and, further south, by the inhospitable Danakil lowlands.

The Ethiopian highlands are dissected from north-east to south-west by the Rift
Valley. Its northern part, a continuation of the Red Sea formation, has already been
noted. Further south, it separates the western highlands around Lake Tana from their
eastern counterpart centred on Harar. The Awash river, draining much of this area, flows
in a general north-easterly direction along the Rift Valley into the lowlands of the
Ethiopia/Djibouti border country where its seasonally substantial waters are lost by
evaporation before reaching the sea. In the vicinity of Addis Ababa, the Rift Valley is ill-
defined; further south it is a clear trough containing a string of lakes.

The climate of this part of equatorial Africa is largely determined by altitude. Large highland areas, although lying entirely within the tropics, have an essentially temperate climate despite their proximity to hotter low-lying zones where tropical diseases are rife. Seasonal variation owes more to rainfall than it does to changes in temperature. As a general rule, higher ground experiences lower temperatures and greater precipitation. The Simien mountains, for example, not infrequently receive heavy falls of snow while the Danakil depression, only about 250 km (150 miles) to the east, is one of the hottest and driest places on earth. The rugged relief results in much climatic variation being experienced within a short geographical distance, and some low-lying areas being well watered by run-off from rainfall in adjacent highlands.

Rain in the highlands falls at two seasons. The 'big rains' occur between June and September, originating to the south-west and thus falling most heavily in that quadrant of Ethiopia, becoming progressively lighter to the north and east. The 'little rains' are significantly less predictable, but often occur at some time between March and May. There is much variation in rainfall from year to year. A wholly different pattern prevails in the coastal lowlands, where such rain as there is falls in January and February.

The highlands (fig. 3 and pl. 1) owe their initial formation to Tertiary earth-movements accompanied by large-scale volcanism. Granites (*sensu lato*) and basalts are the predominant rock types.[3] The volcanic soils, although often exceedingly stony, have high inherent fertility. The present rugged topography has for the most part been brought about by erosion, resulting in valleys and gorges, often with bare rocky sides, and in rugged mountains which include flat-topped plateau remnants (locally known as *ambas*) and steep sided volcanic plugs. Much of the soil removed by this erosion has been carried away by the westward-flowing Nile tributaries, but some has accumulated in highland basins, the largest of which is now occupied by Lake Tana, where the headwaters of the Blue Nile are dammed by a lava flow.

The natural flora and fauna have been greatly modified through millennia of intensive human exploitation.[4] Climatically controlled variation provides the baseline, with tree cover ubiquitous in the better-watered areas. The densely forested areas of the south-west have a comparatively sparse human population. Elsewhere much of the tree cover has gone, being replaced by open grassland or rocky erosion surfaces except where cultural constraints to deforestation (as in the precincts of churches in the Christian highland areas) have resulted in the preservation of isolated pockets of indigenous woodland dominated by *Podocarpus* in the lower regions and by *Juniperus* in the higher. Dense indigenous woodland often survives also in those gorges and steep-sided valleys where cultivation is impracticable. The dominant tree in many highland areas today is the Australian *Eucalyptus*, introduced in the late nineteenth century and now popular both for reforestation and as a source of construction poles and firewood. Above the natural tree line, at altitudes less suited to human occupation, the tropical alpine vegetation often survives with little modification.

Most larger wild animal species have shared the fate of the indigenous trees. Their destruction has been accelerated following the introduction of firearms from the sixteenth century onwards. In the less accessible areas of the south and west, big game –

Fig. 3 Highland scenery in northern Ethiopia. Above: between Aksum and Adwa.
Below: between Adwa and Yeha.

including elephants – have survived in some quantity. Elsewhere, numbers are severely depleted and several species are in danger of extinction. The physical isolation of the Ethiopian highlands results in the fauna and flora including many varieties that are unknown in adjacent regions.

Data are not yet available which could support a view of the extent of environmental change in the Ethiopian highlands during the last 10,000 years.[5] It would, in any event, be difficult to differentiate between natural changes and those brought about as a result of human activity. The extent to which large timbers were used in buildings until a few centuries ago suggests that deforestation did not reach its present extent until comparatively recently. A Byzantine writer recorded the presence of large numbers of elephants on the Tigray plateau where they no longer survive.[6] Pollen analysis in the Aksum and Makelle regions suggests, however, that vegetation some two thousand years ago was broadly similar to that which prevails today.[7] Certainly, as will be shown below, the climate during Aksumite times of the mid-first millennium AD supported the cultivation of a range of crops virtually identical to that which is exploited at the present time. There is evidence that the decline of Aksum around the seventh century AD may have been associated with intensified erosion.[8]

Human geography

Socio-political differentiation is largely a matter of an individual's sense of identity. This may not only change through time, it may also vary according to the circumstances in which people find themselves (fig. 4). There is often a tendency for this degree of fluidity to be underestimated. There are, of course, longer-term factors that are also involved. One of these is language, discussed below. Another, particularly important in the Ethiopian context, is religion. Subsistence is also relevant as a determining factor of traditional lifestyle. All these elements are, to a greater or lesser extent, becoming subordinate to the growth of the modern nation-state.[9]

It is worth noting in this context that the modern borders of Ethiopia are essentially those which resulted from the expansionist policies of the emperor Menelik II around the end of the nineteenth century. Eritrea's borders are those established for the Italian colony at about the same time. Both modern nations subsume far older ethnicities. To some extent these are reflected in Ethiopia's present federal structure.

The border between Eritrea and Ethiopia separates closely-related peoples, especially on the Tigray plateau and in the Danakil lowlands. Agau and Falasha populations (see below) have been recorded almost exclusively from Ethiopian territory.

The languages traditionally spoken by the indigenous populations of Ethiopia and Eritrea are predominantly of the Afroasiatic family. Two principal divisions of this family are represented. The older and more diverse is that conventionally known as Cushitic. The other division is Semitic.[10] In some southern and western regions languages are spoken which belong to the wholly distinct Nilotic group, widespread in Sudan and in parts of East Africa.

Fig. 4 People at Aksum. Above: musicians at the festival of St Mary, 1994. Below: priest at the monastery of Abba Pantaleon, 1996.

Although the territory where Afroasiatic languages are spoken extends (as their name implies) over parts of two continents, their Cushitic division is exclusively African, occurring primarily in a coherent block of territory in the north-eastern quadrant of that continent, in what is now Sudan, Eritrea, Ethiopia, Djibouti, Somalia and northern Kenya, with occasional outliers to the south and west. Within the area with which this book is concerned, the Cushitic languages of the northern highlands are generally classed as Agau dialects. In the southern and central highlands, numerous related

16

languages are in use, the most widespread being Oromo. (Other languages of southern Ethiopia, formerly regarded as Cushitic, are now attributed to the Omotic branch of Afroasiatic.) In the south-east, Somali dialects predominate.

The African Semitic languages are both more homogeneous and more circumscribed in distribution than are the Cushitic ones. Their principal representatives spoken in the northern Ethiopian highlands are Amharic and Tigrinya, closely allied members of the Southern Semitic grouping. Although no longer in secular use, the liturgical language of the Ethiopian Orthodox Church, Ge'ez, should be noted as another member of this group.[11] Also closely related is Tigre (not to be confused with Tigrinya), spoken by a predominantly Muslim population in northern Eritrea. (Arabic, widely spoken in parts of Eritrea and eastern Ethiopia, is a Northern Semitic language, almost certainly introduced at a more recent date.) It may be noted here that the so-called Falasha are not distinguished on linguistic grounds, since they speak Agau, Amharic or Tigrinya languages indistinguishable from those of their neighbours.

Although the historical inferences that may be drawn from linguistic evidence are discussed in subsequent chapters, it should be stressed here that the Cushitic languages of Ethiopia appear to have greater local antiquity than the Semitic ones. The latter are generally considered to have been introduced in an ancestral form from southern Arabia during the first half of the last millennium BC, along with the South Semitic script from which the modern Amharic syllabary (also used with minor modification in Tigrinya) is derived.

Language is a major factor in determining an individual's sense of ethnic and/or national identity. There are thus strong pressures for the maintenance of Ethiopian languages and also for distinctions to be emphasised, sometimes to the extent that what are in linguistic terms closely related dialects are popularly regarded as distinct languages.

Traditionally, post-Aksumite northern Ethiopia and Eritrea have lacked major urban centres.[12] The extent to which such centres existed in Aksumite times is discussed below.[13] In later periods there were religious centres such as Lalibela, great monasteries such as Debra Damo, and markets which grew and flourished as centres of redistribution and exchange. However, for centuries prior to the establishment of Gondar early in the seventeenth century, there were no permanent political or administrative centres. The ruler and his court (like some of their counterparts in mediaeval Europe) essentially lived off the land; and the capital was wherever they happened to be at any given moment. Long-lasting conurbations were thus rare until their growth during the past one hundred years in response to the requirements of governmental administration and commerce. Asmara is essentially a development of the Italian colonial period, while Makelle owes its growth to that of Tigray as a modern administrative unit.

Just as major population centres are (with the exceptions noted) comparatively recent phenomena, so are fixed lines of long-distance communication. The ruggedness of the terrain is a further factor which has contributed to this situation. Wheeled vehicles being essentially unknown until recent times, transport of goods and personnel has traditionally been by donkey, mule or camel, on horseback, or on foot.

17

In most highland areas subsistence has for long been based on agriculture. In the more arid lowlands, notably near the Red Sea coast but also over wide areas of northern Eritrea, nomadic pastoralism is the mainstay of the economy. These divisions are fluid and major differences may occur within comparatively short distances.[14]

In the northern highlands the principal cereal crops include not only wheat and barley which are generally believed to have their ultimate origin in south-western Asia, but also African millets as well as other cereals, notably *teff* and (less certainly) finger millet which are of local Ethiopian derivation. A wide variety of non-cereal crops is also grown, the most important being *ensete* – a banana-like plant, of which the pulp from the base of the leaves forms the staple food of the Gurage and other peoples in the southern highlands. *Ensete* is an exclusively Ethiopian crop; others are *noog* and *chat*, while coffee seems to have been originally cultivated in south-western Ethiopia. The developmental history of Ethiopian agriculture is considered below.[15] The agricultural technology is also of particular interest and significance, not least because this is the southernmost African area where the ox-drawn plough was used in pre-colonial times (fig. 5).

The principal domestic animals of modern Ethiopia are cattle, horses, donkeys and mules, sheep and goats. Chickens are numerous; cats and dogs are also kept. Camels are now encountered in some plateau areas, notably in Tigray, although previously restricted to their preferred lowland environments.[16]

Salt has long been a valued commodity, important in the diet both of people and of livestock. It occurs in enormous quantities in the Danakil depression but is virtually unknown in the much more densely populated highlands. For centuries - probably millennia - it has been traded up the escarpment and throughout the highlands, its value growing markedly with increased distance from its source.[17] Bars of salt also served as currency in many areas, continuing as units of low-value exchange well into the twentieth century.[18]

Despite the clear evidence for international commerce in the Aksumite period,[19] it is likely that such activity was subsequently restricted until its rapid growth from the late nineteenth century onwards. Market centres served for the exchange and redistribution of locally-produced commodities. Items traded over longer distances in post-Aksumite times were largely restricted to metals and a few high-value commodities and artefacts.

Preparation of food and drink was, and in many areas still is, a local activity based largely in the individual household. The preferred staple food is a flat, sour pancake-like bread called *enjera*, produced from *teff* flour and cooked on a flat pottery tray, *metad*, which is sometimes incorporated in a specially made oven (fig. 6). It is eaten with a spiced sauce, *wat*, which may include meat and/or vegetables. Meat is often eaten raw, especially on formal or ceremonial occasions.[20] The numerous fasts of the Ethiopian Orthodox Church impose many dietary restrictions on its adherents. Coffee and, more recently, tea are widely drunk. The traditional alcholic beverages - again domestically produced - are a honey-based brew called *tej* and beer which is generally made from finger millet.[21]

Domestic food production and the general prosperity of the countryside depend on prevailing systems of land ownership and taxation. Both have been extensively changed since the 1974 revolution.[22] Rural land has been nationalised and the taxes previously

Fig. 5 Traditional agriculture at Aksum. Above: ploughing, 1997.
Centre: harvesting *teff*, 1993. Below: threshing, 1996.

levied by the Church and by great feudal landowners have been abolished. Cultivation rights are now allocated more widely and on a more equal basis than previously. Problems of long-term tenure, inheritance and investment in improvements, however, remain to be fully addressed.

Religion occupies a major place in the lives of the Ethiopian and Eritrean peoples. In the parts of those countries with which this book is primarily concerned, three major religions have prevailed in recent times. These are Christianity as practised by the Ethiopian Orthodox Church, Islam, and the religion of the Falasha generally characterised as Hebraic or Judaic. These may conveniently be considered in reverse order.

Much that has been written about Falasha religion has emphasised its connections with Judaism. The label 'black Jew' has been widely misinterpreted.[23] The Falasha, at least for so long as they lived in Ethiopia, proudly maintained their adherence to the religious beliefs and practices set out in the Pentateuch, but not those which had been incorporated subsequently into mainstream Judaism. Their scriptures and prayers were written and spoken, however, not in Hebrew but in Ge'ez apparently indistinguishable from that used by their Christian neighbours. Many traditional aspects of their daily lives were also identical to those of their compatriots, despite their maintenance of crafts and art styles which served to emphasise their separate identity. It seems best, following Edward Ullendorff, to regard the Falasha as descended from, and maintaining at least some of the religious beliefs and practices of, certain of the pre-Christian Semitic inhabitants of the Ethiopian highlands. Their religion would thus share a common ancestry with modern Judaism, whilst not being Jewish in the sense commonly attributed to that term today.[24] Ethiopian Christianity also incorporates many early Judaic features.[25]

Christians in the highlands belong almost exclusively to the Ethiopian Orthodox Church.[26] One of the Oriental Orthodox churches, this was until 1974 the official religion of the Ethiopian state.[27] It still carries great prestige and influence, with almost universal adherence in many areas. It is monophysite, i.e. maintaining belief in the unity of Christ's divine and human natures, having maintained this position since the early centuries of Christianity despite its abandonment by other denominations at the Council of Chalcedon in AD 451. From its initial years the Ethiopian Church, although autonomous, was headed by an *abuna* nominated by the Patriarch of Alexandria; this link was broken only in the 1950s, since when the Ethiopian Church has had its own patriarch, nominally appointed through ecclesiastical and governmental agreement.

The Ethiopian Orthodox Church is dominant throughout the northern highlands, virtually every community having its church building, often an ancient foundation although relatively few examples have escaped drastic modernisation. There are numerous monastic establishments. Prior to the 1974 revolution the Church, both collectively and through individual establishments, was a major landowner. Following the nationalisation of land, this source of income has been largely replaced by a system of gifts and offerings which has enabled the Church to maintain much of its influence.

20

Many important ancient buildings and artefacts are under ecclesiastical control.[28] The application to these possessions of state legislative restraints is contested, resulting in friction and misunderstanding between the ecclesiastical authorities and the government departments charged with the protection of the cultural heritage. The Church nonetheless maintains great influence and is itself a strong factor in maintaining traditional arts, skills and social norms. It also sees itself as in many ways the heir to ancient Aksum and guardian of its traditions.

Despite the long dominance of the Ethiopian Orthodox Church and periods of savage animosity such as the 1530s, there is a very long-standing tradition of tolerance towards the Muslim minority. It is mainly in the northern highlands that Islam occupies a markedly minority position; in both Ethiopia and Eritrea as entities, numbers of adherents to Islam and Christianity are more nearly equal.[29] While churches are widely distributed in almost every community, the placement of mosques is more circumscribed. Although Muslims were in some respects disadvantaged prior to the 1974 revolution, their equal rights are now officially respected in both Eritrea and Ethiopia. Since 1991 there has been a resurgence of certain aspects of traditional culture and religious practice, at least partly as an assertion of national identity.

Traditional material culture (fig. 6) prevails in many areas of everyday life.[30] This may be attributed to several factors: the richness and adaptability of the cultural traditions, the respect and affection with which these traditions are regarded, and the restraints imposed until recently by the difficulty of long-distance transport. The speed of change is now nonetheless accelerating.

Some specialist domestic utensils are remarkably resistant to replacement. Although electrically heated counterparts are available in urban areas, the preparation of the staple food, *enjera*, is in many places still carried out using largely traditional equipment. It is, however, now generally eaten off enamel trays which were until recently imported. Plastic holloware is widely available and there is a thriving industry in the recycling of metal containers to produce a wide variety of domestic utensils. Pottery, produced almost exclusively in the traditional manner without use of a wheel, remains in use mainly for the carrying and storage of water and for brewing beer: its porosity provides welcome cooling of liquids.

Furniture, although often locally produced, generally follows foreign fashions, initially Arabian-inspired and made of wood, now in European styles and increasingly made of metal. An exception is in traditional-type houses where built-in beds, seats and storage facilities often remain in use.[31]

Although most Ethiopians and Eritreans choose European forms of clothing for everyday wear, traditional dress is frequently seen, especially in rural areas and on holidays and ceremonial occasions including attendance at church. Hand-spun and woven cotton is preferred, being generally grown in low-lying areas but processed in households at all altitudes. In the highlands, although spinning is done by women, weaving is men's work. Their principal product, the multi-layered toga-like *shamma*, worn by both sexes, is widely seen, often in conjunction with European-style garments. Many women wear dresses of similar undyed cotton cloth. The male attire of a tunic

Fig. 6 Domestic activities at Aksum, 1996. Above left: cooking *enjera*.
Above right: spinning cotton. Below: weaving cotton.

Fig. 7 Traditional architecture of Tigray, 1996. Above: rural, south of Aksum.
Below: urban, at Yeha.

worn over tight-legged but baggy-seated trousers is now rare, even at festivals and other
ceremonial occasions.

Architecture shows much regional variation (fig. 7). In much of the northern
highlands rough stonework is widely used. In contrast with the practice in Aksumite

23

times[32] stone is only roughly dressed, if at all. Until the advent of European influences (less than one hundred years ago in many areas), lime cement was not used: it is still not widespread except in urban areas.[33] At the beginning of the twentieth century almost all domestic buildings were round, those in Tigray and adjacent highland areas sometimes having two storeys. Farmsteads often have flat earth-covered roofs, other buildings being covered with conical thatch which is now increasingly replaced by corrugated iron. Until the 1930s, it was only occasional ecclesiastical buildings that retained the rectangular plans which had been the Aksumite norm, but most recent construction has reverted to this form.[34]

Outsiders' knowledge

The extent to which the outside world was familiar with the regions which now comprise Ethiopia and Eritrea can be learned mainly through the study of foreign writings and by tracing objects which are of demonstrable Ethiopian origin. Both enquiries face much uncertainty: the first because of ambiguous terminology, the second because most early exports consisted of raw materials which, in contrast with finished products, are rarely precisely attributable.

The word 'Ethiopian' in English versions of the Old Testament is a translation of the Hebrew 'Kush', which was applied to any inhabitant of Africa to the south of Egypt.[35] In the Greek New Testament the term 'Aithiopis' (which was also used to translate the Hebrew 'Kush') had similar connotations. References in the New Testament to Ethiopians therefore probably indicate Nubians or, more generally, black Africans.[36] References to Ethiopians in the fourth-century BC Greek writings of Herodotus are similarly imprecise.

Ancient Egyptian knowledge of the territory that now comprises Ethiopia and Eritrea seems to have been severely limited. By Ptolemaic times the Red Sea coasts were frequented by sailors, some of whom travelled as far as the Indian Ocean.[37] Although the Egyptians not infrequently acquired at these ports products of the hinterland, they obtained very little information about the regions whence these products originally came. Knowledge of the 'Land of Punt', although of long standing, seems to have been restricted to a very small trading fraternity, doubtless with the intention of maintaining the value of imports.[38] These imports appear to have included animals, people, and raw materials which, if and when they have survived in the archaeological record, can rarely be differentiated from those obtained in other regions.

It is remarkable how few are the artefacts of demonstrably Egyptian origin that have been recovered from archaeological sites in Ethiopia and Eritrea (fig. 8).[39] Contacts with the Nile Valley, both in Nubia and further downstream, probably became stronger during Aksumite times, both through trade in raw materials (perhaps accompanied by military subjugation) and through links between Christian Ethiopia and her co-religionists. This was often the route by which Ethiopian pilgrims travelled to Jerusalem, the place where most regular contact was established between Ethiopians and people from other countries.

Fig. 8 The Egyptian *cippus* given to James Bruce. Left: as illustrated by Bruce 1790.
Right: as preserved at the Royal Museum of Scotland.

The historian is faced with similar problems when considering knowledge about Ethiopia and Eritrea in the Roman/Byzantine world. Most literary references date from the fourth century AD or later and are concerned with ecclesiastical matters.

Exports of raw materials are listed by an anonymous Alexandria-based trader in the handbook known as the *Periplus of the Erythraean Sea*, written in Greek around the middle of the first century AD.[40] The *Periplus* notes that Adulis was then an important port and that inland lay 'the metropolis of the people called Aksumites'. Geographers, notably Ptolemy and Strabo, were also familiar with the Red Sea coasts and the immediate hinterland. The former, in the second century, noted Aksum as the royal capital.[41]

There is an increase in written references to Aksum from the fourth century, but most are concerned with ecclesiastical matters. For example, Rufinus and others recount the conversion of the Aksumite ruler and the appointment of Frumentius as first bishop, while Athanasius provides details of the unsuccessful attempt by the Roman Emperor Constantius II to enlist the support of his Aksumite counterpart in a doctrinal dispute.[42] Otherwise, the two most significant accounts are those by Cosmas Indicopleustes who visited Adulis in the early sixth century and left a detailed description of an earlier inscription which he saw there, as well as some detail about Aksum, and by Nonnosus who records the presence of large herds of elephants under royal protection.[43]

South Arabian contacts are better attested archaeologically, for a wealth of inscriptions and other material there extends in date from at least the fifth century BC until the rise of Islam.[44] It seems clear that, not only were the rulers and (doubtless to a lesser extent) the inhabitants of the two areas familiar with each other, there was also regular interaction. This is most clearly seen in the political field, as will be discussed in detail below.[45] Aksumite coins are frequently discovered in South Arabia. Important information about the paintings in the Cathedral at Aksum is preserved in an Arabic source which may be traced to one of the Prophet's wives who, before marriage, had sought the protection of the Aksumite king.[46] After the rise of Islam, such contacts appear to have ceased for many centuries, although it is recorded that a Yemeni envoy was received at Gondar in 1648.[47]

Links between Ethiopia on the one hand and South and East Asia on the other are poorly illustrated by the research that has so far been undertaken. The *Periplus of the Erythraean Sea* records trans-Indian Ocean trade, in which Adulis was a partner, in the first century AD.[48] Indian gold coins of the second–third centuries have been found in a hoard at Debra Damo and it seems that there have been finds of Aksumite coins in India.[49] There are references to the presence of Aksumite trading vessels in what is now Sri Lanka.[50] None of this, however, provides any firm indication that Indians at this time had any clear knowledge about Ethiopia. A similar situation prevails with regard to China. There is one piece of ironwork, found at Aksum, which may indicate trade contact with China, presumably via India, as early as the third century AD.[51] Chinese records have not been comprehensively studied in this respect.[52] It does, however, appear that Chinese geographers possessed detailed knowledge of the eastern shores of Africa at least as early as the eighth century AD.[53] More recently, an Ethiopian mission travelled to India and the East Indies in the seventeenth century.[54]

Jerusalem was the place where Europeans and Ethiopians most regularly came into contact with one another.[55] Despite sometimes being regarded by the Muslim authorities with greater favour than other Christians, the Ethiopians were seen by European Crusaders as potential allies. In later centuries it was more often the Ethiopian Christians who sought European assistance against Islam. During the thirteenth and fourteenth centuries stories of an oriental Christian monarchy, 'the kingdom of Prester John', gained wide circulation in Europe. In the first half of the fifteenth century several emissaries and travellers from Europe – Italian, French and Spanish – managed to reach Ethiopia and, in some cases, to return. The Ethiopian monastic community in Jerusalem ensured that their Church was represented at the Council of Florence in 1441. It was from this same source that knowledge of Ethiopia was obtained by fifteenth-century Italian cartographers.[56] From 1539, Ethiopian ecclesiastics had their own establishment in Rome.

The Portuguese were the principal European visitors to Ethiopia and Eritrea in the sixteenth and seventeenth centuries.[57] Particularly important was a diplomatic mission which landed at Massawa in 1520 under the leadership of Rodrigo de Lima, dispatched in response to an Ethiopian appeal for support against the Turks. The Emperor Lebna Dengel was, by the time the mission arrived, unenthusiastic about a Portuguese alliance; but their prolonged residence permitted the visitors to travel extensively and to record much that was shortly afterwards destroyed at the hands of Muslim invaders led by Ahmad Gran from the sultanate of Adal in what is now eastern Ethiopia.[58] A subsequent Portuguese intervention, in 1543, resulted in Gran's defeat. It was this success, and their resulting influence at the Ethiopian court, that inspired subsequent Portuguese missionary activities leading to the conversion of the then Emperor, Susneyos, to Roman Catholicism early in the seventeenth century. The popular animosity which was thus generated resulted, however, in the formal expulsion of the Portuguese in 1632 by the new Emperor Fasiladas.

There were only brief and intermittent contacts between Europe and Ethiopia for the next one and a half centuries. Throughout this time the Ethiopian capital remained at Gondar, where it had been established by Fasiladas. Contact was re-established by the Scots traveller, James Bruce of Kinnaird, who arrived at Massawa in 1769 and proceeded to Gondar where he remained for about three years. Although Bruce's account of his travels[59] was widely ridiculed, it served as a stimulus for much increased attention on the part of Europeans from several countries during the nineteenth century.[60]

A flurry of diplomatic activity which accompanied these journeys resulted inadvertently in a military operation of long-term consequence. The detention of British envoys and breakdown in subsequent negotiations with the Emperor Theodore led to armed intervention to secure the captives' release. In 1868 a force was landed near Adulis and marched on Theodore's headquarters at Magdala which was captured, along with much treasure that Theodore had accumulated from churches and elsewhere. Magdala having been sacked, the captive envoys released and Theodore having killed himself, the British forces withdrew.[61]

The defeat of Theodore both weakened Ethiopia and encouraged other European powers to reflect on the opportunities for colonial expansion in the region. Italy established a presence in the ports of Massawa and Assab, eventually expanding inland and establishing its colony of Eritrea in 1890. At the same time, Menelik II, ruler of Shewa, was establishing himself as Emperor of all Ethiopia. In 1896 an Italian attempt to expand southwards from Eritrea into Menelik's domains was resoundingly defeated at the battle of Adwa. Menelik began the slow process of transforming his feudal empire into a modern state, with its capital at the new city of Addis Ababa. The process was taken over and accelerated by Menelik's eventual successor, Haile Sellassie I, but interrupted by the Italian conquest of 1937. The Italians having been ejected and Haile Sellassie's rule restored in 1942 through the combined efforts of the Ethiopian resistance and British Commonwealth forces, modernisation continued, the former Italian colony of Eritrea having been federated to, and then amalgamated with, Ethiopia. The process of modernisation was, however, too slow to satisfy some more radical elements in Ethiopia, and the Emperor was deposed in 1974. The revolution was followed by the savage imposition of a marxist government, by famine and by civil war. It was not until 1991 that some measure of peace and prosperity returned, Eritrea and Ethiopia becoming separate nations in the following year.[62]

Historical and archaeological studies

In post-mediaeval times, the first foreign visitors to Ethiopia/Eritrea who recorded material which is of direct relevance to study of the region's archaeology and early history were members of a Portuguese diplomatic mission which arrived in 1520. A remarkably detailed account of their six years' travel and observation, by their chaplain Father Francisco Alvares, was published in Lisbon in 1540. Noteworthy is its account of Aksum, particularly of the Cathedral, for the Portuguese saw this building shortly before its virtual destruction at the instigation of Ahmad Gran. Alvares also visited Lalibela, where he was amazed at the sophistication of the rock-cut churches. Although his architectural descriptions are not always easy to understand, Alvares seems a generally trustworthy guide for a period when no other sources are available.[63]

Subsequent Portuguese visitors were, with some exceptions, primarily engaged in Roman Catholic proselytism. Such data as they recorded concerning the earlier history of the region are often difficult to interpret.

Towards the end of the seventeenth century, works of seminal importance to Europe's understanding of Ethiopia were published in Frankfurt. Their author, Job Ludolf, never visited Ethiopia but derived his information over several years from an elderly Ethiopian monk called Gregory who lived in Rome. Gregory taught Ludolf Ge'ez, this dead language becoming for a time their main means of verbal communication, and imparted also detailed knowledge of the natural and cultural history of his homeland. As a result of Gregory's teaching, Ludolf was able to publish a Ge'ez grammar and lexicon, followed by their Amharic counterparts and two substantial works on Ethiopian history.[64]

As noted above, James Bruce of Kinnaird landed at Massawa in 1769 and spent three years in Ethiopia, based at Gondar. He visited Aksum, producing a disappointingly cursory and manifestly inaccurate account of what he saw. The fact that his account was not published for more than fifteen years after his return may have contributed to this state of affairs: Bruce's five-volume work, *Travels to Discover the Source of the Nile*, is of greater value for its general impressions than for its precise facts.[65]

The nineteenth century saw a substantial increase in the number of foreign visitors to Ethiopia, particularly in the north. A significant number of these have left accounts of their travels, some providing valuable information relative to history and archaeology. Particularly important was Henry Salt, better known today for his collection of Egyptian antiquities now in the British Museum. He first visited Ethiopia in 1805 as a member of an expedition led by Viscount Valentia, by whom he was employed as secretary and draftsman. He returned in 1809, bearing a letter from George III to the King of Ethiopia. Salt has left us a detailed description of Aksum and its monuments, illustrated with engravings which are the oldest reasonably precise pictorial representations (fig. 9).[66] He also conducted the first known archaeological excavation in the country, when he cleared the lower part of the famous Ezana inscription.[67]

Following Salt, an increasing number of European travellers visited Ethiopia and Eritrea, publishing accounts of their observations.[68] Particularly noteworthy are those of Rüppell and Lefebvre.[69] The Magdala expedition of 1867/8 resulted in important

Fig. 9 Lithograph of Aksum by Henry Salt 1809.

publications, relating not only to the history and monuments, but also to the geology and natural history; it was also the means whereby substantial collections of Ethiopian manuscripts and other artworks came to the British Museum and other institutions.[70] Study of these, together with classical sources, resulted in detailed accounts of Aksumite history, most notably by A. Dillmann.[71]

A more specifically archaeological publication is that of J. Theodore Bent who travelled to both Yeha and Aksum, producing a summary but illustrated description of his observations.[72] Bent was the first to note the distribution of ancient sites extending from Adulis inland to Aksum.[73]

The first major (and, to this day, the most comprehensive) attempt at recording the ancient monuments of Aksum and other sites in Tigray and Eritrea was made in by a German team officially designated the Deutsche Aksum-Expedition (D.A.E.). The work of the expedition was fully published in 1913 in four large volumes.[74]

The D.A.E. was sponsored by the German Kaiser. Its leader was Dr Enno Littmann, assisted by the architect Daniel Krencker and by Theodor von Lüpke. The expedition was in Aksum for a total of 84 days. The amount of work that was achieved can only be described as remarkable (fig. 10). Its primary aim was to record the extant ancient monuments and, for comparison, traditional Tigray architecture both ecclesiastical and vernacular. Littmann, as a linguist, took particular interest in coins and in ancient inscriptions, both formal and *graffiti*. All the Aksumite inscriptions then extant were

Fig. 10 The work of the Deutsche Aksum–Expedition in 1906
(Littmann *et al*. 1913). Above: Stela 6. Centre: excavations at Ta'akha Maryam.
Below: base of colossal statue.

recorded and discussed in meticulous detail in volume IV of the D.A.E. publication. Stratigraphic archaeological excavation was not undertaken for its own sake, although very considerable digging was done to clarify the plans of early buildings and to expose part-buried monuments.

The architectural drawings which Krencker produced, notably of the stelae and throne-bases, are of wholly exceptional quality: more recent investigators have for the most part felt unable to improve on them and they have been reproduced on many occasions. A reasonably full photographic record was also made, but the quality of reproduction in the published volumes does not do this justice.

The expedition's departure from Aksum was apparently hurried. On its return journey to Asmara and Massawa, records were made of monuments at Yeha, Debra Damo and sites in Eritrea. Their work is of particular importance both because of its precision and because much of what was recorded is no longer extant. All subsequent researchers at Aksum and related sites have acknowledged their debt to the D.A.E.

At virtually the same time that the D.A.E. was engaged on inland sites, two separate expeditions worked at the Aksumite Red Sea port of Adulis, revealing buildings and evidence for prolonged ancient occupation.[75] Thereafter until 1936, when Italy annexed Ethiopia, remarkably little archaeological or historical field research appears to have been undertaken either in the Italian colony of Eritrea or in independent Ethiopia.[76] Important historical studies were, however, published by A. Kammerer in the 1920s.[77]

During the five years of Africa Orientale Italiana, archaeological recording and publication advanced rapidly,[78] but there was also much destruction, notably when the great 'palace' of Ta'akha Maryam at Aksum was effectively obliterated by road building. In 1937 the second largest of the Aksumite stelae was removed to Rome on the personal orders of Mussolini. Following the liberation of 1942 it was some years before significant research could be undertaken, although restoration and detailed recording was carried out at the monastery church of Debra Damo in 1948 under the direction of Derek Matthews.[79]

The next significant development came in 1952 when the Ethiopian government established an Institute of Archaeology with the co-operation of French interests. The organisation was directed for some twenty-five years by Francis Anfray. Preliminary accounts of its work were published in a journal, *Annales d'Ethiopie*, which appeared intermittently in fifteen volumes between 1955 and 1990. The Institute's sphere of activity extended into Eritrea, which at this time had been formally incorporated with Ethiopia. Major investigations were at Aksum (particularly in the stelae area, around the Cathedral and at the Dungur 'palace' to the west of the modern town), Yeha, Hawelti-Melazzo, Matara and Adulis. It is tragic that, although summary accounts of this work were published fairly promptly,[80] in no single case has a detailed definitive report been made available. The value of this extensive research is thus very greatly reduced, and subsequent investigations have been severely hampered.

The post-liberation period also saw increasing involvement of Ethiopians in the active study of their country's past. Profound historical consciousness and respect for the past is characteristic of very many Ethiopians. Their culture preserves strong memories of the past and there is a long-standing tradition of committing these memories to writing in a form suitable to prevailing circumstances. For centuries, such traditions have been firmly rooted in the Ethiopian Orthodox Church. With the establishment of a university[81] at Addis Ababa in 1951, study of the Ethiopian past broadened, accepted versions were questioned, and methods which had been developed in other countries began to be applied by Ethiopians themselves to the study of their own past. Some of the researches undertaken in Ethiopia and Eritrea at this time were carried out in collaboration between local and foreign scholars.

Archaeology has been slower than other historical disciplines to achieve Ethiopian and Eritrean involvement. The Ethiopian Institute of Archaeology had disappointingly little success in training local members of its professional ranks. To some extent this was because of the greater glamour and resources obtained by researches into palaeolithic archaeology, which resulted in some degree of neglect for the later periods despite their more direct relevance for understanding Ethiopian and Eritrean history and culture.

Shortly before the 1974 revolution, the archaeological research base began to expand. Italian-sponsored work was conducted at several sites in the vicinity of Aksum, directed by Lanfranco Ricci and Rodolfo Fattovich.[82] Joseph Michels from the United States undertook a detailed archaeological survey of the region between Aksum and Yeha with a view to illustrating the overall settlement pattern through time.[83] The British Institute in Eastern Africa began large-scale excavations at Aksum itself under the direction of the late Neville Chittick, aimed primarily at establishing the age and associations of the principal stelae.[84]

The investigations noted above were all curtailed by the revolution, by the civil war that ensued, and by the concurrent famines. Foreign-based work was abandoned. The Ethiopian Institute of Archaeology withered. Many Ethiopian scholars left their country or were incarcerated. The northern regions, including Eritrea, with which this book is principally concerned, were most seriously affected.

With the return of peace and some measure of prosperity from 1991 onwards, research has resumed and expanded. There is greater participation by Ethiopian and Eritrean scholars. Foreign-based projects are according a much higher priority than previously to providing training and experience for local people at all levels. In Tigray, the British Institute in Eastern Africa has resumed its work at Aksum with a five-year campaign directed by the present writer: many of its results are discussed in the chapters which follow. Rodolfo Fattovich, now with the collaboration of Kathryn Bard, has undertaken parallel research at Beta Giyorghis near Aksum.[85] There is discussion of further investigations being undertaken at Yeha. The pace of research is clearly accelerating: it is hoped that the ideas offered in this book may serve as a stimulus and guide.

Chapter 2

ETHIOPIA BEFORE AKSUM

Prehistory

Ethiopia can claim the longest archaeological record of any country in the world. Two regions, the Omo Valley in the south-west and the Afar lowlands in the north-east, have yielded evidence for the early development of hominids and of stone-flaking technology more than two million years ago.[1] The survival and discovery of this material is due to a combination of circumstances favourable to the preservation of bone, lack of subsequent geological disturbance until erosion re-exposed the remains, and accessibility by researchers. By additional good fortune, both these regions saw volcanic activity broadly contemporary with the early hominid occupation; and this has provided means whereby the age of the sites may be ascertained with reasonable precision by means of potassium/argon analysis. There is, however, no reason to believe that the territories of the early hominids were necessarily restricted to those areas where their remains have so far been discovered. The following account is intended to show how Ethiopia and Eritrea fit into the emerging picture of early African prehistory; where necessary it draws on evidence from other parts of the continent.

The oldest and most complete remains are found in the Afar, a region which has given its name to a species of early hominid, *Australopithecus afarensis*, whose fossil skeletal remains have been found both there and in Tanzania in contexts dating between 4 and 2.5 million years ago.[2] The most complete skeleton known comes from Hadar in Ethiopia and is about 3.6 million years old - roughly twice the age of the famous fossils from Olduvai Gorge.[3] These hominids walked upright and were about 1.2 m (4 ft) tall. There is no evidence that they had mastered the skills of making sharp tools by flaking stone, but they may have selected naturally broken stones or other items for use, and/or made tools out of materials such as wood which have not survived in the archaeological record. The world's earliest recognisable stone tools have likewise been found in the Afar; they are simple, unstandardised flakes which come from a context dated to about 2.6 million years ago.[4] Although sparse, such evidence does permit a tentative reconstruction of the early hominids' behaviour patterns.

During the following one million years important developments took place, albeit almost imperceptibly slowly.[5] Hominid evolution resulted in the appearance of several lineages (expert opinion is divided as to how many), including some which have been identified as belonging to our own genus, *Homo*. During this period there were

33

significant technological advances. More refined and standardised stone tools were made, including a small number of distinct types presumably intended for particular purposes. With increased adaptability, hominids seem to have been able to exploit a wider range of environments; and archaeological evidence for their presence is for the first time found in highland areas, as at the important site at Melka Kontoure not far to the south of Addis Ababa.[6] Adaptability and specialisation led to the search for raw materials best suited for making stone tools. These were now sometimes transported for considerable distances from their source to the hominids' encampments, where traces of social patterning and interaction may be discerned in the archaeological record.

No convincing evidence has yet been found for the presence of very early hominids in the regions of northern Ethiopia and Eritrea which are the main focus of this book. It must be recognised, however, that very little relevant research has yet been undertaken there; and it may well be that important discoveries are yet to be made.

About one million years ago, early hominids – now all, so far as we know, of the species *Homo erectus* – greatly extended their territories, penetrating into most parts of Africa and for the first time moving outside that continent into Eurasia.[7] Technology and food-getting skills were further developed and diversified. By about a quarter of a million years ago, these processes had resulted in regional cultural differences which are an essential hallmark of what archaeologists in Africa generally call the 'Middle Stone Age'.[8] Many types of specialised tools were produced for particular purposes; they were often smaller and more finely made than previously, permitting the more economical use of selected raw materials. Caves were sometimes sought as desirable places in which to live or to take temporary shelter, and there is evidence for the controlled use of fire. It was probably at this general time, if not before, that speech developed to the extent that abstractions and future plans could be expressed, greatly facilitating the transfer of knowledge and ideas and thus the improvement of group co-operation.[9] One effect of this was a steady acceleration in the rate of cultural change.

These highly significant developments probably took place in several regions, but appear to have been generally earlier in Africa than elsewhere. They are seen as fundamental to the attainment of the complex cultures of more recent times. Their early attestation in Africa is in accord with the genetic and fossil evidence that it may have been in that continent that anatomically modern humans, *Homo sapiens sapiens*, first evolved.[10] It is in fact in the Omo Valley of Ethiopia that one of the oldest known fossil skulls of this type has been discovered.[11]

Tantalisingly, despite the richness of its evidence for early hominid development, Ethiopia and Eritrea comprise one of the least-known parts of Africa in terms of later prehistoric archaeology. A bare outline may be proposed, based on the scanty research that has yet been undertaken and by drawing parallels with neighbouring regions. The trends already noted towards smaller and more specialised tools continued. Increased adaptability and inventiveness led to more varied activities and cultural diversification, including the seasonal exploitation of contrasting environments. In the so-called 'Late Stone Age', beginning perhaps as long ago as 40,000 years, evidence may be recognised of ritualised disposal of the dead, and of varied artistic expression, providing opportunities for the study of additional aspects of human culture. Although archaeological sites of this general period have been noted in several parts of northern Ethiopia and Eritrea, the only one which has yet been investigated in any detail is the rock shelter at Gobedra, 4 km (3 miles) west of Aksum.[12] Here, it seems that pottery was first used about 5000 years ago.

Farming

Throughout the huge span of prehistory that has been rapidly surveyed in the foregoing paragraphs, humans obtained their food through the gathering of wild plant foods, hunting and - in some areas - fishing. New developments of fundamental importance were the domestication of plants and animals. Ethiopia may be shown to have played a vitally important role in these processes.[13]

The initial domestication of both plants and animals was doubtless a slow and hesitant process. Although modern cultivated plants and domestic animals are generally clearly distinct from their wild prototypes, this differentiation has come about very slowly through repeated selection. For animals, control of breeding, provision of food and water, protection from predators and restriction of range will have been important factors. For plants, a similar role will have been taken by weeding, protection from birds and animals, harvesting, seed storage and deliberate planting or transplanting. For both, humans may have been instrumental in moving species to areas where they did not occur or flourish naturally. As humans grew increasingly dependent upon farming, so the plants and animals concerned became reliant upon human protection and intervention.[14]

With the range of environments which their country provides, Ethiopians today make use of a great variety of cultivated plants.[15] These include varieties which appear to have been domesticated locally from indigenous wild species, and others which were almost certainly introduced from elsewhere before diversifying in response to local conditions. Of the local crops some, such as *teff* and *enset*, are effectively restricted to Ethiopia, while others such as coffee have passed to many other parts of the world. The two most important crops of foreign origin traditionally grown in Ethiopia are wheat and barley, both of which are represented by numerous local varieties, indicating that they must have been used in the region for a very long time - perhaps as much as several thousand years.

Unfortunately, little archaeological research has yet been directed at questions of prehistoric Ethiopian plant cultivation.[16] Most of the information currently available is derived from botanical studies of recent crops.[17] Such work can prove informative, and is indeed an essential component of any investigation into ancient farming. However, historical reconstruction is very rarely a primary concern of its practitioners. Furthermore, such botanical research cannot establish an absolute chronology or link developments in husbandry with particular human populations.

Teff (*Eragrostis teff*) is of particular interest.[18] It is a tiny-grained but highly nutritious cereal, the preferred basis for Ethiopia's traditional and preferred staple food – a flat sour pancake-like bread known in Amharic as *enjera*. *Teff* is extensively grown and has wide environmental tolerance (fig. 11). Its numerous varieties and their differences from its

Fig. 11 Traditional crops. Left: *teff*. Right: emmer wheat.

wild relatives suggest that its cultivation is of considerable antiquity, although it has not yet been traced back in the Ethiopian archaeological record beyond the Aksumite period. Similar arguments about diversity apply equally to wheat and barley;[19] although these crops were almost certainly initially introduced to Ethiopia from the north, most of the varieties grown in the region today are not known elsewhere, leading to the view that their local antiquity may be analogous to that of *teff*.

Wheat is used primarily for making bread, barley for beer. Both can be used as a substitute or adulterant for *teff*. Another important cereal crop in the Ethiopian highlands is finger millet (*Eleusine coracana*), locally known as *dagussa*, which is particularly valued for making beer.[20] It is an indigenous African crop, probably originating in or near the modern Uganda.

In parts of the southern Ethiopian highlands the remarkable *enset* plant (*Ensete edulis*) is intensively cultivated and supports a very high population density. It is a vegetatively-propagated banana-like plant with fleshy stems at the base of the leaves which are made into a heavy, bread-like food. The leaves themselves are also put to a variety of uses. *Noog* (*Guizotia abyssinica*), grown for its oil-yielding seeds, is another exclusively Ethiopian cultigen. Flax, probably introduced from Egypt, is used for similar purposes. Indigenous cotton (*Gossypium spp.*) occurs in both wild and cultivated varieties distinct from the types introduced in modern times.[21] No discussion of Ethiopian traditionally cultivated plants would be complete without mention of two stimulants. Coffee (*Coffea arabica*) is indigenous to the forested areas of the south-west but is now widely grown elsewhere. The narcotic *chat* (*Catha edulis*) is grown in the eastern highlands.[22]

The summary presented above, although brief, serves to demonstrate the richness and diversity of Ethiopian cultivation as well as its many unique features. It seems almost inconceivable that its antiquity, at least in substantial part, should not extend back for a very long time - perhaps several thousands of years - beyond the Aksumite period of the first millennium AD. Definite proof of this is so far lacking and should be a focus for future research. Historical linguistic studies tend to confirm the possibility that agriculture may be of very great antiquity in parts of Ethiopia.[23]

The archaeological data concerning domestic animals are somewhat more plentiful, although many important matters require further illumination.[24] Animal bones in archaeological deposits are more easily recovered and identified than are remains of plants. Animals, both wild and domestic, are not infrequently depicted in rock paintings, although such representations can rarely be dated with any precision. The main species with which we are concerned are cattle, donkeys, sheep, goats, dogs, camels and chickens. There can be little doubt that cattle, sheep and goats have, like dogs, been in Ethiopia longer than the others; none of the four is indigenous and they must therefore have been introduced from elsewhere in an at least partially domestic state.[25] Cattle and sheep are shown in rock art and cattle bones have been recovered at several sites, including Gobedra near Aksum, in contexts of the first millennium BC.[26] In the Chercher mountains near Harar cattle bones have been recovered which date from the second millennium BC.[27] The donkey is the only domestic animal which was probably indigenous to north-east Africa. It was known in Egypt as early as the third millennium BC.[28] The camel, which was almost certainly introduced from Arabia, is not attested in Nubia until the first millennium BC.[29] Nubian evidence is not necessarily relevant to Ethiopia; and there are indications that the coming of the camel to parts of north-eastern Africa may have taken place earlier than is commonly supposed.[30] The date at which horses, and hence mules, were first available in the region is not known. The few data that are available relating to chickens suggest that they are unlikely to have been present before the early centuries AD.[31]

Such is the lamentably sparse information that is available about early Ethiopian farming. It is clear that both cultivation and herding are of considerable local antiquity, extending back in something approaching their modern complexity to at least the last millennium BC, while many components are probably much older.

The third and second millennia BC in Eritrea and northern Ethiopia

It cannot be emphasised too strongly that modern political boundaries did not exist in prehistory. Names of countries or provinces often provide a convenient means of geographical reference, but to consider the distant past within the framework of recent politics can only be misleading. Thus, so far as this book is concerned (and notwithstanding its title) no distinction is made between the territories now comprising Ethiopia and those included in Eritrea. For the period to which we now turn our attention - the third and second millennia BC - the most relevant information comes in fact from a site near Kassala, across the Eritrean border in what is now Sudan.

At Mahal Teglinos near Kassala, Rodolfo Fattovich and his colleagues have unearthed settlement and mortuary remains which, when comprehensively published, will provide a framework for understanding the later prehistory of a very extensive region.[32] There is evidence for large nucleated settlements supported by a mixed farming economy. It is claimed that the pottery from this site shares features both with the Nile Valley to the west and, in the opposite direction, with the Red Sea coastlands and northern Ethiopian plateau. Small standing stones, stelae, were used to mark graves. It seems that a very extensive culture area may be discerned, including the Tigray and Eritrean highlands, in which were present at an early date many features from which aspects of later Ethiopian civilisation derived.[33]

It was possibly at this general time that knowledge of metal working first appeared in northern Ethiopia. Both in the Sudanese Nile Valley and in south-western Arabia it is clear that copper and some of its alloys were utilised, along with gold (at least in the Nile Valley), long before iron.[34] It is plausible to suggest, but cannot yet be proven, that the same may have been true of the Tigray/Eritrea highlands where, as will be shown below, iron is not attested prior to the first millennium BC. It is unprofitable to speculate on the degree to which such cultural developments may have been due to the transfer of knowledge from adjacent regions rather than to independent invention.

There are numerous references in ancient Egyptian writings to the 'Land of Punt', which was an important source of exotic materials such as gold, timber, aromatics and skins that were traded to Egypt at various times during the third and second millennia BC. It is clear from Egyptian records that part of the journey to Punt was made by water – almost certainly along the Red Sea. It has often been assumed that Punt lay on the Red Sea coast, probably on the African side; and various regions between Port Sudan and Cape Guardafui have been proposed. It now seems likely that inland parts of the Eritrea/Sudanese borderland may have been, or have been included in, the territory which the Egyptians conceptualised as 'Punt'.[35] The term 'Punt' may have been a very general one which did not necessarily always refer to the same place.

It is possible to offer only a very provisional picture of northern Ethiopia/Eritrea during the second millennium BC. Such an attempt is necessary, however, if we are fully to understand the significance of the later developments with which this book is primarily concerned. The region probably supported a moderate density of population, concentrated in the better-watered and more fertile areas where a mixed-farming lifestyle was already established. This may be reflected in the remains attributed to the poorly known Ona culture of highland Eritrea and eastern Tigray.[36] The more mountainous environments, such as those of Simien, and the arid lowlands, such as Danakil, if inhabited at all, may respectively have retained the hunter/gatherer economy that had been ubiquitous in earlier times, or seen the development of nomadic pastoralism. The extent to which settlement on the plateau was nucleated remains unknown but, especially in the more rugged terrain where communication between fertile areas will have been difficult, it must be imagined that scattered homesteads and/or small villages were the norm. Caves and rock shelters probably continued as foci of shelter, at least in some areas. No houses of this period have yet been excavated in Ethiopia or Eritrea. In view of the environment, and of contemporaneous examples at Mahal Teglinos and in South Arabia,[37] it is likely that dry-stone construction was preferred. Timber for roofing may have been more readily available than was the case in more recent times prior to the introduction of *Eucalyptus*.

As noted above, the basic features of traditional Ethiopian cultivation and herding were probably already established by the second millennium BC, if not before. In the highlands of Eritrea and Tigray cereal agriculture may have made use of *teff*, wheat, barley and finger millet. It is possible that the ox-drawn plough was already in use at this time.[38] Further to the south, *enset* may have been long established as a staple crop: it may at one time have been grown over a wider area than is the case today, but there is no evidence that it ever achieved importance further north than Gondar, beside Lake Tana. Cattle, sheep and goats may have been kept, along with dogs. It is not known whether camels, horses and/or donkeys were already available. If they were not, cattle would have been the only animals available for transport purposes, thus limiting facilities for movement of goods. Chickens were probably a later arrival.

The main technological features of this time have already been noted. Pottery was exclusively hand-made and unglazed. In view of its commonness, weight and fragility it was probably rarely transported over any distance, except as a receptacle for valuable contents. Similarities between the wares of different areas are thus likely to have been due to derivation from common traditions and to mobility of the potters themselves. It is possible, as noted above, that the working of copper began here at around this time, although iron remained unknown. Whether or not metal was available, there can be no doubt that the 'Late Stone Age' tradition of producing small flaked stone tools continued. The only form of artistic expression[39] for which evidence survives, and which may have been practised at this time, is rock painting, described below.

In the absence of any form of writing, there is no direct archaeological indication of the language or languages which may have been spoken in northern Ethiopia during this period. However, historical linguistic studies leave little doubt that these belonged to the Cushitic family of Afroasiatic, directly ancestral to such modern languages as Agau, Dankali and, more remotely, Somali.[40]

Rock art

The study of ancient rock art has great potential for elucidating many aspects of past society, including such areas as belief systems that are rarely accessible through other forms of archaeological investigation. Rock art has the additional advantage that it is relatively conspicuous; and this serves to explain why the known rock-art sites of northern Ethiopia and Eritrea significantly outnumber other archaeological occurrences apart from historical stone structures. Unfortunately, rock art is extremely difficult to date other than by circumstantial means that require knowledge of the relevant archaeological sequence more detailed than is, in this particular case, currently available.

Rock art's distribution depends on two factors: the former presence of people with a cultural inclination to execute it, and the natural occurrence of rock surfaces suitable both to receive it and to ensure its subsequent preservation. Recent accessibility to those interested in recording its presence is also, of course, relevant. In the region with which this book is primarily concerned, rock art is mainly found on the eastern side of the plateau extending northwards from the vicinity of Adigrat into Eritrea.[41] Most sites are small rock overhangs or shelters, well within reach of daylight, rather than dark inaccessible caves. Weathering and natural destruction have undoubtedly taken their toll; and it cannot be assumed that the oldest art has necessarily survived. Motifs cut or pecked into the rock (petroglyphs or, loosely, engravings) are less prone to destruction than are paintings, but the few examples known from this region appear to be of late date.[42]

The subject matter of the extant rock art appears at first sight to fall into two distinct categories. The first and, in this area, by far the larger comprises motifs which are readily recognisable as representations of people, animals and inanimate objects or accoutrements such as weapons. The second class, often ignored because less easy to describe or interpret, includes signs or symbols not obviously representational, which may occur alone or in direct connection with motifs of the first class. Research in other regions, most especially in South Africa;[43] has shown that the second class of motifs may be of great significance in understanding and interpreting the art as a whole.

Representations of animals, people and their accoutrements may provide valuable opportunities for linkage with, and augmentation of, the archaeological record. The depiction of, for example, domestic animals or metal tools must indicate that the artist was at least familiar with the existence of such things. In Ethiopia and Eritrea (fig. 12)

Fig. 12 Rock paintings. Left: cattle and herders at Sekama near Dire Dawa (after Clark and Williams 1978). Right: ox-drawn plough at Ba'ati Facada near Adigrat (after Drew 1954).

there are frequent representations of men armed with spears, and of domestic cattle as well as wild animals.[44] Breeds of cattle may sometimes be recognised by the forms of horns and the presence or absence of humps.[45] The manner in which udders are depicted may serve to indicate the significance of milking.[46] To the south-east, around Harar, fat-tailed sheep are clearly depicted. A particularly interesting painting at Ba'ati Facada near Adigrat shows a man guiding a plough drawn by a pair of yoked oxen.[47] The absence of certain representations in the art does not, of course, indicate that the items concerned were necessarily unknown, merely that the artists had no desire to depict them.

Study of symbolism in South African rock art, linked with knowledge of traditional belief-systems that have survived into recent times, has permitted an understanding of non-representational motifs and an appreciation of the position and significance of the art in the society which executed it.[48] In Ethiopia and Eritrea this is an exciting opportunity for research of a type that has not yet been attempted. The varied and abundant rock art of this region remains a largely untapped resource for understanding the past.

South Arabia

No meaningful evaluation of the first millennium BC in northern Ethiopia and Eritrea could be presented without reference to contemporaneous developments on the other side of the Red Sea. The highlands of the two regions have much in common physically and environmentally. The cultural traditions of their inhabitants have been closely linked for at least three thousand years, only superficially obscured by the rise of Islam.[49] On several occasions – as this and later chapters will show – there have been close political connections also. The Red Sea itself and the inhospitable nature of its coastlands seem to have been no great impediment to contact. Indeed, archaeological evidence (supported to some extent by linguistic reconstructions) has been cited for cultural similarities in even earlier times; and it is remarkable that the earliest attestation of certain African cultivated plants comes, not from Africa at all, but from sites in the Yemeni highlands.[50]

Although many details, including the chronology, remain uncertain, there can be little doubt that by early in the third millennium BC settled farming communities were established in the highlands of what is now northern Yemen. Villages comprised clustered houses with round rooms, some of which were used for special purposes. Domestic animals that were kept included cattle, sheep, goat and pig. Although the archaeozoological evidence is inconclusive, it was probably at around this time that the one-humped camel was first domesticated in the Arabian peninsula. Tools were made of flaked stone (some of the materials for which were transported over considerable distances) and, more rarely, of copper or bronze. The hand-made pottery has been claimed to share affinities both with materials from far to the north and with certain African wares. By about 2000 BC there appears to have been a collapse of agricultural productivity in this area.[51]

The crucial period of the second millennium BC remains poorly understood. The rise of urbanism may be traced to the middle centuries but, both in the Hadhramaut and in the highlands near Marib, there are signs of continuity – most clearly seen in the typology of the associated pottery – with the earlier agricultural communities. By the first millennium BC individual states were known as Ausan, Hadhramaut, Ma'in, Qataban and Saba, with Himyar apparently a later development. Although the probable capitals of most of these kingdoms have been located, their detailed chronologies and inter-relationships remain to be fully elucidated.[52] Major towns were defended by monumental stone walls and gates. It is not known to what extent the kingdoms were differentiated by dialect, religion or material culture, although many of these features were undoubtedly shared. A distinctive art style arose, represented mainly in monumental sculpture and in large-scale bronze-casting. Massive stone architecture (fig. 13) was developed both for buildings associated with the elite and/or religious functions, and for complex irrigation works.[53] The latter are best known (both today and in ancient times) from the great dam at Marib, with its complex and finely constructed system of sluices and water-channels.[54] At some stage scripts came into use for recording the local South Semitic languages. Although there is no incontrovertible evidence for the use of these scripts prior to the eighth century BC, their rapid development and sophistication suggest earlier beginnings.

The fertility and prosperity of southern Arabia has for millennia provided a contrast with the arid, more northerly regions of that peninsula: hence its ancient designation as 'Arabia Felix'. In incense it produced a commodity that was greatly valued, readily transportable and available nowhere else, except in adjacent parts of the Horn of Africa. These factors enabled southern Arabia to establish a strong economic position for itself, whilst retaining its cultural distinctiveness. By the first millennium BC if not before, overland trade routes were developed northwards through Arabia,[55] while maritime contacts were established along the northern shores of the Indian Ocean linking South Arabia with the Indian subcontinent on the one hand and the Horn of Africa on the other. To facilitate these trading activities coinage was adopted around the fourth and third centuries BC: the designs of the earliest South Arabian coins were based on somewhat earlier Athenian issues which circulated widely around the eastern Mediterranean and which were also imitated around the Persian Gulf.[56]

The subsequent history of South Arabia is best viewed in a broader context. Since it falls outside the chronological framework of this chapter, only the basic features will be briefly noted. The establishment through the Red Sea of regular maritime trade based in Ptolemaic Egypt diminished South Arabia's involvement in international trade.[57] Roman interest was, in contrast with more northerly parts of the Arabian peninsula, minimal.[58] As subsequent chapters of this book will show, South Arabia's later connections were primarily with Aksumite Ethiopia. This is reflected at the site of Shabwa, where recent excavations have revealed material with strong Aksumite affinities.[59] The Aksumites may have exercised political control over parts of southern Arabia as early as the third century AD, and certainly did so for periods of the fourth and sixth centuries. These cultural links lasted until the rise of Islam in the seventh century, when the Red Sea came once more under the control of peoples living on its eastern shore.[60]

Yeha and the 'pre-Aksumite' cultures

At some time during the third quarter of the last millennium BC strong connections were established between South Arabia and some highland areas of Tigray and Eritrea. These are marked in the archaeological record by the sudden appearance in the latter areas of features not known there previously - notably writing, monumental stone architecture

Fig. 13 Ancient architecture at Marib, Yemen. Above: the dam.
Below: the moon temple now popularly known as Mahram Bilqis.

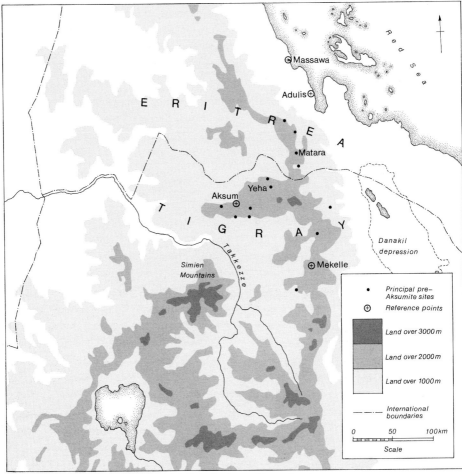

Fig. 14 Principal pre-Aksumite sites.

and sculpture - the earlier development of all of which may be recognised in South Arabia. It is possible, but cannot yet be proven, that the working of iron also began in Ethiopia at this time.[61] These new traits occurred suddenly and in closely circumscribed areas. The date at which this took place is generally attributed to the sixth or fifth century BC, but epigraphic evidence could support a somewhat greater antiquity.[62]

The best known occurrence of these features is at Yeha, some 30 km (20 miles) north-east of Adwa. About 30 additional sites are known (fig. 14), notably the complex known collectively as Hawelti-Melazzo about 15 km (10 miles) south of Aksum. These locations seem to have been selected on account of their exceptional fertility.[63] Yeha, for example, lies in a broad, well-watered valley with deep fertile soils, surrounded and sheltered by mountains (pl. 2). Each of these settlements appears to have been tightly circumscribed in area. They may be regarded as having been established by small numbers of colonists from South Arabia. The observation that some features of the material culture, notably the domestic pottery, appear to have strong local antecedents does not invalidate this interpretation. For a short while, some form of over-arching political system may have linked several or all of these sites; this may have been the polity named in unvocalised inscriptions as the kingdom of D'MT (perhaps Daamat).[64] Its rulers were apparently local, implying partial or total autonomy from Arabia. The physical presence of immigrants from across the Red Sea is demonstrated by the seemingly simultaneous first appearance of several specialist crafts and items which must have been locally produced using highly developed styles and technologies whose formative stages are known exclusively from South Arabia. The fact that these settlements did not maintain their separate identity for more than a few generations points to the small numbers of colonists and the fact that links with their Ethiopian neighbours soon became stronger than those with their Arabian kin.

Yeha is the site of a remarkable monument - the so-called temple (fig. 15) - which comprises a rectangular building measuring 18.5 x 15 m (60 x 50 ft) whose plain walls without apertures other than a single entrance still survive to a maximum height of more than 11 m (35 ft). It is constructed, without the use of mortar, from regular rectangular blocks of silicified sandstone up to 3 m (10 ft) in length; the outer faces, edges and corners are superbly dressed with great precision. The temple undoubtedly owes its good preservation to the fact that it was subsequently (perhaps about a thousand years after its initial construction) converted into a Christian church.[65] Today, a modern church stands next to it on the same rocky hillock, the whole being surrounded by a wall as a sacred precinct. The walls of the modern church incorporate two finely carved stones depicting a frieze of stylised ibex figures in characteristic South Arabian style.[66] These carvings were probably once part of the temple structure, as may have been three stone slabs, now kept in the church treasury, which bear South Arabian texts. Two of these come from the same inscription with raised lettering; the other is incised.

Some 200 m (200 yds) to the north-east of the church enclosure, on another low hill, stand the remains of a monumental structure known as Grat Beal Gebri. Its most prominent feature is a series of massive square-sectioned monolithic pillars of a type also known not only at the contemporary Ethiopian site at Hawelti-Melazzo but likewise in South Arabia - most famously at the moon temple at Marib, the capital of the South Arabian kingdom of Saba.[67] Grat Beal Gebri has been investigated archaeologically both (briefly) by the Deutsche Aksum-Expedition of 1906 and (more intensively) by Francis Anfray in the early 1970s.[68] It was shown that the structure was broadly contemporary with the temple described above, but no convincing information was obtained which might indicate its original function. Sadly, Anfray's work has not been fully published and no adequate conservation works were undertaken following these excavations; the monument is now badly deteriorated.

A series of rock-cut graves was also investigated by Anfray on the lower south-western slopes of the outcrop on which the temple stands. Vertical shafts lead to one or more tomb-chambers, the contents of which included abundant pottery, copper-alloy sickles and other tools, and an alabaster vessel of Nubian affinity. Rodolfo Fattovich has suggested that one of these graves may have belonged to one of the D'MT rulers.[69] A

Fig. 15 The temple at Yeha. Above: the exterior, seen from the north-west. Centre: the interior, seen from the south-east. Below: stone with frieze of carved ibexes, now built into the west wall of the modern church adjacent to the temple.

Fig. 16 The pre-Aksumite site at Hawelti, south-east of Aksum.
Above left: distant view of the site. Below left: square-sectioned monoliths.
Right: detail of the stone throne (after Gerster 1970).

claim[70] that Yeha was a town covering some 7.5 hectares (18 acres), and with a population in the order of 10,000 must be regarded as speculative, even unlikely, since there is no evidence that occupation was continuous either in space or in time; furthermore the population density remains completely unknown.

The site-complex of Hawelti–Melazzo lies amid vast fertile plains (fig. 16). A low dome-shaped hill is marked by monolithic square pillars remarkably similar to those at Grat Beal Gebri. Excavations directed by Henri de Contenson in 1958-59 on behalf of the Ethiopian Institute of Archaeology revealed an extremely fine covered throne of carved limestone, its sides bearing low reliefs and a frieze of ibexes in typical South Arabian style. There was also a small statue of a seated figure, the hair and facial features of which are depicted in a manner for which very close parallels may be found in South Arabia.[71]

As noted above, the D'MT kingdom seems to have been short-lived. Later inscriptions are interpreted as referring to a range of smaller polities, each with its own ruler. It is unfortunate that the archaeology of the later first millennium BC is so poorly known.[72] Until more research is undertaken it will not be possible adequately to document the processes by which the old D'MT kingdom broke down, to be replaced by local successors having much weaker links with South Arabia. It must have been at this time that the foreign influences attested in D'MT, including writing and architectural styles previously unknown on the African side of the Red Sea, became fully incorporated in Ethiopian culture.

Until the results of ongoing research are fully published, knowledge of this intermediate period will remain tantalisingly incomplete. Use of stelae to mark burials is attested, and substantial nucleated settlements appear to have been established in several areas, including that around Aksum where the capital subsequently arose. Such long-distance trade links as were developed were with the Nile Valley rather than with countries bordering the Red Sea. Continuity from earlier times is marked by the use and development of scripts originating in South Arabia (fig. 17), and by certain artefact types including metal openwork badges or 'identity marks'. It was from this base, in which successive pre-Aksumite and proto-Aksumite stages are conventionally recognised but not clearly defined, that true Aksumite civilisation arose.

There is no evidence that the actual site of Aksum was occupied before the first century AD. It lies on the edge of the broad fertile Hatsebo plain, where the Mai Hedja

Fig. 17 Stone inscriptions. Above left: pre-Aksumite, incised South Arabian script, from Seglamen. Below left: pre-Aksumite, raised South Arabian script, at Yeha. Above left: Ge'ez inscription of King Ezana, at Aksum. Below right: Greek text of the same inscription.

stream emerges from between the hills of Beta Giyorghis and Mai Qoho (fig. 18).
During the early centuries AD, Aksum rapidly became the centre of a major urban
civilisation, as the following chapters will describe.

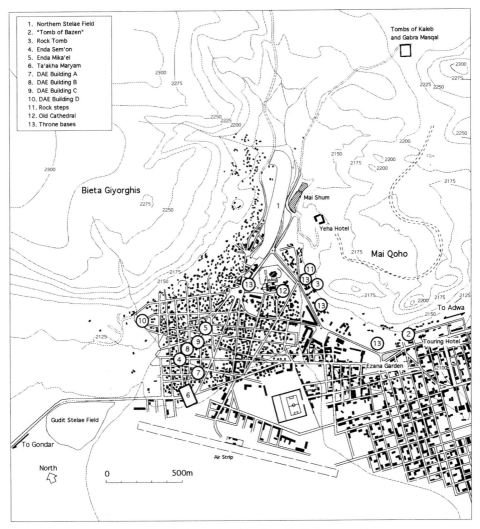

Fig. 18 Plan of Aksum showing the principal ancient sites
and other features mentioned in the text.

Chapter 3

AKSUMITE CIVILISATION

Political history

The sources from which we may learn about Aksumite political history are scattered and diverse. Traditional sources were generally committed to writing long after the events to which they purportedly relate: they have thus been subject to re-interpretation in accordance with the circumstances prevailing not only at the time of transcription but also earlier.[1] There are a surprisingly large number of references to Aksum in Graeco-Roman and Byzantine writings,[2] but it is not always easy to differentiate first-hand observation from hearsay, or to make appropriate allowance for prejudice, ignorance or misunderstanding on the part of the chronicler. The coinage provides an independent source, although firm correlations between the numismatic sequence and that recorded in documentary media are disappointingly rare.[3] Archaeology offers evidence which is often of a different nature. Only through inscriptions (including those on coins) can it supply the names and titles of individuals. Its anonymous data nonetheless include much that is relevant to the reconstruction of past political systems: datable buildings and tombs which can be placed in hierarchies of wealth and power (to the extent that these can be differentiated), monuments and artefacts illustrative of socio-political practices and beliefs. All these sources of evidence will be utilised in the discussion that follows.

It is widely accepted that the florescence of Aksumite civilisation spans the first seven centuries AD. The view formerly held that it continued into the tenth century is generally but not universally discounted.[4] Much of our more detailed knowledge comes from study of the coinage which was issued from around the third quarter of the third century. The period prior to this, which saw the establishment and rise of Aksum as the centre of a major polity, remains very poorly known.[5]

Although material dating from the last four hundred years BC has been recorded from the immediate vicinity, there is as yet no evidence for human settlement on the site of Aksum itself until around the beginning of the first century AD.[6] It is not until the third century that we have plentiful data for great prosperity and the centralisation of resources. By the fourth-century reign of Ezana there are inscriptions which record the titles and exploits of Aksumite kings, demonstrating that Aksum was by then at the centre of a complex political system.[7] The formative processes of that system, however, remain very poorly known. The fourth century was also the time when the rulers of Aksum adopted Christianity.

A second fixed point in the sequence occurs in the early sixth century when the activities of King Kaleb are recorded in inscriptions from Aksum, from South Arabia (whither his rule extended), and in written sources both foreign and local; Kaleb's reign is also attested by his coins. Christianity was by this time a major factor both in the conduct of foreign policy and in the interests of chroniclers.

Aksum's political control extended at several times to regions beyond the modern borders of Ethiopia and Eritrea. Large areas of southern Arabia were ruled from Aksum at intervals between the third and the sixth centuries.[8] It is likely that Meroe in the Sudanese Nile Valley was conquered by an Aksumite army under King Ezana, but the nature and consequences of this episode remain poorly understood.[9]

The decline of Aksum is represented archaeologically by the abandonment of settlement areas, by the cessation of monument construction, and by the end of the coinage series. Historians note that the capital was at this time moved elsewhere.[10] It seems increasingly likely that the rise of Islamic control of the Red Sea, and the resultant isolation of Christian Ethiopia, was a major contributing factor.[11]

There can be no reasonable doubt that Aksum was a monarchy. Tradition, foreign writers, inscriptions and coins all refer to the rulers as 'MKRB', 'negus' or 'basileus'. That hereditary principles played at least some part in determining the succession seems likely but cannot be proven incontrovertibly: the terms 'son' and 'brother' were sometimes used to signify 'protégé' or 'close colleague' respectively.

The monumental tombs and their associated ostentatious stelae, described below,[12] include several examples that can be dated within a comparatively short period in the third and fourth centuries AD. This suggests several things. Very substantial resources of organised labour must have been available to achieve such construction within the period indicated. These resources were markedly greater than those which had been available in earlier times. If, as seems highly probable but cannot be proven, the tombs are royal, there may have been marked increases in ostentation with each successive reign. On the other hand, the stelae in the central area, numbering over 140 and showing much variation in size and elaboration,[13] cannot all be those of monarchs. This, and the presence of several large 'élite residences' in and around Aksum,[14] suggests that there was a substantial upper class, presumably occupying the higher part of a politico-economic pyramid below the monarch. Whether and to what extent this élite represented the monarch's kin, howsoever defined, we do not know.

There are occasional suggestions that Aksum may sometimes have been ruled by two co-regents. Constantius II addressed his message of AD 357 to Ezana and Saizana.[15] These two individuals are conventionally identified with the Abraha and Atsbaha of Ethiopian tradition.[16] The contemporary Aksumite inscriptions and coins, however, seem to imply a single ruler.[17]

Although the tombs and other monuments of Aksum clearly demonstrate the wealth, sophistication and organisational power of which the Aksumite rulers could dispose, most of our primary evidence for regalia and the trappings of authority comes from depictions on the coins.[18] It is noteworthy that the earliest ruler depicted, Endybis, is invariably shown wearing a simple head-cloth and not accompanied by symbols of

Fig. 19 Aksumite coins depicting regalia. (Type-numbers follow Munro-Hay and Juel-Jensen 1995.) Top: Ousanas, *c.* AD 300, gold of type 20. The bust on the obverse is crowned while that on the reverse wears a head cloth. Above both busts is the pre-Christian crescent-and-disc symbol. Below left: Ousas, *c.* AD 500, gold of type 86. The Christian cross may be seen over the crowned bust, the arm wears bangles and holds what appears to be a fly-whisk. Below centre: Anonymous (type 76), probably late 5th century AD, copper. A long-handled cross is shown in front of the crowned bust. Below right: Armah, early 7th century AD, copper of type 153. The crowned king sits on a throne and holds a long-handled cross.

authority. Later rulers are generally shown wearing a crown which becomes progressively more grandiose. This process began before the conversion to Christianity under King Ezana and continued without interruption afterwards. On coins where the royal portrait is shown on both obverse and reverse, it is sometimes crowned only on the former, the reverse portrait retaining the head-cloth shown on earlier issues. From the late fourth century, the ruler is often shown carrying a sceptre or fly-whisk; in the sixth century its place is sometimes taken by a hand-cross or, possibly, a processional cross (fig. 19).[19] In more recent times, the latter attributes have been restricted to the clergy. An additional indication of the appearance of an Aksumite ruler is provided in the account of a Byzantine embassy of *c.* AD 540, in the reign of Justinian I, which describes King Kaleb wearing a costume of linen and gold adorned with pearls or beads, and riding in a golden chariot pulled by four elephants.[20]

There are preserved at Aksum more than two dozen monuments which are interpreted as the stone bases of thrones.[21] Each comprises a granite slab approximately 2.0 – 2.5 m (6 – 8 ft) square which, in at least some instances, was set on a stepped base. In the centre of each slab was a further square stone (sometimes integral, sometimes separate) with rectangular grooves around three of its sides. These features are interpreted as settings for vertical sides and back. At the corners of the basal slab of some thrones (but probably not all of them) were 'L'-shaped blocks with recesses to receive the base of a stone column. In the case of two thrones in the Cathedral precinct, these columns still stand.[22] They presumably originally supported some form of canopy. The illustration (fig. 20) shows the

Fig. 20 Stone thrones at Aksum. Left: a throne base in the Cathedral precinct.
Right: reconstruction by D. Krencker (after Littmann *et al.* 1913).

detailed layout of a typical throne as it now survives, together with an attempted
reconstruction.

The thrones at Aksum fall into two groups. One extends along the foot of Mai Qoho
hill on the north-western side of the road leading from the east into the central area of
Aksum; the other forms a compact cluster in the Cathedral precinct. The first group,
although there are now many gaps and displacements through erosion, probably retains
its original configuration. There are indications that some or all of the thrones in the
second group could have been moved from elsewhere in early times.[23] Tradition records
their use in post-Aksumite times in connection with coronations and other ceremonies.[24]

Comparable thrones are attested elsewhere. There is one at Matara[25] and another,
apparently already ancient, was described at Adulis in the sixth century AD by Cosmas
Indicopleustes.[26] An inscription records that King Ezana set up a throne at the
Nile/Atbara confluence to commemorate a military victory.[27] There is no independent
corroboration for a sixteenth-century Portuguese account which mentions possible
further examples in the vicinity of Lalibela.[28]

There are at Aksum several inscribed stone slabs, the dimensions of which are
concordant with their having originally formed the sides of thrones. The nature of the
extant inscriptions[29] agrees with the view that these thrones were erected to
commemorate royal exploits.

Some of the inscriptions are, however, too large to have formed the sides of thrones.
One of these has been known for many years: it formerly stood beside the road at the
entrance to Aksum from the east,[30] but was unfortunately moved during Italian road-
widening operations of the late 1930s and is now in a public park nearby. It bears a text
in one Greek and two Ethiopic versions recording the titles and military exploits of King

Ezana.[31] A virtually identical inscription (fig. 17) was discovered in 1981 on the north side of Aksum, beside the road leading up the valley between Beta Giyorghis and Mai Qoho hills to the Tombs of Kaleb and Gabra Masqal.[32] There were thus inscribed stones set up beside two of the principal entrances to ancient Aksum. A similar inscription was described at Adulis, likewise beside the road leading out of the town, by Cosmas Indicopleustes who unfortunately did not record the name of the ruler responsible.33 The erection of grandiloquent commemorative inscriptions at the entrances to towns is thus attested at two Aksumite sites. The following excerpt from the Adulis inscription may be cited as an example of their content:

> I entered valiantly into battle and subdued the following peoples: I fought the Gaze, then the Agame and the Siguene and, having conquered them, reserved for myself half their lands and people....I am the first and only of the kings my predecessors to have subdued all these peoples.[34]

The configuration of Aksumite settlements can provide some indication of security and its military implications. Aksum and, so far as we can tell, other agglomerations seem never to have been circumscribed by defensive walls.[35] Indeed, the location of the sites (often overlooked by nearby hills, as at Aksum and Matara for example), and the dispersed nature of the settlement that is suggested archaeologically, combine to indicate that defence was not an important consideration. The length of the route from Adulis to Aksum (cf. fig. 2, above), along which valuable commodities were regularly transported, is a further demonstration of settled and secure conditions in the Aksumite heartland.

The situation seems to have been markedly different in more peripheral regions. The evidence for this comes primarily from the inscriptions which record a warlike relationship between the Aksumites and their neighbours on both sides of the Red Sea, notably in the reigns of Ezana and Kaleb.[36] Unfortunately the peoples named as adversaries can rarely be identified with precision. The usual aim of these military operations was subjugation, pacification and the exaction of tribute. Herds and foodstuffs are the commodities most commonly recorded in the latter category: it is clear that the Aksumite rulers commanded prolific supplies for the use of their own forces. Slaves were also captured; their presence in large numbers at Aksum would help to explain the provision of the manpower that must have been available for the erection of stelae and other monuments.[37] The probable presence of a substantial slave population makes the absence of defensive structures all the more noteworthy.

Social history

It is usual for archaeological and historical knowledge to emphasise the upper strata of ancient societies. Aksum is no exception to this generalisation. Funerary and residential monuments attributable to the élite are comparatively well known: some (though we are not always sure which or how many!) may confidently be regarded as royal. As noted above, it seems that there was a fairly numerous élite class enjoying great material prosperity.

The middle ranks of Aksumite society are less clearly represented. Nonetheless, excavations at Matara, Adulis and Aksum have revealed areas of domestic occupation with evidence for agricultural and industrial production.[38] The buildings were of undressed or roughly dressed masonry significantly less substantial than that of the élite structures. In most cases there was evidence for repeated alteration and modification, and for the direct association of domestic occupation with production above the subsistence level.

Clay models of smaller houses,[39] both rectangular and round, usually thatched, have been found. They appear to represent simpler and smaller structures than have yet been recognised archaeologically. It could be that such houses occurred mainly in the countryside where little excavation has yet been conducted. Wherever they resided, very large numbers of people must have been engaged both in erecting the buildings and monuments of Aksum and other settlements and in producing food for the numerous builders, artisans and dominant élites. However, living quarters have not yet been investigated archaeologically on a scale commensurate with such numbers. The presence of large numbers of slaves may also be inferred: a human skeleton excavated at Matara wore iron shackles,[40] but there is otherwise no primary archaeological trace of the accommodation or management of slaves.

The archaeological materials provide abundant testimony for the presence in Aksumite society of numerous specialist artisans. The evidence of the stone buildings and monuments has already been cited as indicating the existence of a large and well organised labour force. No less striking is the requirement for skilled masons capable not only of carving the elaborate designs on the storeyed stelae but also of calculating the angles and dimensions of the huge interlocking stone blocks used in tomb construction.

Timber is known to have been an important component of much Aksumite architecture, although one that has rarely survived in the archaeological record. Post-Aksumite buildings, notably the church at Debra Damo,[41] provide clear indications of how it was used. Many architectural features represented in stone on the storeyed Aksumite stelae were generally of wood. Structural timberwork was thus extensively employed and carpenters would have contributed significantly to Aksumite building work.[42] Much finer woodwork was also undertaken: some traces have survived in tomb deposits but the greater part of our evidence consists of nails and elaborate metal fittings including hinges, handles and applied decoration.[43]

Pottery was produced and used in great quantity and variety. This craft is traditionally practised by women, but there is no conclusive evidence whether the division of labour was the same in Aksumite times. It appears that all local pottery was produced without use of the wheel. Most types are highly distinctive: a summary description is offered on pp. 74-7, below. Occasional clear instances have been noted of imported forms being imitated by local potters.[44] There is remarkable standardisation and specialisation, although most fabrics appear to utilise clay sources in the immediate vicinity.[45] Pottery production thus seems to have been largely in the hands of local specialists. Observation of the work of modern potters suggests that little in the way of dedicated equipment or premises would have been employed.[46]

The wide variety of metalwork known from Aksumite sites is evidence for a rapid proliferation of skills during the early centuries AD. If we are to believe the *Periplus of the Erythraean Sea*, much metalwork was being imported through Adulis during the mid-first century, suggesting that local supplies and skills were not then able to meet demand.[47] By the end of the third century, the quantity of fine metalwork that was available strongly suggests that local production was not only firmly established but displayed great variety and skill.[48] It is not always easy to differentiate between imports and local products; very few items however have stylistic affinities sufficiently clear to place them firmly in the former category. Iron and copper alloys were worked and, in some instances, combined.[49] Techniques of gilding and glass-inlay were understood and executed with considerable expertise[50]. *Cire perdue* casting appears to have been practised;[51] and inscriptions of King Ezana mention metal statues, their presence being supported by the recording of a stone pedestal for a statue which may have been about 5 m (16 ft) high (fig. 10).[52] There can be no reasonable doubt that the Aksumite coinage was produced locally, and therefore that both gold and silver were available.[53]

It has long been recognised that ivory may have been a major export commodity. Recent archaeological research has for the first time revealed that it was also carved locally, at least in Aksum itself, to a very high level of artistry and technological sophistication.[54] The standardised steeply flaked stone scrapers which are found in large numbers on the western side of the modern town may have been used in the preparation or working of ivory and/or wood.[55] Experimental comparisons confirm that this may have been the case, but it seems that much of the finest ivory carving must have been done with metal tools.[56]

The textile industry must also have involved a considerable number of operatives. This may have been largely a rural activity. Whether or not cotton was grown in the immediate vicinity of Aksum[57], it was clearly brought there for processing as is indicated by the presence in domestic occupation horizons of cotton seeds, spindle-whorls and loom-weights. In Tigray today, the initial processing and spinning of thread is done by women, but weaving is a male task. There is no evidence to show whether this division prevailed also in earlier times. Other fibres may have been processed, as well as skins; but firm evidence is lacking.[58]

A further population element which may be assumed to have existed is that involved in the community's religious life. From the fourth century onwards there would have been an increasing number of Christian priests, perhaps initially concentrated in the urban areas, subsequently in the countryside also.[59] In pre-Christian times, the old religion/s doubtless involved a priesthood of some sort, although we are ignorant of the details. At least from the late fifth century, monasticism took root in several parts of the Aksumite realm. Religious practices would also have supported numerous craft specialists such as painters, producers of vestments, vellum-makers and scribes, makers of sistra and other instruments, all of whose activities may be inferred directly or indirectly from historical references.[60]

In addition to those enumerated above, Aksumite society must have supported numerous other specialists whose products have been preserved archaeologically or may confidently be inferred. Included here are the carvers of small stone objects, such as lamps and seals, and makers of the (?leather) ropes that must have been used in quantity in the erection of stelae as well, probably, as in the transport of these and other building materials. Flaked stone tools, noted above, seem at least in some instances to have been made and used by different specialists.[61] Glass makers and/or re-workers appear to have been represented and there may well have been numerous others, working in perishable materials which have not survived in the archaeological record.

The specialists and other inhabitants of urban centres, noted above, would have exerted substantial demands for food and other rural produce. The research of Joseph Michels, who has undertaken the only substantial systematic survey of the Aksumite countryside, has provided evidence for numerous rural settlements, thus strengthening the view that potentially productive areas were intensively exploited.[62] It is only very recently that archaeologists have sought detailed evidence for the Aksumite food-producing economy.[63] Such evidence as has been recovered suggests an economy strikingly similar to that which prevails in rural Tigray today: details are summarised in the following section.

The density of population, perhaps analogous to that which prevails today, must have exerted considerable demands for fuel. Diminishing supplies of wood are currently supplemented with dried cattle dung; the antiquity of this practice is unknown. Some industrial activities, notably metal-working, will have required large quantities of charcoal. This was probably produced in wooded areas which may have been found at progressively greater distances from the urban centres. The necessary transport will have been provided by people (doubtless mostly women) and by livestock; the numerous transport animals mentioned in Aksumite inscriptions were probably mules and/or donkeys although the presence of some camels cannot be discounted.[64]

Transport animals are not the only domestic stock recorded in the inscriptions as having been obtained from subject peoples either by capture or as tribute. Large numbers of cattle and some sheep/goats are noted in this context. How these royal herds were managed is not known. They may have been retained for the use and support of the military, they may have been reserved as resources under state control, or they may have been distributed in some way through the rural population. In any event, their management must have had a major impact on the inhabitants of the Aksumite countryside.

Maintenance of the population and economic activities that have been noted above must have necessitated exchange mechanisms and transport arrangements on a substantial scale. It is probable that the trade in salt from the Danakil lowlands to the plateau has been conducted from Aksumite times if not before.[65] Itinerant traders may also have transported other commodities whose use was widespread. In cases where demand was more restricted, transport may have been organised by the consumer. Commodities in the latter category will have included metals, most of which have restricted geological occurrence.[66] This is particularly true of gold and silver. Cosmas Indicopleustes has left an account of sixth-century Aksumite trade for gold with the peoples of Sasu (probably south-west of Lake Tana in the land encircled by the Blue

Nile.[67] Although it seems that Cosmas relied on hearsay and never saw these activities himself, the statements that beef, salt and iron were exchanged for gold and that the trade was controlled by the Aksumite state may reasonably be accepted, even if the details of silent barter are apocryphal.

Another class of commodity that was transported or traded over variable distances comprised the raw materials for fine stone-carving and for flaked stone artefacts.[68] The occurrence of nodules and primary flaking debris in areas where such artefacts were used far from their natural occurrence suggests that the materials were transported in rough unworked form.

It is also necessary to consider the way in which international trade was organised. This trade comprises an area of Aksumite studies which has received a disproportionate amount of attention in the past. Imports and (to a much lesser extent) exports have been identified and listed, but very little attention has been paid to ascertaining how these transactions were actually organised. The first point to emphasise is that almost all Aksumite long-distance trade seems to have passed through the Red Sea port of Adulis, which would have rendered it susceptible to centralised control. Aksumite settlement was, however, mainly based on the plateau at least 2000 m (6500 ft) above the sea. Aksum itself, moreover, was located far to the south-west, close to the further limit of the main settlement area, some 170 km (100 miles) in a straight line, or twelve days' journey, from Adulis.[69] The route by which goods had to be transported between the coastal entrepôt and the principal metropolis was thus long and arduous, involving the ascent or descent of a difficult and precipitous escarpment.[70] Two principal conclusions follow from this observation. The first is that there must have been some strong reason why the principal metropolis was located so far inland, in a position by no means central to the polity as a whole. Access to produce and raw materials was probably the principal factor.[71] The second conclusion is that both imports and exports would have acquired considerably enhanced value at their destination by virtue of the care and effort expended on their transportation.

Domestic economy

Information about the Aksumite domestic economy may be obtained from various sources. In approximately decreasing order of reliability these include: (a) primary archaeological materials such as firmly dated and identified remains of crops, animals or other relevant commodities; (b) artefacts depicting or used in activities relevant to the enquiry; (c) inscriptions – problematic both because they may record the exceptional rather than the everyday and because the precise meaning is not always clear; (d) ancient written accounts or illustrations by outsiders, to which the same difficulties apply; and (e) evidence from recent traditional practices for the antiquity of which there are archaeological, botanical, zoological, linguistic, written or oral indications.

The traditional subsistence practices of northern Ethiopia and Eritrea have been summarised above on pp. 18-20. Regional differences have been emphasised. It will be convenient to return to consideration of their relevance to the present enquiry after the archaeological and written evidence has been surveyed.

Recovery of identifiable plant remains from stratified and datable archaeological contexts is so far restricted to sites in the immediate vicinity of Aksum. Seeds of cultivated finger millet recovered in 1974 at Gobedra rockshelter about 4 km (3 miles) west of Aksum were at first thought to date from the fourth or third millennium BC and thus to be the earliest known example of any indigenous African cultigen.[72] Subsequent research has shown that the seeds are actually post-Aksumite, being approximately 1000 years old, and that they must therefore be intrusive in the horizon from which they were recovered.[73]

The *Periplus of the Erythraean Sea* records that grain was imported to what is now Somalia during the first century AD. Its omission from the list of imports to Adulis suggests that northern Ethiopia and Eritrea were self-sufficient in cereal produce at that time.[74] Representations of cereal ears on Aksumite coins are, as noted below, generally interpreted as emmer. Irrigation seems to have been employed where necessary to boost agricultural production.

On-going research to the north-west of Aksum at the settlement site called Ona Negast and its associated burial ground at Ona Enda Aboi Zague, both on Beta Giyorghis hill, has yielded remains of wheat and barley in contexts apparently dating to the first four centuries AD. Later, between the fourth and seventh centuries, these same crops continued to be cultivated, alongside *teff*, lentils and grapes.[75]

Closer to Aksum itself, excavations were conducted in 1995 and 1996 at an area of domestic occupation immediately to the north of the modern town. Deposits dated to the sixth century AD were preserved. Wet-sieving of samples from securely stratified contexts yielded archaeobotanical samples in which the following crops have, at the time of writing, been identified: wheat, barley, probable *teff*, sorghum, oat, pea/bean, lentil, cotton, linseed/flax, *noog*, gourd and grape.[76]

The presence of grape is of interest. Vines with bunches of grapes are represented on the front base-plate of Stela 3 at Aksum, probably dating to around AD 300. A rather similar, better preserved but undated stone carving is built into the fabric of the Old Cathedral nearby.[77] At the Tomb of the Brick Arches, vines and grapes are depicted on ivory carvings which were almost certainly manufactured locally during the third century AD. Two sets of large rock-cut tanks at Atsafi (fig. 21) are interpreted as fruit-presses, perhaps for the production of wine.[78] Thus, whilst it is possible that the seeds recovered at Aksum came from imported raisins, there is evidence to support the view that grapes were locally grown and used for making wine.[79]

As with archaeobotany, it is only around Aksum itself that archaeozoological research has been undertaken. A few provisional identifications of excavated bones, mostly of cattle and sheep/goat, were made in the course of the 1972-74 excavations directed by Neville Chittick, but circumstances did not permit their detailed investigation.[80] At Gobedra cattle remains seemed to date from the last millennium BC and a camel tooth to an even earlier period:[81] it has unfortunately not been possible to obtain radiocarbon (AMS) dates on the specimens themselves so as to ascertain whether, like the finger millett seeds mentioned above, they were in fact intrusive from more recent levels.[82]

Animal bones from Beta Giyorghis include specimens identified as from cattle,

Fig. 21 The Aksumite rock–cut tanks at Atsafi, interpreted as fruit–presses.

sheep/goat and dog.[83] Study of archaeozoological material from the 1993-96 excavations in Aksum and its immediate vicinity has not, at the time of writing, been completed; so only preliminary and tentative conclusions may be offered. Most of the material so far examined comes from contexts dating to the fourth and sixth centuries AD. It seems probable that the same species were present, with the addition of some wild ungulates, and possible camels and donkeys.[84]

Other studies offer some amplification of the archaeozoological data. Particular interest attaches to a small series of pottery figurines, each representing a pair of yoked oxen (fig. 22). The yoke is similar to that employed in the region today for ploughing, which is the only use for which oxen are currently yoked. Three such figurines come

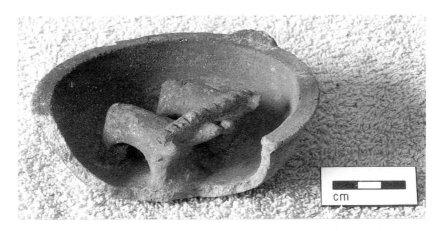

Fig. 22 Figurines of yoked oxen from the Tomb of the Brick Arches, Aksum.
The scale is in centimetres.

from the third-century Tomb of the Brick Arches. One was definitely and the other two probably set integrally in the base of a pottery bowl. Similar examples come from other locations at Aksum.[85] Further afield, there is a specimen from Baroca and two from Hawelti, one of which may belong to the earlier phase of occupation.[86] Whatever the original use or symbolism of these artefacts may have been, they may safely be interpreted as demonstrating that yoked oxen were used, presumably for ploughing, in the third century AD if not significantly earlier. These figurines, like others of bronze from Mahabere Dyagwe and Zeban Kutur, confirm that both humped and humpless varieties of cattle were present in Aksumite times.[87]

An iron sickle or reaping hook was recovered in 1974 from a tomb in the Gudit Stelae Field at Aksum which probably dates to the third century AD or thereabouts. It is remarkably similar to those used locally today. Several copper alloy sickles come from Hawelti and from burials at Yeha which probably date to a significantly earlier period.[88]

It is noteworthy that grindstones and other artefacts are markedly more numerous on the domestic occupation site that has been investigated on the outskirts of Aksum than in the central areas. This implies that the primary processing of plant foods may have been concentrated in rural areas to a somewhat greater extent than is the case today. Unfortunately, comparable data for Matara have not been published, so it is not known whether the same pattern applied at the only other Aksumite site where areas of domestic occupation have been excavated on a significant scale.

Little detailed information may be gleaned about culinary processes. The results of analysing cut-marks and differential representation of body parts as indicators of butchery practices are not yet available. Much of the domestic pottery recovered was doubtless used in connection with storing, transporting, preparing, cooking or consuming food and drink. Large vessels, often with handles, and remarkably similar in overall shape to modern examples, were probably used for carrying or storing water, or for brewing. Heavy open ceramic objects, sometimes with signs of burning, are conventionally interpreted as stoves. There are numerous bowls or necked vessels which may have been used for cooking. Large flat platters such as have been used in recent times for cooking *enjera* may be recognised only at a late stage in the Aksum sequence.[89]

The inscriptions provide additional evidence for Aksumite diet, as supplied on military expeditions. Bread, apparently made of wheat, was evidently an important component, at least in the fourth century.[90]

The overall impression gained from the very incomplete evidence currently available for the domestic economy during the Aksumite period is remarkably similar to that which has traditionally prevailed in rural parts of Eritrea and northern Ethiopia in recent times. The temptation must be resisted to assume that this similarity extended also into areas where there is no independent substantiation. Differences undoubtedly existed. There are areas of the modern economy for which no data are available to indicate whether or not they existed in Aksumite times. It seems probable that the Aksumites maintained a more highly centralised political system than prevailed subsequently, with a correspondingly larger proportion of the population not directly involved with subsistence activities. There may thus have been a greater degree of exchange in the ancient economy. From the late third century such exchange would have been facilitated by the circulation of copper coinage. The presence of base-metal coins on domestic occupation sites, and in outlying areas as well as in population centres, shows that such denominations circulated locally; their numbers suggest that many, if not most, transactions involved the use of coins.[91] Despite mention in the *Periplus of the Erythraean Sea* of first-century coinage imports to Adulis, and very occasional finds of Roman and South Arabian coins,[92] it seems that there was no extensive use of coined currency in the Aksumite realm prior to the third century.

International economy

Although the place of the Aksumite kingdom in the international economy of the early centuries AD is a topic which has long received a large – possibly disproportionate – amount of scholarly attention, it remains imperfectly understood. Contemporary written accounts are almost invariably expressed from an external viewpoint, usually set in the eastern Mediterranean; and the precise nature of relations with Aksum was often coincidental to the principal topic. Aksum's other partners rarely feature in the documentary sources that are available. A similar imbalance affects our understanding of the archaeological evidence. Mediterranean (and Egyptian) manufactures tend to be far better known, and thus easier to recognise, than those from other areas. This has almost certainly resulted in Mediterranean imports being over-represented in accounts of Aksumite international trade. Items from other parts of Africa, from Arabia, the Indian subcontinent or more distant eastern sources have been harder to recognise or to identify with precision. Even more basic has been the emphasis on Aksum's imports rather than her exports.[93] At the time of the *Periplus*, the general pattern was for raw materials to be exported and manufactures imported; this pattern probably continued throughout the Aksumite period – indeed, it is still a feature of trade between Africa and the rest of the world. Many raw materials – skins, ostrich feathers, tortoiseshell, ebony – will rarely be preserved in the archaeological record and, when they are (either as waste or as a component in a manufactured article), their place of origin will hardly ever be identifiable. The same is unfortunately still true of ivory, which appears to have been one of ancient Aksum's principal exports.[94] Even more fugitive, because of their nature and the uses to which they were put, are aromatics and spices. Living exports – slaves or wild animals – are equally problematic.

It has been the fashion to ascribe most movements of commodities between one region and another to 'trade'. This is misleading. It can result in the less tangible effects of inter-regional contact being effectively ignored. Even when manufactured goods are involved, it can give rise to excessive emphasis on commercial arrangements at the expense of other transfer mechanisms: gifts, loot or tribute, for example, whether or not made in recognition of a social or political connection.[95] Equally unsatisfactory is use of an overall but unspecific term like 'exchange'. Wherever possible the historian should go beyond these generalisations and seek to investigate the nature of the relationship represented.

It is extremely difficult to compile a balanced picture of Aksumite imports. Our knowledge depends on such factors as archaeological visibility and the extent to which commodities were deemed noteworthy by ancient chroniclers, whether Ethiopian or foreign. What was considered important by Aksum's trading partners may seem insignificant in the context of modern research: for example, the Romans sought on more than one occasion to control or prohibit the transfer of precious metals to Aksum and India, although it appears that the former was never a major recipient.

This section on imports has so far dealt exclusively with material culture. It is important not to ignore the less tangible aspects of international contacts. Expertise and learning may also have been transferred in either direction. Several attempts have been made to show that certain aspects of Aksumite architecture may be of foreign inspiration. These are now largely if not entirely discounted, if we ignore the South Arabian inspiration for some Aksumite expertise in monumental stone architecture. Brickwork, formerly seen as possibly inspired from overseas, is now recognised as an integral part of the Aksumite architectural tradition. Far more important intellectual imports may be demonstrated. The idea of coinage is one, being clearly derived directly or indirectly from the Graeco-Roman world. The weight standard of the Aksumite gold coinage, not only at its inception but for at least one hundred years subsequently, was based on those prevailing contemporaneously in the Roman Empire.[96] Use of the Greek language, not only internationally (as in the coinage inscriptions) but also internally in inscriptions, is another obvious import from the first century onwards.[97]

From the fourth century the developing history of Ethiopian Christianity provides the context for much external influence, although it would be wholly wrong to underestimate its specifically local aspects. The fact remains that Christianity was a religion whose earliest developments took place elsewhere before being transferred to Ethiopia: the Ethiopian Church retained its organisational link with the Patriarchate of Alexandria until the mid-twentieth century. A second phase of religious contact occurred in the second half of the fifth century, recalled in Ethiopia as instigated by the 'Nine Saints' from the Byzantine empire. It seems that Syrian influences were strongest at this phase, and that a lasting result of the 'Nine Saints'' activities was the inception of Ethiopian monasticism.[98]

The most detailed primary account of imports through Adulis is the *Periplus of the Erythraean Sea*.[99] This document has now been shown to date from the mid-first century AD and thus to predate by some two centuries the rise of Aksum as a major participant in international trade. It belongs to a period for which the local archaeology is poorly known. We cannot even be certain that the imports described as arriving at Adulis were destined for the plateau area which subsequently became the Aksumite heartland. Care must therefore be exercised in comparing the evidence of the *Periplus* with that of archaeology, much of which belongs to a significantly later period. That said, it is appropriate here to quote the *Periplus*' summary of Adulitan imports. They comprised various types of clothing and textile, glass, silver and gold vessels 'for the king', brass 'for ornaments as well as cutting up for coins', copper pans and drinking vessels 'and for cutting up to make armlets', iron for spears, axes, adzes, knives, 'a little

Plate 1 The highlands of Tigray, north of Aksum.

Plate 2 The temple and church of Yeha in their mountain setting.

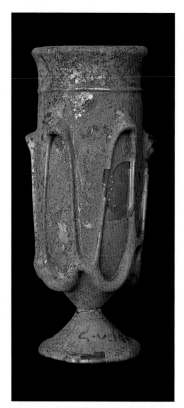

Plate 3 Imported glassware from tombs at
Aksum: a) Egyptian goblet of the third century
AD, one of a set of six found together in a large
pottery bowl, from the Gudit Stelae Field.
b) Small beaker from the Gudit Stelae Field.
c) Goblet fragment, from the Tomb of the
Brick Arches.

a

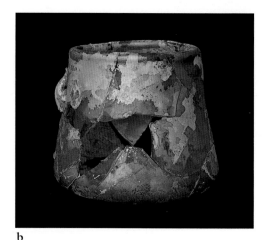

b

5   10

cm

c

Plate 4 Detail of ivory panel from the Tomb of the Brick Arches at Aksum, showing a human-headed animal.

Plate 5 The 517-tonne Stela 1 at Aksum.

Plate 6 Inside the Tomb of the Brick Arches at Aksum. *Above*: General view from Chamber B towards the entrance. *Left*: Loculus H in course of excavation. Pottery bowls are in situ on the bench; a smashed glass vessel lies in the silt below.

Plate 7 Inside the Mausoleum at Aksum, looking west.

Plate 8 Eighteenth-century mural painting of the Trinity and crucifixion at Gebra Berhan Selassie church, Gondar.

Plate 9 Inside the rock-cut church of Mary, Lalibela: capital and arches.

Plate 10 The rock–cut church of St George, Lalibela.

Plate 11 Wall painting in the rock–cut church of Merkurios, Lalibela.

Plate 12 Procession at the Festival of St Mary, Aksum, 1993.

Roman money for the resident foreigners', as well as small quantities of wine and olive oil.

Trade from the eastern Roman empire through the Red Sea into the Indian Ocean was on a substantial scale.[100] Aksum's geographical position relative to this route must have provided great economic advantage.

Of all the archaeological data relating to Aksum's international trade, perhaps the easiest to interpret are those relating to imports from Egypt and the Nubian Nile Valley. Much of the material of Egyptian or Nubian origin that has been recorded from Eritrea and northern Ethiopia appears to be of pre-Aksumite date and has been considered on pp. 24-5. From a cache at Addi Gelamo on the edge of the escarpment south-east of Adigrat came four metal bowls, one of them decorated with lotus plants and frogs: they probably originated in the Meroitic state during the very early centuries AD.[101] The carving of an Egyptian ankh symbol on a stela at Aksum[102] cannot be dated: the age of the stela itself has not been ascertained, and the carving could have been added at any subsequent time. Occasional sherds of coarse pottery from late Aksumite contexts seem to be related to material in the Sudanese Nile Valley; it cannot yet be ascertained whether the pottery was itself imported or whether it was made in Ethiopia/Eritrea by potters who originated in what is now Sudan. Definitely imported, however, is a pottery flask found in 1996 during industrial excavation on the western edge of Aksum: it was made near Aswan in Egypt between the fourth and sixth centuries AD.[103]

Imports from the *circum*-Mediterranean world are most readily identified in the form of pottery and glassware. Some pottery and most if not all of the glass vessels were probably brought as luxury tableware (or its equivalent). Glass is mentioned in the *Periplus* as an import through Adulis; and excavations at Aksum and related sites have revealed examples which appear to have been manufactured between the first and the third centuries AD.[104] The pottery in this category mainly comprised so-called African red-slip ware (*terra sigillata Africana*), produced in Roman North Africa. Bowls and platters are the usual forms; they are wheel-made, sometimes elaborated with moulded relief decoration. This pottery was introduced to Aksum at a rather later date than the glass, being generally attributed to the fourth and fifth centuries. It is noteworthy that two tombs at Aksum, which are dated to the third century and which contained large numbers of artefacts, both yielded imported glassware (pl. 3) but no recognisably foreign pottery.[105] A second type of imported pottery, which occurs in quantity at several sites, consists of amphorae, easily distinguished even in small sherds by their distinctive cream/buff-coloured fabric, wheel manufacture and generally ribbed texture (fig. 23). Such vessels were produced in many areas, generally as containers for wine, oil or a salty fish paste called *garum*. The examples that were brought into the Aksumite realm seem mostly to date between the fifth and seventh centuries.[106] Detailed study as to their sources has not yet been completed, but there are indications that North African, Cypriote, Egyptian and Syrian manufactures may be represented, perhaps with others.[107] They were presumably brought to Eritrea and Ethiopia as receptacles, by virtue of their contents. We have as yet no direct evidence as to what this may have been; amphorae were frequently reused in ancient Mediterranean trade, so there is no reason to suppose that they necessarily came to Adulis directly from their place of original manufacture, or with

Fig. 23 Imported pottery from Aksum. Above: bowl–rim of African red-slip ware from North Africa. Below left: amphora from the eastern Mediterranean. Below right: flask from the Aswan area of Egypt. The scales are in millimetres (above) and centimetres (below).

their original contents.[108] Once arrived at Aksumite sites, they or their broken sherds were sometimes put to completely different purposes such as directing water to a baptismal tank, making spindle whorls, or burying dead babies.[109]

Wheel-made pottery, often glazed, has been recovered from several Aksumite sites. None is demonstrably of local manufacture. At least one (unglazed) example[110] may be paralleled in the Aswan area of the upper Egyptian Nile Valley. A much larger group appears to have originated in Arabia, more specifically in the area around the Persian Gulf.[111] These vessels mainly comprise bowls and fairly small jars, rarely if ever exceeding 30 cm (12 ins) in height. While the former were presumably brought to Aksumite sites as prestigious utensils, it is not known whether the latter were similarly valued, or treated primarily as receptacles for contents which we cannot now identify. These materials seem to date from the sixth and seventh centuries, to judge from the contexts in which they are mostly found.

Evidence that objects of Indian origin were imported to Ethiopia/Eritrea remains inconclusive. The strongest contenders for such status are some of the numerous beads of glass and semi-precious stone, bangles and other decorative items that have been recovered in some quantity both from tombs and from occupation sites.[112] (There is some evidence for a local glass industry at Aksum but we do not know whether it was engaged in primary manufacture or merely in the reworking of imported glass, a fair proportion of which was doubtless broken in transit. It is not yet possible to differentiate its products from imported ones.) The suggestion that clay figurines found at Hawelti may have been Indian imports is unconfirmed.[113]

The archaeological evidence for possible trade-contact between Aksum and China consists of a single piece of iron from the third-century Tomb of the Brick Arches. It comprises an angled strip or bracket, the two ends joined by a silver rivet (fig. 24). Superficial examination (not yet confirmed by expert analysis) suggests that it may be of cast iron: the only place where the technology of casting iron is attested as early as the third century AD is China.[114] The tentative identification of this piece as being of Chinese origin is strengthened by the style of its decoration. Although expert confirmation is awaited, this specimen must be regarded as a possible indication of contact – albeit perhaps indirect – between Aksum and China around the third century of our era.[115]

Ivory seems to have been a major export. Need to control, and/or have access to, sources of ivory may have been one of the reasons for the location of the principal metropolis, Aksum, in such a westerly position and far from the Red Sea port at Adulis.[116] Although ivory was locally worked into a wide variety of objects, there is no evidence that it was primarily exported in this form, rather than as tusks.[117] Ivory was extensively used in Egypt, the Mediterranean world, Arabia, the Indian subcontinent and China.[118] (It was also imported, from sources as yet undetermined, into early mediaeval Europe.) In several of these areas ivory was locally available, although it appears that material of African origin was preferred because of its colour and working qualities. Little research has yet been undertaken to differentiate elephant ivory by geographical source, although techniques are becoming available which will permit this and throw considerable new light on the ancient ivory trade.[119]

Fig. 24 Iron object which may be of
Chinese origin, excavated from the
Tomb of the Brick Arches at Aksum.
The scale is in millimetres.

Fig. 25 Frankincense.
Left: *Boswellia* tree in the Takkezze
Gorge. Right: Blaze for extraction of
the resin.

Spices and aromatics are likewise noted in documentary sources as Aksumite exports. The Takkezze Gorge is still an important source of frankincense (fig. 25) and this may have been a further factor in determining the western location of the Aksumite metropolis. These are commodities that were very greatly valued in the ancient world, both in the *circum*-Mediterranean lands and in the Orient.[120] It is extremely unlikely, however, that they will be detected in the archaeological record until such time as techniques are developed and implemented specifically for their recovery and identification.

Ebony and other timbers, skins and tortoiseshell are other commodities which the *Periplus* records as exports from Adulis. They may have been obtained in many parts of the Aksumite realm and are known to have been valued elsewhere, but will rarely be detected or identified archaeologically.

A final commodity which – by contrast with those considered above – is readily identifiable as Aksumite, is coinage. There is no reason to believe that this was exported as a trade item *per se*, but its distribution does provide some indication of the extent of Aksumite commercial activity. This is, perhaps, particularly true of the base-metal issues since gold, once exported as a medium of commercial exchange, is likely to have been treated and transported as bullion irrespective of its Aksumite origin. Aksumite bronze coins have been recovered from archaeological sites in the Nile Valley at Meroe and at several locations in Egypt.[121] Further east they have been found in Israel and in stratified contexts at Aqaba.[122] By contrast, finds of Aksumite gold coins come primarily from South Arabia and, less certainly, India.

Despite the numerous lacunae in our knowledge, it is possible to offer a map (fig. 26) showing the geographical coverage of Aksumite commercial activity. This inevitably presents a minimal view, being largely restricted to information concerning the sources

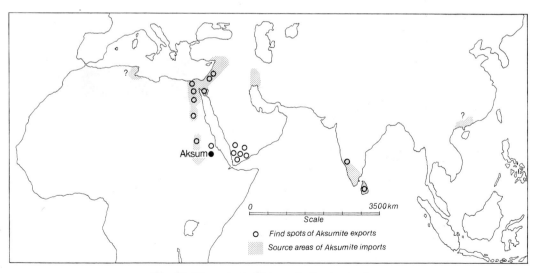

Fig. 26 The extent of Aksumite foreign trade.

of manufactured goods recovered in the course of archaeological excavations at Aksumite sites. Although it is known that other goods – primarily raw materials – were exported through Adulis, we have virtually no information as to their ultimate destination.[123] The nature of Red Sea commerce at this time clearly involved substantial trans-shipment and the destination of exports could have been significantly different from the sources of imports.

Chapter 4

AKSUMITE MATERIAL CULTURE AND BELIEFS

Coinage

Coins were struck in gold, silver and copper/bronze in the names of the kings of Aksum from, probably, the third quarter of the third century AD until the first quarter of the seventh.[1] These coins circulated far beyond the modern borders of Ethiopia and Eritrea; probably more Aksumite gold coins have been discovered in southern Arabia than on the African side of the Red Sea.[2] Study of several thousand coins, taking account of such factors as style, epigraphy, weight and fineness, die-links and overstrikes, has permitted the various issues to be ordered with a fair degree of confidence.[3] A total of 149 types is currently recognised, of which 68 are in gold, 35 in silver and the remaining 46 in copper.[4] The large number of minor varieties that are recognised indicates that, despite the present rarity of most Aksumite coins, many dies were in use and the coinage must originally have been produced on a substantial scale. The coinage preserves the names of some twenty Aksumite rulers; only two or three of these names are incontrovertibly attested from other sources. These links are sufficient, however, to anchor the chronology of the coinage series reasonably precisely (see fig. 27). There were also issues in all three metals which do not bear a ruler's name; these anonymous issues, dated to the fourth and fifth centuries, are among the commonest Aksumite coins.

The date at which the Aksumite coinage began cannot be determined precisely. The weight standard adopted for the Aksumite gold seems to have been based on that which prevailed in the Roman Empire shortly before the coinage reform under Diocletian during the last decade of the third century. Taking Roman gold-coin weights into account,[5] and noting the rulers named on Aksumite issues prior to the independently-dated reign of Ezana,[6] it seems most likely that coins were first struck at Aksum around AD 270 or slightly before. The independent coinage of South Arabia had probably come to an end a few decades earlier; and it may be that Aksum was able to exploit the commercial opportunity thus created. The anonymous *Periplus of the Erythraean Sea*[7] indicates that small amounts of Roman coinage were imported into Adulis from the first century AD for use by merchants. Both Roman and South Arabian coins have sometimes been found on Aksumite sites.[8]

Date AD	Ruler	Note	
c. 270	Endybis		
	Aphilas		
	Wazeba		
	Ousanas		
c. 330-360	Ezana	*	1
	Ouazebas	*	
	Eon	*	
	MHDYS		2
	Ebana	*	
	Nezool/Nezana	*	
	Ousas/Ousana/Ousanas		
c. 520	Kaleb		3
	Ella Amidas		
	Wazena		
	Ella Gabaz		
	Ioel		
	Hataz/Iathlia		
	Israel		
	Gersem		
c. 630	Armah		4

* Anonymous coinage issues are also attributed to this position in the sequence.

1 King Ezana's name is known from stone inscriptions at Aksum. It was in his reign that Christianity was officially adopted at Aksum. In AD 356 a letter was addressed to him by the Roman Emperor Constantius II.

2 This ruler is named only in unvocalised Ge'ez.

3 Kaleb's name is also preserved on stone inscriptions at Aksum and in Yemen, which he invaded c. AD 519.

4 The ruler of Ethiopia in the time of the prophet Mohammed is recorded in Muslim tradition as the father of a king Arma (Taddesse 1972:34). His identity with the ruler named on the coins is, however, disputed.

Fig. 27 Chronology of Aksumite coinage (based on Munro-Hay and Juel-Jensen 1995).

The first Aksumite coins bear the name of King Endybis, who is otherwise unknown.[9] These coins set a general pattern which was to continue for several centuries. Both sides bear profile portraits,[10] framed (on the gold coins) between ears of corn.[11] It has generally been assumed that both portraits represent the king, but the depictions are not sufficiently individual to prove this, and the possibility should be considered that a close associate of the king is also portrayed. The inscriptions on all coins of this reign are in Greek. Use of Greek on coins of all metals was continued under King Aphilas, apparently Endybis' successor; thereafter Ge'ez began to be used, generally but not exclusively on the copper. Greek continued on the gold coins until the final issue in that metal, under King Gersem at the beginning of the seventh century.

The reign of Aphilas, probably late in the third century, was a period of expansion and innovation. In addition to the gold currency unit introduced under Endybis, gold coins were struck in half, quarter and eighth units, each carefully differentiated by type as well as by weight. There were also at least two denominations struck in silver and two in copper. Such complexity is restricted to the one reign and was evidently not deemed a successful innovation.

For some seven or eight decades almost all Aksumite coins bore a portrait on both obverse and reverse (fig. 28).[12] On both obverse and reverse of those of Endybis a close-fitting head-cloth or cap is worn; this was retained on the reverse of subsequent issues, where the obverse portrait was crowned. The early issues all incorporated within their inscriptions the crescent-and-disc symbol of the pre-Christian religion.[13] During the

Fig. 28 Aksumite coins. (Type numbers follow Munro-Hay and Juel-Jensen 1995.) Top row: the first Aksumite coin, the gold issue of Endybis (type 1) *c.* AD 260–270, showing a bust wearing a head-cloth on both obverse and reverse. The smaller coin is the reverse of a silver issue (type 10) of Aphilas, Endybis' successor, showing selective gilding around the bust. Centre row: Anonymous copper issue (type 52), *c.* AD 350–400. The reverse bears the Greek inscription TOYTO APECH TH XWPA around a cross. Gold issue of Ebana (type 71), mid/late 5th century AD. Bottom row: copper issue of Ioel (type 132), *c.* AD 550.

reign of Ezana this symbol was replaced by the Christian cross. By about the third quarter of the fourth century, greater variety was introduced to the reverse types, particularly on the copper. The usual motifs were based on the cross, in a wide range of forms; pious propaganda typified the accompanying legends, such as 'joy and peace to the people' or 'he conquers through Christ'.[14] The gold issues, on the other hand, maintained throughout the series their traditional two-portrait designs with legends often restricted to royal names and titles. The general pattern of Aksumite coin types shows considerable stability. Although the weights of the gold coins were generally maintained, their fineness and that of the silver decreased fairly steadily, although the copper coins were larger from the end of the sixth century.

A remarkable technological feature of the Aksumite coinage is the presence of localised gilding on several silver and copper issues as a means of accentuating sections of the design such as parts of the cross when used as a reverse type, or the crown on a royal portrait. On the earliest examples gold foil seems to have been applied during the striking process; subsequently a gold-amalgam firing technique was employed after

73

striking.[15] The methods used have not been investigated in detail, but were evidently extremely effective for the gilding appears to have been a standardised feature of certain coinage issues and one which has only rarely been obliterated through the passage of time. So far as is known, no other coins anywhere in the world have ever employed localised gilding in this way.

What was the purpose of the Aksumite coinage? Why did no other polity in sub-Saharan Africa issue its own coins until the closing centuries of the first millennium AD?[16] It is noteworthy that the first Aksumite issues, those bearing the name of Endybis, were predominantly of gold and silver, the gold coins following the weight standard then prevailing in the Roman Empire;[17] furthermore, they were inscribed in Greek. These points all suggest that the first Aksumite coins were primarily intended for circulation in the context of international trade. Subsequently, Aksumite coins in copper were issued in far greater numbers and were often, at least from the late fourth century, inscribed in Ge'ez, a language that was only occasionally employed on the gold. It is reasonable to conclude that the copper coins were intended mainly for local circulation, as is supported by the nature of the reverse inscriptions and by the frequent occurrence of these coins (and their debased silver contemporaries) on domestic occupation sites at Aksum.[18] By contrast, the gold coins, although progressively debased,[19] generally followed fluctuations in Roman/Byzantine weight standards; they continued to circulate more commonly overseas, notably in South Arabia, than in the Aksumite heartland itself. The conclusion to be drawn is that coinage was originally issued at Aksum to support involvement in international trade; this remained the basic function of the gold, although use of copper denominations subsequently expanded locally, especially through the urbanised population.

It is noteworthy that this pattern continued to the end of the Aksum coinage series. Gersem, apparently the penultimate king to issue coins, is named on gold (in Greek) as well as on silver and copper (in Ge'ez). His successor in the early seventh century, Armah, appears not to have issued gold coins, although the use of gilding continued on his silver and copper, inscribed exclusively in Ge'ez.[20] Armah's relatively common copper shows a marked increase in size and weight over the sixth-century issues. It thus seems likely that the end of the Aksumite coinage was shortly preceded by abandonment of the international gold currency and emphasis on domestic circulation.[21]

Technology and material culture

Most of our information about Aksumite material culture and technology comes from Aksum itself. In the account which follows, use will, wherever possible, be made of data from other sites, although the generally incomplete publication of this material presents substantial difficulties. At the same time, an attempt will be made to set Aksumite culture in its chronological context, drawing comparisons with its predecessors as well as with subsequent developments. There are also infrequent relevant references in written documents.

The pottery used by the Aksumites may conveniently be discussed under two heads: that which was produced locally and that which was imported from overseas.[22] The first category is very much the larger, representing effectively the whole of pottery assemblages excavated at Aksum from contexts dating before the fourth century AD, while in later contexts the proportion of locally produced wares is around 99 per cent.[23] All locally produced pottery (fig. 29) seems to have been made without use of a potter's wheel; although surfaces were often finely burnished, true glazes appear to have been unknown, except on imports.[24] Firing was at comparatively low temperatures, probably in an open fire rather than a constructed kiln. Indeed, Aksumite ceramic technology seems to have been remarkably similar in its technological aspects (and, from later Aksumite times, in its typological features also) to that traditionally practised into recent times.[25]

A potential distortion of the apparent sequence results from the fact that excavated early Aksumite assemblages come predominantly from funerary contexts, whereas domestic occupation is known mainly for later periods. This division does not permit us confidently to conclude that specifically funerary pottery differed significantly from that which was in use for domestic purposes.

Bearing in mind this last point, we may observe that earlier Aksumite pottery, until around the late fourth century, was predominantly of a red fabric, often rather sandy, but with carefully smoothed surfaces.[26] A wide variety of bowls, flasks and beakers was produced. Decoration was often based on surface relief, motifs including parallel fluting and broad bands of shallow impressions from a stamp 'walked' with a rocking motion over the surface of the soft clay. The insides of bowls often bore elaborate moulded geometrical designs. Rims were occasionally elaborated with applied figures of birds, etc. Jars surmounted with naturalistic representations of human heads are characteristic. Handles were almost always tiny, sometimes applied strips of clay in a crescent or cross-shape,[27] or a loop through which a thread or thong could be passed; in many cases it seems unlikely that these could have been used to support the weight of the vessel when full.

Two unusual vessel forms of this period are those conventionally designated foot-washers and stoves. The former are bowls, generally 45-50 cm (17-20 ins) in diameter, with a platform in the centre supported on two or more pedestals. The upper surface of the platform was often deeply scored. The conventional designation offers one plausible interpretation of these objects, but is not based on any firm evidence: it could be argued that some are rather too small to have been used conveniently for this purpose. The stoves are massive rectangular objects produced from slabs of clay with buttress-like reinforcements and, sometimes, crenellated upper edges. While they could have been used to support a cooking pot over a charcoal fire, it is somewhat surprising that few examples show signs of exposure to intense heat.

In later times there is a preponderance of grey or black wares.[28] These often have a more gritty temper and lack the sandy texture of some of the red wares. Vessels tend to be larger and more crudely made: this may be due to the fact that most assemblages of this period come from domestic rather than funerary contexts. There are large water pots and storage vessels, often with massive load-bearing handles. Occasional flat

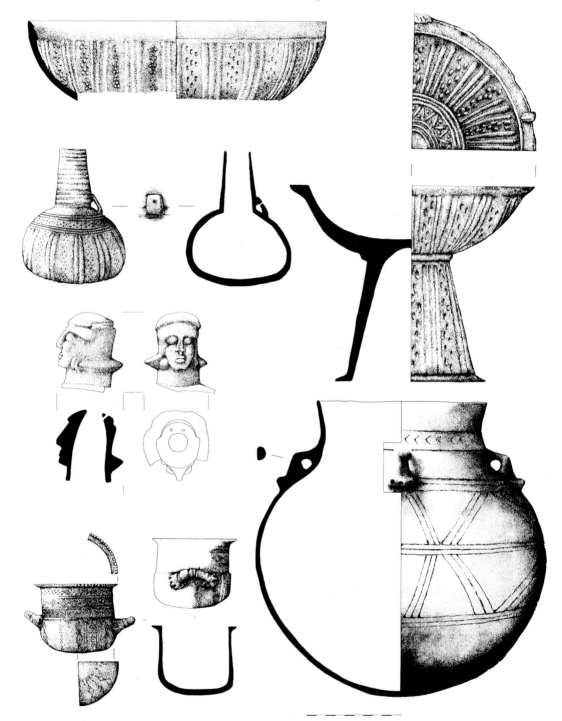

Fig. 29 Aksumite pottery. The vessel at the bottom right is from a domestic occupation site of about the sixth century AD; the other specimens are from the Tomb of the Brick Arches. The scale is in centimetres.

platters, resembling the *metad* used for cooking *enjera*, make their appearance. The small beakers and narrow-necked jars of earlier assemblages are now rare. The break between red and grey/black wares does not appear to have been a sudden one. At the time when grey/black wares were predominant, some of the need for fine wares seems to have been met by imports. Some imported wares, notably bowls of African red–slip ware,[29] were locally imitated. Clay was also used for the production of small items such as stamps, lamps and boards with rows of hollows used for playing the game known as *gebeta*.[30]

Although most Aksumite pottery was probably produced close to its place of intended use, the general features and sequence outlined above seem to have been mirrored in other parts of the Aksumite realm. The assemblages most intensively studied come from Aksum and from Matara. Ceramics from other Aksumite sites have been examined in less detail. Studies of pottery fabrics are being undertaken in the expectation that precise clay sources may be identified.

There is evidence from Aksumite sites for the working of iron, copper and its alloys, silver and gold (fig. 30). The sources of the ores or metals that were utilised have not been precisely ascertained, although there is good reason to believe that all were available within Aksumite territory. The record in the *Periplus*[31] that iron was imported to Adulis by sea in the first century AD may be seen as a reflection more on the available technology than on the absence of raw materials. We shall be in a much better position to comment on Aksumite metallurgical technology and to differentiate between imports and local manufactures when workshops have been identified and excavated.

Iron was mainly used for a variety of tools and weapons, including knives, billhooks, sickles, saws, spearpoints and hammers, as well as a variety of nails and tacks.[32] Where appropriate, tools and weapons were hafted by means of a tang rather than a socket. There is evidence that iron tools, examples of which have not yet been identified, were used at least for the final stages of carving both ivory and stone.

A very wide range of artefacts was made of copper alloys. Most were decorative in at least part of their function, and some incorporated other materials such as glass inlay, ivory, or plating with more precious metals. Fittings included tacks, hinges, clasps and handles as well as decorative strips and plaques. (Coins and personal accoutrements are discussed separately.) Both casting and hammering were employed. Castings included items of very large size: although none has survived, there are documentary references to large statues of bronze (and other metals).[33] A carved stone has been described from Aksum which appears to have been the pedestal for a metal statue of between two and three times life-size. Castings which have survived include figurines and a figurative metal plaque which may have been intended to adorn the top of a stela.[34]

Coins were struck in gold, silver and bronze. Die varieties suggest that minting took place on a substantial scale. It is possible that more than one mint was operated: no dies or minting-places have been discovered. Technologically, the process of gilding selected areas of the designs on bronze and silver coins is of considerable interest.

Silver has been recovered only rarely, in the form of pins, rings and decoration on base metal items such as a copper-alloy buckle. Despite frequent documentary mention, gold is likewise only rare in archaeological contexts, being limited to beads, gilded

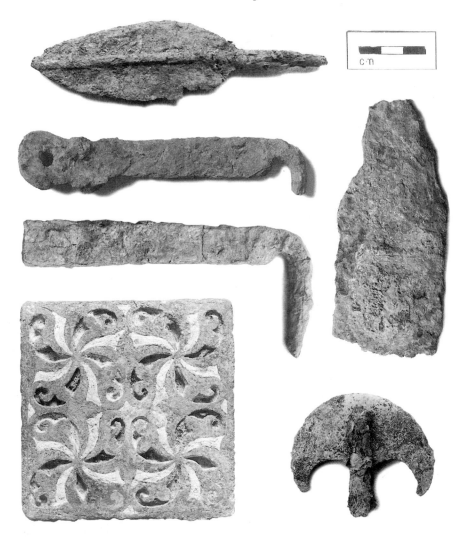

Fig. 30 Aksumite metalwork from the Tomb of the Brick Arches at Aksum.
The four upper items are of iron; the plaque at bottom left is of copper alloy
over an iron base, the floral design being of coloured glass paste; the projectile
point at bottom right has a copper alloy blade set in an iron shank.

bronzework, and fragments of foil and thread used either in embroidery or woven as cloth of gold.[35] To some extent this scarcity may be a result of gold's inherent value and the assiduity with which it has been sought by tomb-robbers, but it may be that documentary references to its large-scale use are exaggerated. Gold was almost certainly an important export commodity, both as raw material and, from the third century onwards, as coinage.

The most impressive use of stone in ancient Aksum was as a building material or for monuments, discussed below. It was, however, also employed in a range of smaller artefacts, most commonly grinders and pounders used in food preparation and for other purposes. Small stone carvings include lamps, beads and seals (fig. 31).[36] Breccia was lathe-turned to produce highly decorative bowls.[37] A variety of stones was also flaked into tools; there are clear stratigraphic indicators that this practice continued into Aksumite times.[38] The most extensive use of such tools seems to have been concentrated in an area on the west side of Aksum where there are huge numbers of very standardised steep scrapers; although detailed use-wear studies have not yet been completed it has been demonstrated that these so-called Gudit scrapers were used for some specialised industrial purpose such as wood-working or the preliminary working of ivory.[39]

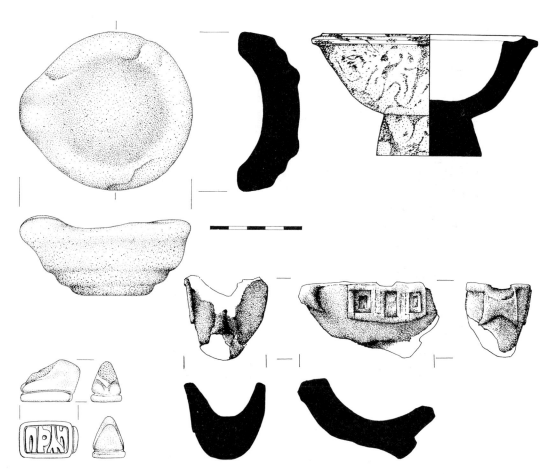

Fig. 31 Carved stone artefacts from fifth/sixth-century contexts at Aksum.
Above left: lamp. Above right: bowl turned from breccia (after Munro–Hay 1989a). Below left: stamp seal. Below right: lamp in architectural style. The scale is in centimetres.

Although there are several documentary references to ivory as an important Aksumite export,[40] it is only recently that physical evidence for its working has been found on sites of this period in Ethiopia/Eritrea. It is now apparent, mainly from discoveries in the third-century Tomb of the Brick Arches at Aksum, that ivory was not merely collected for export, it was also worked to a very high standard of artistry and technological competence.[41] Ivory artefacts (figs 32, 33) include lathe-turned plaques decorated with concentric rings, which probably originally adorned a wooden box or chest, an exquisitely carved cylindrical box and a tiny female figurine with long straight hair. Most remarkable of all is a pair of ivory panels found close together, each measuring some 490 x 160 mm (19 x 6 ins), which must have come from exceptionally large tusks. They are carved with elaborate designs of vines and human-headed animals, the African physiognomy[42] of which is strongly indicative of local manufacture (pl. 4). The two panels are approximate mirror images of one another and the placement of the animals suggests that they were set with their points uppermost. This positioning, the holes for fixing, the carefully-cut joints and the presence of other ivory fragments including rectangular-sectioned slats all suggest that these objects are best interpreted as having adorned the back of an elaborate chair or throne.[43]

Glass was available to the Aksumites in a number of forms. It was formerly believed that all glass found on Aksumite sites was imported, but this no longer appears to have been so. There is increasing evidence for local working; but whether this involved primary manufacture or merely the reprocessing of materials originally imported is not yet clear. Many imports consisted of glass vessels of high but (in Mediterranean terms) not the highest quality. Some were extremely fragile: transport from Adulis up the escarpment and across the plateau must have added greatly to their eventual value and one must imagine that there were numerous breakages in transit. Vessels were sometimes imported as sets, as is shown by the six matching beakers from third-century Alexandria found in a tomb at Aksum's Gudit Stelae Field.[44] (This same discovery, incidentally, shows that ownership of fine imported glass was not restricted to the highest echelons of Aksumite society.)

Glass was used for inlaid decoration, both as trimmed fragments (presumably recycling of broken vessels) and as paste.[45] The parent objects in which the inlay was set were doubtless made of several different materials, but it is only the metal examples that have survived.[46]

Other glass artefacts include bangles, labrets, ear-studs and numerous beads. These are discussed below with other articles of personal adornment. Discoveries in the Tomb of the Brick Arches, however, suggest that beads were regarded as a valuable commodity in their own right and were hoarded as such.

The commonest use of wood was in building construction, discussed below. Only rarely has it survived in the archaeological record. Iron nails and bronze fittings, some retaining in their corrosion traces of the wood to which they were attached, provide some indication of the numerous wooden objects which have not survived.[47] These must have included substantial boxes or chests, to judge from the size of the inlaid metal plaques with which they were decorated.

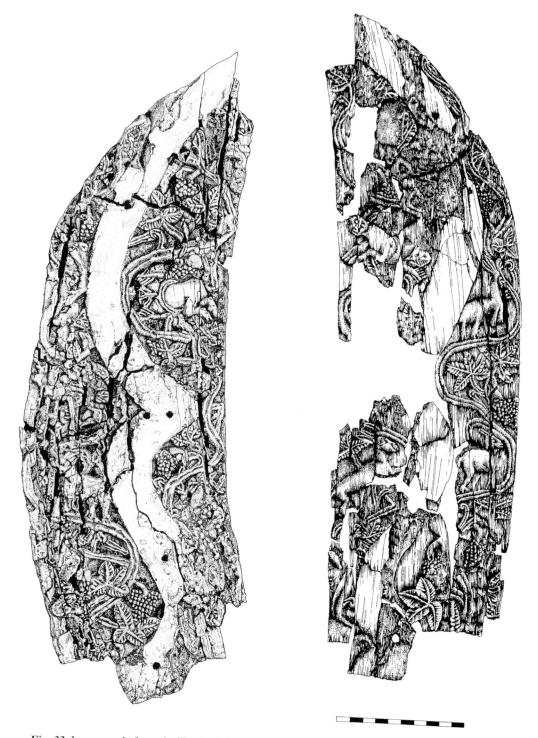

Fig. 32 Ivory panels from the Tomb of the Brick Arches at Aksum. The scale is in centimetres.

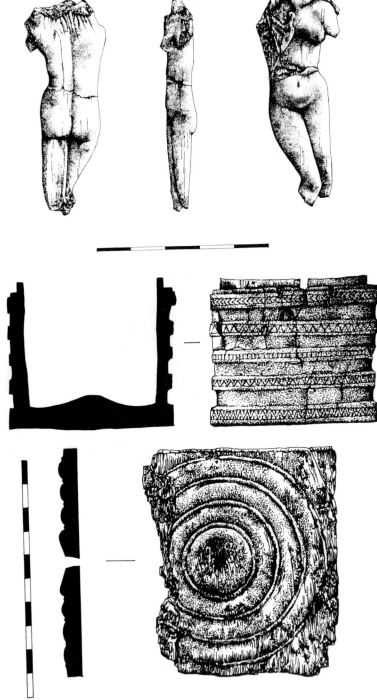

Fig. 33 Ivory artefacts from the Tomb of the Brick Arches at Aksum.
The scales are in centimetres.

Evidence for textiles in ancient Aksum is largely indirect. Cotton seeds have been recovered from deposits dating to the sixth century. Spindle whorls ground from sherds are additional testimony for the processing of thread.[48] Loom weights have also been recovered.[49] Tiny fragments of gold thread from the Mausoleum may have been preserved from embroidery or from weaving as cloth of gold.

The fact that metal and other imperishable items of personal adornment are virtually all that have survived ensures that we have only a very incomplete picture of the appearance of Aksumite people. Graphic representations are few: royal portraits on coins, human-headed pottery jars, rare figurines and engravings in bronze.[50] The evidence noted above for the local production of cotton cloth may be compared with the account in the *Periplus of the Erythraean Sea* that luxury textiles, including manufactured clothing, were imported through Adulis, at least in early Aksumite times.[51] The coinage portraits seem to represent some form of draped cloth apparel, but there is no way of knowing from what this was made, or even whether it presents an accurate picture of what Aksumite people actually wore and, if so, on what occasions. The regalia represented on the coins has been discussed on pp. 51-2, above.

Items of personal adornment which have been preserved include metal rings, bangles, buckles and hairpins. Fine bronze instruments resemble those which have been used in more recent times for the application of antimony and other cosmetics.[52] There is evidence that extract of civet may have been processed as perfume.[53] Bangles and beads occurred also in glass and, more rarely, stone which was apparently chosen for its fine texture and decorative quality: some may have been imported. Perforated clay cones and crosses, often found together in considerable numbers, may have been worn by individuals unable to afford more costly adornment.[54]

No account of Aksumite material culture would be complete wthout consideration of what has not survived. Despite the advances made by recent archaeological studies, there is no doubt that our current picture is very inadequate. It is, for example, recorded that in the seventh century the paintings in the Cathedral excited the admiration of visitors from Arabia,[55] yet no trace of them or of any other Ethiopian paintings from the first millennium AD has survived.[56] There is documentary mention of metal statues but the only trace that has survived is a single stone base. It would be reasonable to assume that vellum was used in scrolls and, perhaps, books; but the oldest extant examples are provisionally dated to the tenth or eleventh century.[57] Literacy, in both Greek and Ethiopic, is indicated in foreign documentary sources, on stone inscriptions and on coins, so it may be fairly supposed that writing was also executed on more perishable materials. Tradition attributes invention of the unique Ethiopian musical notation to a priest, Yared, in the sixth century;[58] but archaeology so far tells us nothing about the whole subject of Aksumite music.

Architecture

This section will begin with accounts of those buildings that appear to have been occupied by the Aksumite élite, whether as residences or for other purposes. The architecture of funerary and other monuments is discussed elsewhere.[59] Most of our knowledge of these buildings comes from Aksum itself: these examples will be described first, followed by comparative observations from other Aksumite sites.

Three large élite structures located in the south-western part of Aksum have been known since early this century, when they were investigated and described by the Deutsche Aksum-Expedition.[60] These structures, Enda Mikael, Enda Semon and Ta'akha Maryam, were partly obscured beneath recent buildings and had been much affected by stone robbing. Enough remained, however, to enable the German team to ascertain much of the original plans, although detailed research was not directed at investigating chronological matters or the purposes to which the buildings and their constituent parts had originally been put. It will not be easy for future researchers to remedy these shortcomings, since robbing and overbuilding have continued on a more intensive scale and, in the case of Ta'akha Maryam, much of the site was destroyed during the Italian occupation when a main road was realigned so as to pass straight through its central area. The difficulty of conducting further excavation in this western part of Aksum town was demonstrated in 1973-74 when it was only possible to open small test-trenches in roadside areas to investigate buildings which may have been part of the complexes previously recorded.[61]

A much better preserved example of a similar, if somewhat smaller, structure was excavated at Dungur, further to the west and outside the modern built-up area in the 1960s.[62] A detailed plan was recorded and the building, excavated in its entirety, may still be seen although marred by some insensitive restoration. It is tragic that the detailed results of this work have never been published. Traces of another building of this type have recently been located in a comparable peripheral position on the northern side of Aksum.[63] Extant fragments and reports of chance discoveries suggest that more structures of this type wait to be revealed.

Ta'akha Maryam (fig. 34) comprised a building complex extending over an area some 120 x 80 m (390 x 260 ft) in extent. In the centre stood a square building with tower-like projections at each corner, its angles made of massive, finely dressed granite blocks.[64] The intervening walls were of typical Aksumite style, recessed at intervals from their straight alignment and stepped back (rebated) with increased height, built of smaller undressed stones set in a timber framework. There was a basement area with pillared supports for the main floors; traces of internal stairs show that this central building had more than one principal storey. The reconstruction published by the Deutsche Aksum-Expedition,[65] however, almost certainly exaggerates its original height. It was approached by grand monumental stairs on the north and south sides. Around this central building, 24 m (80 ft) square, extended a series of courtyards, some with porticos of stone columns standing on elaborate stepped bases. The whole complex was surrounded by massive walls incorporating towers and ranges of rooms. It had two principal entrances, each approached by a broad staircase of finely dressed stone slabs.

At Enda Mikael and Enda Semon only the central buildings were investigated.[66] They measured 28 and 34 m (90 and 110 ft) square respectively, the former being somewhat better preserved than either of the others.

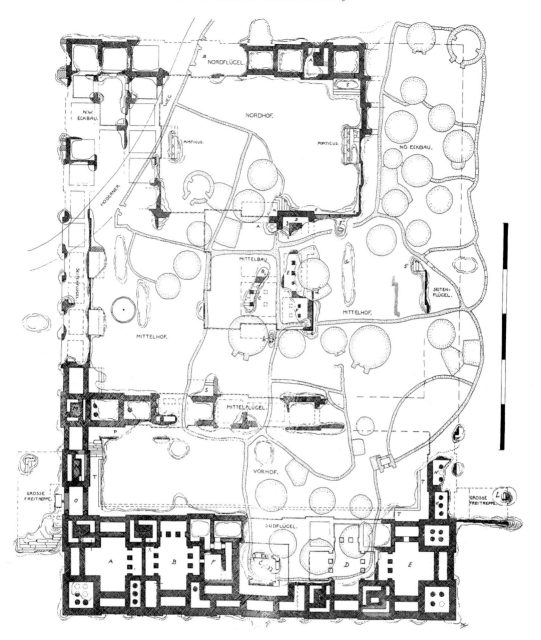

Fig. 34 Aksum: plan of Ta'akha Maryam, as revealed by the Deutsche
Aksum-Expedition (after Littmann *et al.* 1913).

Although precision and certainty are impossible, the datable features recorded by the
Deutsche Aksum-Expedition would support a date for the Ta'akha Maryam complex in
the fourth or fifth centuries AD. A similar date has been proposed for Enda Semon, with

evidence that the original building had fallen into decay by the sixth century.[67]

Dungur presents interesting contrasts. The overall plan resembles that of the structures described above. The central building seems to have been similar both in size (18 m or 60 ft square) and in layout, but the surrounding wings were smaller and closer, so that the complex measured only 55 x 52 m (180 x 170 ft) overall. The structure as it now survives shows much less use of timber than was observed at Ta'akha Maryam. If and when a detailed report is published, it may be possible to learn more about the function of the Dungur complex and its constituent parts, as well as its chronology. Such information as is available suggests that the coins recovered during the excavations were of types that are now dated to the sixth century. If this date is confirmed, Dungur would be shown to be later than Ta'akha Maryam or Enda Semon.

At Matara, an edifice broadly similar to that at Dungur is dated to the sixth or seventh century.[68] It is smaller than those at Aksum, with a central building 18 m (60 ft) square set in a single courtyard surrounded by a simple range of rooms, the whole complex measuring 61 x 50 m (200 x 160 ft). Less use was also made of massive dressed blocks. Investigations at other Aksumite sites have not been sufficiently intensive to ascertain whether similar buildings were present.[69]

Information about the buildings used by lower levels of the socio-economic hierarchy is less plentiful. The most intensive excavations have been those directed by Francis Anfray at Matara.[70] Although the final report has not yet been published, a reasonably clear picture is available. Buildings were of roughly dressed or undressed stone, with rooms rarely exceeding 12 sq. m (125 sq. ft) in size. Two or three such rooms seem to have formed a unit. The units were closely set in blocks separated by narrow streets. The layout of these areas showed far less regularity and precision than is apparent at the élite structures described above. A small area of commoner occupation was also excavated by Anfray at Adulis in 1961-62.[71]

At Aksum, two areas of non-élite occupation have recently been excavated on a small scale, respectively inside and outside the main built-up area.[72] Both seem to date around the sixth century. At the former, substantial walling was preserved, built of small roughly dressed blocks, apparently without extensive use of timber or of massive dressed corner-blocks. The excavations were not sufficiently extensive to reveal details of the overall plan. The external area, to the north, preserved a complex of rectangular rooms and courtyards, the whole subject to repeated alterations and modification to the general layout (fig. 35). The general picture, as in the case of the élite architecture, is of greater prosperity at Aksum than at Matara. It seems unlikely that, at either site, settlements of the lowest social strata have yet been investigated.

The use of stelae as grave-markers is discussed elsewhere, in the context of Aksumite funerary customs. Stelae are known in great variety, from unworked stone slabs less than a metre (3 ft) in length to a huge and elaborately carved example at Aksum which originally weighed some 517 tonnes and, had it ever been successfully erected, would have stood about 30 m (97 ft) high. This monument exceeds in bulk, if not in height, the largest ancient Egyptian obelisk still extant and is a strong candidate for consideration as the largest single monolith which humans have ever attempted to erect.[73] Here, we are

Fig. 35 Buildings excavated at Aksum in 1995-96 (scales in 10-cm units).
Above: élite structure to the north of Aksum. Centre: domestic structure to the
north of Aksum. Below: domestic occupation in the main built-up area.

87

concerned with the representations of buildings which they provide, and with the manner in which they were produced, transported and erected.

The second largest stela, long fallen and broken, was taken to Rome in 1937-38,[74] but study of plans prepared by the 1906 Deutsche Aksum-Expedition[75] has allowed its former position to be located. Excavations in 1994 revealed the stone slabs which apparently formed the base and south side of the pit in which the stela had originally been erected.[76] Indications that the stela may have been intentionally destabilised many centuries ago are of particular interest in view of persistent traditions that stelae were cast down by invaders around the tenth century.[77] It appears that the lower levels in this area are essentially undisturbed, so detailed excavation of the site may in future prove exceptionally informative.[78]

Six of the stelae at Aksum are carved in representation of multi-storey buildings.[79] Following fanciful attempts in the nineteenth century to compare them with Indian pagodas,[80] they have been recognised as depicting in solid stone an exaggerated form of the architecture that prevailed at Aksum around the time of their erection in the third to fourth centuries AD. Comparison with surviving buildings of later date, especially churches such as that at Debra Damo,[81] permits recognition of most if not all of the architectural features that are represented.

The stelae depict buildings of up to thirteen storeys. There is, however, no evidence that actual buildings at Aksum ever achieved more than two or, at the most, three storeys. Taller buildings in a related style have, however, been erected in South Arabia.[82]

The principal characteristics of the multi-storeyed stelae (fig. 36) may be summarised as follows. Their cross-sections are either simple rectangles or have central recesses on one, two or four sides resembling those on the ground-plans of known Aksumite buildings. At the foot there is on the front, and in three cases on the back also, a false door whose frame is a faithful representation of a wooden doorway, complete with the projecting ends of square beams passing through the thickness of the wall. In some instances the false door is provided with a representation of a lock or ring-handle. Above some of the false doors is carved a horizontal band marked with evenly spaced vertical dentils: this is a schematised representation of the setting of vertical planks which was sometimes inserted in this position, as may be seen at Debra Damo. The walls themselves show recessed horizontal bands representing wooden beams, above each of which are rows of round bosses which are clearly representations of the projecting ends (colloquially known as 'monkey heads') of beams laid at right angles to the line of the wall in order to bind and strengthen it and also, in some cases, to provide anchoring for internal floors. Upper storeys are marked by rows of windows, their outer frames similar in construction details to those of the doorways, but with internal divisions. The windows of the mezzanine storey are characteristically shorter than the upper ones. On the largest and most elaborate stela (pl. 5), the windows on the uppermost three storeys depict elaborate tracery virtually identical to that preserved in wood at Debra Damo.[83] The rounded top of each stela is demarcated by single or double concavities on its narrower sides, and has one or two recessed areas on the front which appear originally to have housed metal plaques held in place by pegs.[84]

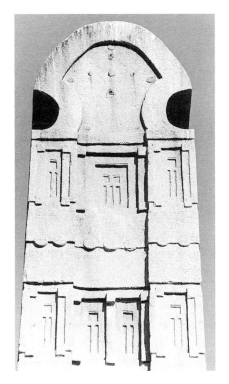

Fig. 36 Stela 3, still standing at Aksum, 20.6 m (67 ft) high.
Left: details of the stela's south face. Above right: general view from the south-east.
Below right: detail of base-plate (scale in 10-cm units).

The dimensions and principal features of the six multi-storeyed stelae are summarised in fig. 37. All were set on gently sloping ground, facing southwards towards the main urban centre. It is noteworthy that the area immediately upslope from each of

Stela number	Storeys	Faces carved	Overall length	Section at ground level	Estimated weight	Notes
6	4	3	15.3m	1.47 x 0.78m	43 tonnes	
5	6	4	15.8m	2.35 x 1.00m	75 tonnes	In stream
4	6	4	18.2m	1.56 x 0.76m	56 tonnes	Enda Yesus
3	10	3	20.6m + *c* 3m	2.65 x 1.18m	160 tonnes	Erect
2	11	4	24.6m	2.32 x 1.26m	170 tonnes	Taken to Rome
1	13	4	*c* 33m	3.84 x 2.35m	520 tonnes	

Fig. 37 Comparison of the six multi-storeyed stelae at Aksum.

the major stelae is unencumbered by earlier features. Ramps could have been constructed here to facilitate erection. The fallen remains of Stela 4 (fig. 38), near the churchyard of Enda Yesus, are particularly informative.[85] It seems that vertical stone slabs were set in the ground as liners to a pit. The stela was raised to a near-vertical position by means of some sort of ramp, and its foot toppled into the pit. This would have been a difficult and dangerous operation; any subsequent adjustment may have been impossible or extremely difficult. It is known from elsewhere at Aksum that the space between the stela foot and the pit lining was filled with tight stone packing to hold the stela in place. Finally, two base-plates were installed, each being recessed to fit closely around the stela in front and back at ground level.

In addition to the multi-storeyed examples, other stelae at Aksum bear decoration of varying complexity. One roughly shaped example bears the representation of an Ionic column surmounted by a house-like structure with a pitched roof. Another has a circular, shield-like design just below the apex.

The only Aksumite buildings of which clay models are extant are small rectangular thatched structures (fig. 39).[86] No indentifiable physical traces of such buildings have been identified in the archaeological record: it is not known whether they were rural or urban buildings or whether they occurred in both milieux. Models from Hawelti, possibly of pre-Aksumite date (c. 200 BC – AD 100), include both round and rectangular examples.[87]

Stone was used as a building material in a variety of ways. It was used undressed or roughly dressed, set in mud mortar, for building walls that were freestanding, or for infilling a wooden framework or set between corner-settings of dressed blocks.[88] Architectural components such as the bases, capitals and shafts of columns, drainage channels and water spouts, architraves, steps and paving were made of dressed stone.[89] Dressed blocks and slabs, some of gigantic size, were used in the construction of tombs and as monuments such as stelae, thrones, inscriptions and statue-bases.

Fig. 38 Stela 4, near Enda Yesus churchyard at Aksum. Above: the base of the stela, showing the inter-relationship of the various components (scale: 50 cm). Below: the front base-plate.

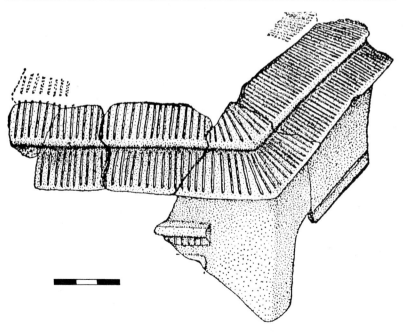

Fig. 39 Clay model from Aksum, representing a thatched house (after Chittick 1974). The scale is in centimetres.

Building stone was obtained from a variety of sources. Small pieces were collected from fields or broken by simple percussion from boulders or outcrops. Larger blocks were extracted from quarries, the principal locations near Aksum being on Gobedra Hill some 4 km (3 miles) west of the modern town.[90] Intended breaks were demarcated by pecked lines, along which were cut series of rectangular sockets (fig. 40). These may still be seen in areas of the quarries where work was abandoned, and also on stelae which were removed to Aksum and erected without the marks being fully obliterated by subsequent dressing. The tools used in these processes have not yet been identified. It is likely that wooden wedges were inserted into the sockets and made to expand by percussion, by the insertion of metal wedges, or by the application of water, thus fracturing the rock. In many instances it seems that the blocks thus extracted from the quarries were transported to their intended usage site without much subsequent preparation. The presence of several unfinished stelae in the area where such monuments were erected,[91] the unfinished state of the Nefas Mawcha capstone,[92] and the way in which blocks were dressed to fit particular configurations at the Tombs of Kaleb and Gabra Masqal[93] all suggest that final shaping and dressing were carried out at the final construction site rather than at the quarries.

Stone constructions either used no mortar at all or were held together with mud. Lime mortar was known in Aksumite times but seems only to have been used in two ways: for setting brickwork and as render for covering the interior walls of the Mausoleum.[94] On the comparatively rare occasions when it was felt necessary to fix stone

Fig. 40 Ancient quarries at Gobedra Hill, west of Aksum.

blocks firmly to each other, metal clamps of various designs were employed. In most instances, as at Nefas Mawcha and Ta'akha Maryam, only the sockets for these clamps remain;[95] but there is one place at the Tomb of the False Door where a ferrous clamp has survived *in situ*.[96]

Brick seems to have been used quite extensively in Aksumite architecture, but for clearly defined purposes. Its presence was noted in a circumscribed area at Ta'akha Maryam as long ago as 1906, but its use there was not precisely ascertained.[97] Further areas of brickwork were discovered during the excavations at Dungur: sadly, their details have never been published and the brickwork itself has been incomprehensibly rearranged during inexpert attempts at restoration so that, again, its original use remains unknown. A further brick-built installation has been found in a low-status area of Matara.[98] It now seems that, contrary to earlier opinion, brickwork was widely used in Aksumite times. However, it is only in élite tombs excavated since the 1970s that well preserved brickwork has been recovered and described (pl. 6). Three tombs are involved. The Tomb of the Brick Arches and the Mausoleum are both described in some detail below: they include respectively three and twelve brick arches in varying states of preservation. Less completely known is the Brick Vaulted Structure located in 1973 and not yet fully investigated.[99] Aksumite bricks generally measure 27 – 28 cm (11 ins) square and 6 – 7 cm (2.5 – 3 ins) in thickness, but are remarkably unstandardised. They appear to have been moulded in reddish brown clay containing impurities, and fired to a low temperature. They were set in a lime cement such as was not normally used in the construction of dry-stone walls.

As noted above, timber was an important component of Aksumite buildings. Large trees seem to have been significantly more plentiful than has been the case subsequently. Doors were, to judge from more recent examples, made from single planks up to a metre (3 ft) wide.[100] Door and window frames were massive wooden constructions. Wood also featured prominently in the construction of walls, especially in those large élite buildings not equipped with massive dressed stone corner blocks. Beams provided a structural framework to which door- and window-frames were attached and which were infilled with stone rubble (fig. 41).[101] Traces of this method of construction were preserved at Enda Semon and a nearby building excavated in the 1970s: both probably date around the fifth century.[102] The same technique is represented on stelae of the third to fourth centuries. It continued in use subsequently, in built churches such as that at Debra Damo (perhaps very late in the first millennium AD) and is represented at rock-cut churches like those at Lalibela.[103] Interestingly, much less wood seems to have been used in buildings at Aksum which are dated to the sixth or seventh centuries, whether these be of élite type as at Dungur, or attributed to lower levels of the hierarchy.

The only roofing method for which there is clear archaeological evidence is thatch, depicted on house models. It was layered, pitched, and presumably applied over a wooden framework. The large élite buildings may also have been roofed in this way, or have had flat earth-covered roofs. Both types have continued in local use into recent times. No trace has been recovered of the use of tiles, slates or other durable roof coverings.

Fig. 41 Aksumite
architecture (after Buxton
and Matthews 1974).
Above: diagram to show
the use of timber. Below:
reconstruction of a room at
Ta'akha Maryam.

Despite the generally poor preservation of ancient buildings other than the most substantial, a reasonably comprehensive picture has emerged of Aksumite buildings and their construction. Not surprisingly, more is known about urban buildings than about rural ones, and least of all about those belonging to the lowest levels of the social hierarchy. Permanence seems to have been a more important consideration for those near the top of the hierarchy, and to have been stressed more in the abodes of the dead than in those of the living.

Burial

A disproportionate amount of our current knowledge about ancient Ethiopia relates to the burials of the dead, particularly those attributable to the élite. This is due not only to the permanence and grandeur of the élite tombs and associated structures, which have ensured their preservation and prominence, but also to the emphases of archaeologists.[104] Only recently has research shown equal concern for the burials of the non-élite members of ancient society, and for illustrating the conditions in which people lived as well as the ways in which they disposed of the dead.

The burial places of the Aksumite élite present at first sight a bewildering variety. As more information becomes available about chronology and the status of the deceased, some patterning is beginning to emerge, although many matters require further clarification.

In pre-Christian times (and probably later) many burials were marked by the standing monoliths now generally known as stelae. The Amharic and Tigrinya term applied to them, *hawelti*, appears to be a loan-word of Cushitic origin which now refers generally to any sort of monument.[105] In some modern Cushitic languages such as Somali, however, it means specifically a funerary monument such as a cairn. There is good evidence that the erection of stelae as grave-markers was a widespread practice over much of north-eastern Africa during the last 5000 – 2000 years BC.[106] This accords with the probability that the word *hawelti* has been borrowed into Ethiopian Semitic languages from a Cushitic source.

It has often been tacitly assumed that the small plain stelae are earlier than the large finely decorated examples.[107] While this view may be partly true, it undoubtedly requires modification to take account of variations in the status of the deceased.

The subject is best introduced with a description of the ancient stelae fields at Aksum itself. Three areas are recognised. Close to what was probably the edge of ancient Aksum, at the south-westernmost foot of Mai Qoho hill, a small group of stelae was recorded by the 1906 Deutsche Aksum-Expedition and some earlier writers.[108] Today, only one stela survives: a roughly dressed example some 6.5 m (20 ft) high which still stands upright, despite its hillslope location, through having been erected in a rock-cut socket. Although no definite relationship can be demonstrated, this stela may have been intended to mark the position of the subterranean tomb known today as the Tomb of Bazen,[109] which lies some 10 m (10 yds) to the south, cut into the soft rock at the foot of the hill.

The Tomb of Bazen was located and cleared by J. Doresse in 1954. Only an exceedingly cursory account of the work has been published,[110] but it appears that the tomb was empty – presumably following ancient robbing – and that no dating evidence was recovered. The tomb is approached by a rock-cut adit, 9.5 m (30 ft) long, with sixteen steps (fig. 42). This opens through a round-topped doorway to a transverse room 7.5 – 8.5 m (24 – 28 ft) below the steeply-sloping surface. A total of four burial *loculi* lead off this room; seven additional *loculi* leading off the adit itself are generally smaller and less regular in shape.

Nearby is a rock-cut rectangular pit with probable burial *loculi* in its sides, some of them unfinished. There are also a number of shaft-tombs and other surface indications which, coupled with the records that further stelae were formerly present, suggest that this burial area may have been quite extensive.[111] There is, however, insufficient evidence to judge how it may relate to the others.

On the northern side of Aksum town, a large stelae field extends for some 700 m (750 yds) along the foot of Beta Giyorghis hill to the west of the Mai Hejja stream.[112] The southernmost area, where the largest and most elaborate tombs and stelae occur, has been most intensively investigated. The earliest archaeological evidence there apparently dates from the first two centuries AD.[113] What had previously been the foot of a rocky hillside was built up into a series of terraces, the whole eventually retained by a massive stone wall which still survives, albeit much altered and almost totally rebuilt.[114] Behind the wall, the now flat ground surface covers a 4 m (13 ft) thickness of stony infill incorporating the remains of earlier platforms and terraces on which stelae had been set.[115] Excavations in 1973-74 revealed traces of several such features, but without sufficient detail to permit the presentation of an overall plan or detailed chronology. The accumulation of deposits was so great that in some areas stelae which remained upright became completely buried.[116] The present flat and open appearance of the south-western part of the area is due to landscaping carried out around 1960, when several houses were demolished to create a so-called 'Stelae Park'.[117]

This large area now preserves the visible remains of some 120 stelae,[118] but their original number will have been much greater. Some, as noted above, are now completely buried; others will doubtless have been removed for reuse.

The extant stelae in this area show great variety, although most are of the same material – a metamorphosed nepheline syenite.[119] They range in height from 1 to 30 m (3 to 98 ft). Some – indeed the majority – are unmodified slabs of stone. Others are partly or completely dressed to a generally rectangular or subrectangular cross-section with flat sides and a rounded or conical apex, devoid of other decoration. A number of these plain stelae retain signs of the wedge-sockets cut during the quarrying process.[120]

There is a tendency for the smaller and plainer stelae to be concentrated in the more northerly parts of the area and for the larger and more elaborate ones to be in the south and west. In particular, the six stelae that are finely carved in representation of multi-storeyed buildings show a steady increase both in size and in elaboration as one passes southwards and westwards.[121] This observation has given rise to the hypothesis that, for this area, the earliest stelae are those in the north and that the burial area was gradually extended southwards and westwards. Albeit plausible, this view cannot be proved

Fig. 42 The burial area at the south-western foot of Mai Qoho hill, Aksum.
Above left: the standing stela. Above right: the Tomb of Bazen, looking up the adit
through the arched entrance to the main chamber (scale in 10-cm units).
Below: burial *loculi* in a rock-cut pit near the Tomb of Bazen.

conclusively through lack of excavation and precise dating evidence. Although the date of its features remains unknown, it may be significant that this area lies virtually adjacent to the one place in the immediate vicinity of Aksum where material has been found apparently dating from the pre-Aksumite period.[122]

The stelae area was used extensively for human burials. In the absence of large-scale excavations designed to illustrate the associations of numerous stelae, it cannot yet be demonstrated whether all stelae were originally erected to mark individual graves.[123] There are also some burials, apparently dating to the general period during which stelae are known to have been erected, which cannot be linked with any particular stela or stelae now extant. Among these are the so-called catacombs, located in 1973-74 in the area some 50 x 45 m (160 x 145 ft) in extent lying to the north-west of the standing storeyed stela (Stela 3).[124] The catacombs, reaching depths up to 9.5 m (30 ft) below the modern ground surface, comprised three apparently independent complexes of tunnels and chambers cut from the soft clayey bedrock, each reached by a vertical shaft which was stone-lined in its upper parts. They have been incompletely investigated but are known to contain artefacts, apparently disturbed by robbers, suggesting a funerary purpose. Their contents may be dated to the fourth to sixth centuries AD, but it is uncertain whether this date relates to the original deposits or to subsequent robbing.

More precise information is available concerning the Tomb of the Brick Arches (figs 43, 44), which is located east of the standing storeyed stela, but does not appear to have been directly associated with any particular stela now surviving.[125] Its date is provisionally estimated as falling around the late third century AD. The tomb is approached by means of an adit with eighteen surviving stone steps. The adit, 12.0 m (39 ft) long by 1.5 m (5 ft) wide, was originally roofed horizontally with rough stone lintels. At the foot of the steps, a horseshoe-shaped brick arch gives access to the tomb, which comprises four rock-cut chambers extending over a total area some 10 x 12 m (33 x 40 ft), their floor being almost 10 m (33 ft) below the modern ground surface. The complex was roughly carved out as a whole, then subdivided by the insertion of stone cross-walls incorporating brick arches built with lime-mortar (pl. 6). Recesses in the walls of the second and third chambers lead to burial *loculi*; the latter pair has been excavated and found to contain stone-built benches, on one of which eleven pottery bowls were still in their original position.

The tomb contained large quantities of archaeological material, generally well preserved, despite having suffered some disturbance in ancient times. Disarticulated human remains probably represented no more than two skeletons. Large numbers of complete and broken pots were mixed with fragmented glass vessels, metalwork and finely carved ivory.[126] A pit in the floor of the first chamber contained a mass of bronze scrap, comprising remains of several artefacts including panels formerly set with coloured glass inlay. Particular interest attaches to fragments of a cast circular plaque, some 35 cm (14 ins) in diameter, depicting a facing human head surrounded by an Ethiopic inscription.[127] It is tempting to suggest that this plaque, which retains holes for fixing, may have been intended to adorn the top of a stela.

The stelae themselves have been discussed in the previous section. The largest (Stela

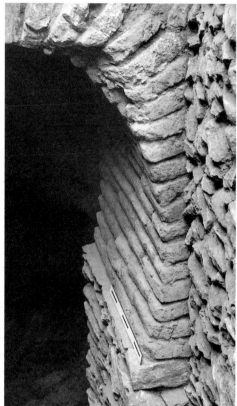

Fig. 43 The Tomb of the Brick Arches at Aksum, excavated 1993-96. Above left: looking up the stepped adit (scale in 10-cm units). Above right: detail of the main brick arch giving entrance to the tomb at the foot of the adit. Below left: *Loculi* with stone-built benches (scales in 10-cm units). Below right: pottery on the floor of the tomb (scale in 5-cm units).

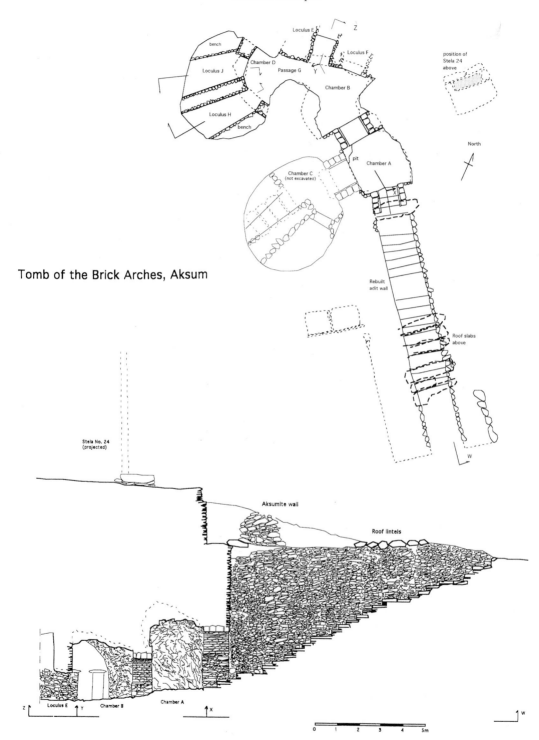

Tomb of the Brick Arches, Aksum

Fig. 44 Plan and section of the Tomb of the Brick Arches at Aksum.

1) was carved on all four sides in representation of a multi-storeyed building. At its foot, both front and back, false doors are carved; that on the former south side, which was hidden from view when the stela fell, retains its finely carved handle. By contrast, the former northern door remained exposed to view, and its handle was found to have been carefully chipped away; that this took place in ancient times may be demonstrated by the patination of the scar. It seems that when the stela fell its symbolism was no longer valid, so the exposed door was – as it were – cancelled by removal of its handle.[128]

When Stela 1 fell, its top hit the north-western corner of the unique megalithic tomb known as Nefas Mawcha.[129] Covering a total area 16 x 23 m (52 x 75 ft), this monument comprised a rectangular central chamber, presumably funerary in purpose, surrounded on three sides by a passage (fig. 45). This bald statement does no justice to the huge size of the monument and of the stones from which it was built, nor to the sophistication of its construction. The passage was roofed with a double series of stone slabs, joined by metal clamps. A similar technique was used for the outer walls. The central chamber was roofed with a colossal capstone, 6.4 x 17.3 m (21 x 56 ft) and up to 1.2 m (4 ft) thick, weighing about 360 tonnes, which rested on top of the passage roof-slabs. The capstone is very carefully dressed on the underside but still uneven on the top and edges, which suggests that some of the working was done *in situ*. Its unfinished state could be due either to a decision to cover the structure with earth rather than finely finish areas which would be hidden, or to the interruption of work on Nefas Mawcha by the collapse of the great stela. In any event, it is clear that Nefas Mawcha was in place before Stela 1 collapsed, and that no attempt was made to repair it subsequently.

Two tombs, clearly associated with the largest stela, were located but not excavated in 1974.[130] That on the east side was investigated in 1993 and found to have a collapsed roof, so subsequent work was concentrated on the westerly tomb, which had been designated the Mausoleum (figs 46, 47). This tomb was entered through a monumental portal carved from a single slab of granite and closely resembling the configuration of the false doors on the stela above. This portal led into a passage 16.7 m (54 ft) long and 1.9 m (6 ft) wide, roofed with dressed granite slabs in which were cut three square apertures connected to stone-lined shafts that originally led to the ground surface. The passage is 2.3 m (7 ft) high, its stone-flagged floor being 5.9 m (19 ft) below the modern surface (pl. 7). At its western end, the passage leads to a brick arch set upon upright slabs of dressed granite. It is likely that a similar arch was originally located immediately inside the entry-portal. Outside the western arch was located a second, broken, megalithic portal nearly identical to the eastern one: the two entrances to the tomb thus appear to have been symmetrical. The outer wall of the Mausoleum extends northwards from the brick arch for almost 1.0 m (3 ft), where another wall abuts it at right angles: the junction between the two walls has, at some unknown date, been disfigured by robbers who dug obliquely through the 1.5-m (5 ft)-thick masonry into the tomb.[131]

On each side of the Mausoleum's central passage are five side chambers, making ten in all, each 6.6 m (21 ft) long and 1.7 m (6 ft) wide. At the entrance to each of these there was originally a brick arch springing from dressed stone slabs: none remains intact although the slabs and substantial remains of the brickwork survive. Like the central

Fig. 45 Aksum: Nefas Mawcha. Above: general view from the south-east, with Stela 1 in the background. Below: wall on the northern side, showing holes for metal clamps (scale in 10-cm units).

Fig. 46 The Mausoleum at Aksum, excavated in 1993-95 (scales in 10-cm units). Above left: western portal. Above right: entrance to a side chamber. Below: walling outside the fallen western portal, showing robber-tunnel.

103

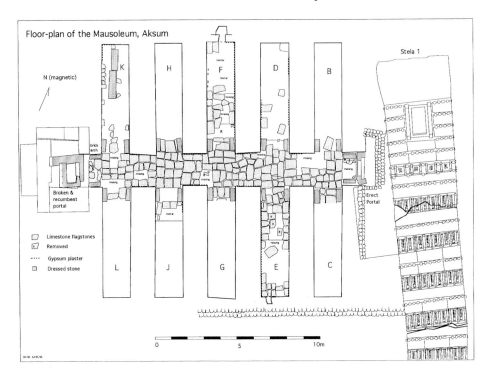

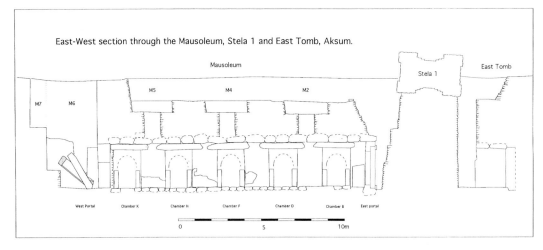

Fig. 47 Plan and section of the Mausoleum at Aksum, relative to the fallen Stela 1 and the largely unexcavated East Tomb.

passage, the side chambers had been largely but not completely cleared in antiquity before being filled with debris and rubbish; some materials apparently dating to the original deposit have, however, been recovered. Examination of the roof slabs in one of the southerly side chambers revealed a single inscribed Ge'ez letter.[132]

The internal walls of the Mausoleum, constructed of rough stones set in mud-mortar, were originally thickly plastered with a coarse, gritty lime-based render: there is no trace of painted or other decoration. This render was also applied to the cracks between the roof slabs and seems to have covered all areas of the Mausoleum's interior except those made of dressed granite, presumably so as to give the appearance of solid stone construction.

There is good evidence that the largest stela was never successfully set up, but that it fell and broke while in process of erection.[133] It seems likely that this catastrophe happened in the second quarter of the fourth century AD, at about the time of the coming of Christianity. It may be conjectured that the simultaneous destruction of Aksum's two greatest pre-Christian monuments in a single event before either was completed may have appeared to observers as an act of God comparable with the legendary collapse of the Tower of Babel. Coinciding as it seems to have done with the advent of Christianity, it may have been a contributory factor hastening that religion's adoption.[134] In any event, the erection of stelae seems thereafter to have been abandoned. Later élite tombs were of distinct but related types, exemplified by the Tomb of the False Door, described below.

Building on the results of previous work, it is now possible to offer a much amplified understanding of the central stelae area. During the first three centuries AD, it was gradually built up in a series of terraces and platforms, in and under which were subterranean tombs, many of them marked by stelae. The finely carved storeyed stelae were probably the latest, dating to around the beginning of the fourth century AD. The largest of all was associated with tombs of great complexity and magnificence. There can be little doubt that these were the burial places of Aksum's élite – presumably royal. They symbolise not only the power, authority and technological expertise of the ancient kingdom, but also demonstrate its capacity for the organisation of manpower. In Yuri Kobishchanov's words:

> the mania for the gigantic reflected the tastes of the Aksumite monarchy and the monuments were the concrete realisation of its ideological purpose, which was to instil awe-inspiring admiration for the greatness and strength of the potentate to whom the monuments were dedicated.[135]

At the western extremity of the main stela area, some 65 m (70 yds) west of the Mausoleum, is the so far unique structure known in the archaeological literature as the Tomb of the False Door.[136] It was discovered in 1972, when erosion in what was then a road revealed the top of a carved stone slab, and was completely excavated under Neville Chittick's direction in the following two years.[137] It was found to have been completely robbed in antiquity, then filled and eventually buried by natural silt and hillwash.

In order to prepare the site, either because it lay beyond the area previously terraced or because it was recognised that the made-up ground provided an inadequate foundation for such a massive construction, a large pit was dug deep into the natural clay. Into this pit a huge stone slab was placed horizontally; it was subsequently covered and can now be seen in only a few places, but it must measure at least 7 x 5 m (23 x 16 ft). On this slab was built the tomb's substructure, comprising an antechamber and inner chamber, both surrounded on three sides by a passage.[138] The inner chambers and the passage were reached by separate stairs; there was originally no intercommunication between them. The roof of these structures was roughly level with the ancient ground surface; above it was erected a squat structure some 12 m (39 ft) square and 2.8 m (9 ft) high, probably flat-roofed (fig. 48). A slab carved with a false door virtually identical to those on the stelae was set vertically in the middle of its south wall directly above the stairs leading into the tomb. In front of this was a paved courtyard, the two stairs each covered with a massive capstone. The large blocks of which the entire structure was built were carefully dressed and fitted only on the surfaces that would have been visible, those comprising the substructure being exceptionally massive.[139]

At some time after its construction, the substructure was entered by robbers. The capstone covering the stair leading into the tomb itself was broken up and removed, but attempts to deal similarly with its neighbour failed and the passage was entered by breaking through the thick stone wall from the antechamber. The inner tomb chamber itself was entered and the single stone sarcophagus which it contained was severely

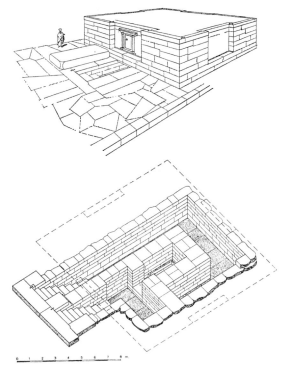

Fig. 48 The Tomb of the False Door at Aksum, excavated in 1973–74. Above left: the entrance. Below left: detail of metal clamp (scale in cm). Right: reconstructions (after Chittick 1974).

mutilated. Although the archaeologists recovered no trace of the original contents, these must have been (or at least believed to be) of great value, to judge from the lengths to which the robbers went in order to gain access.

The thoroughness of the robbing makes it difficult to ascertain the date of the tomb's construction. There is increasing evidence, however, for attributing it to the late fourth or early fifth century AD.[140]

On the western outskirts of Aksum, immediately beside the road leading to Shire and south of the Dungur ruins,[141] is another stelae field, locally named after Gudit, the queen who is said to have sacked Aksum in around the tenth century AD.[142] It was already known by this designation at the time of the German visit in 1906.[143] The Gudit Stelae Field extends over an area some 500 x 200 m (540 x 220 yds), sloping slightly downwards to the south, despite being built up behind a low terrace which has been shown by excavation to have been faced with a stone wall. The continuing cultivation of the site has resulted in much modification but traces remain of several hundred stelae, mostly small and undressed, only about a score of which are still upright.[144] The fallen stelae include a few larger, dressed examples with rectangular cross-sections and rounded tops, otherwise undecorated.

Small-scale excavations were conducted in 1973-74 and again in 1994-96.[145] It appears that at least some of the stelae had been erected to mark graves, but no built or rock-cut tombs have been found analogous to those in other burial grounds at Aksum. The Gudit Stelae Field may be interpreted as a place used for the interment of less prominent or wealthy members of Aksumite society. One tomb, apparently comprising a single pit or chamber, contained an extensive series of grave goods including pottery, ironwork and a fine set of six matching glass goblets, probably of eastern Mediterranean manufacture and of early third-century date.[146] Other graves, comprising simple pits, had far fewer accompaniments and were filled with stones before being marked by a stela. The Gudit Stelae Field may have remained in use for a long time before and/or after the date of the one burial for the age of which we have some indication. Religious belief and practice, status and date are all unknown variables. The fact that a stela base-plate was reused in constructing the adjacent Dungur edifice of probable sixth-century date may suggest that the Gudit Stelae Field had fallen out of use by that time.

Two further monumental tombs are located side by side beneath a shared superstructure about 2 km (1 mile) north of Aksum town. The site, on a saddle between two low hills, offers spectacular views southwards over Aksum to the fertile plains beyond, northwards towards the Mareb valley and what is now Eritrea, and eastwards to the mountains around Adwa. There is evidence for other Aksumite tombs, and for domestic occupation, in the immediate vicinity.[147] The two tombs are basically similar, although differing in detail. Both are approached by a stepped adit, fully roofed, constructed of huge, carefully-dressed granite blocks of irregular shape, each individually worked to fit its desired place. The northern tomb, traditionally attributed to King Kaleb, comprises a longitudinal chamber from which three rooms open eastwards. That to the south, attributed to Gabra Maskal, is more complex and better preserved (fig. 49).[148] There is a similar longitudinal chamber and three rooms to the east,

Fig. 49 The Tomb of Gabra Masqal at Aksum (scales in 10-cm units). Above left: the foot of the stepped adit. Above right: portal leading to the central burial chamber. Below: Looking out from the central burial chamber showing three sarcophagi in the foreground and the stepped adit beyond the portal.

that in the centre retaining three sarcophagi. There are also two rooms extending westwards, on either side of the entrance stair. Three of the five rooms are entered through portals cut in vertical monolithic slabs. That leading to the room with the sarcophagi is particularly fine and well preserved, being carved to represent a wooden construction as were the eastern portal of the Mausoleum and the false doors of the stelae.

The superstructure comprises a central raised courtyard reached from the west by a flight of six steps, 12 m (39 ft) wide. This court links two wings, one erected over and aligned on each of the underground tombs. The two wings are not absolutely identical; and it is possible that they were separate structures subsequently linked by construction of the central raised courtyard.[149]

The two tombs have been open since at least the sixteenth century, when they were described by Alvares,[150] so no contents have survived such as might provide an indication of their age. The plan of Gabra Maskal's tomb shows strong similarity with that of Bazen described above. The German investigations of 1906[151] were limited to clearing of the tombs and ascertaining the original configuration of the superstructure: no datable artefacts were recorded. The only primary (as opposed to circumstantial) evidence for the date of these tombs consists of numerous informal low-relief carvings on their interior walls,[152] including several crosses. These are clearly of Christian type and date, being closely paralleled on Aksumite coins; and there is no reason such as differential patination to suggest that the carvings significantly post-date the construction of the tombs. The superstructure, clearly of an integral design with the tombs, shows ecclesiastical features that are likewise suggestive of a Christian date.[153] None of this evidence is conclusive, but it combines to suggest that the traditional attribution of these tombs to a ruler known to have lived in the early sixth century, and to his successor, is not seriously misleading. A remarkably similar tomb and single superstructure have been unearthed at Matara.[154]

On the edge of the Hatsebo plain west of Aksum are the remains of the ancient structure traditionally known as the Tomb of Menelik.[155] It is not well preserved and there must be some doubt as to whether it was indeed a tomb. Shortly prior to the arrival of the Deutsche Aksum-Expedition in 1906, priests dug into the ruin and found bones, which they removed to the Cathedral.[156]

Around Aksum are various simpler tombs comprising vertical shafts from the base of which extend up to four underground chambers. Examples may be seen near the Tombs of Bazen and Kaleb/Gebra Maskal, and adjacent to the Tomb of the False Door. The tomb on the west side of Aksum traditionally attributed to Etiopis, founder of the Ethiopian nation, may have been of this type. Shaft tombs have also been found on Beta Giyorghis, and at Yeha and Matara.[157]

Some provisional conclusions may now be drawn concerning the variation and sequence of Aksumite burials. Most of the available information relates to the royal and élite members of society. Here, it appears that significant changes took place following the adoption of Christianity and the collapse of the giant stela at broadly the same time. Non-élite burials probably continued, with only minor changes, the pattern of earlier times. Although the data presented in this chapter are derived from Aksum itself, similar burials are recorded from several other sites, notably Matara in Eritrea.[158] One feature recorded at Matara but not, so far, at Aksum is the interment of infants or stillborn babies beneath house floors, often in pots, following a very widespread African custom.[159]

Understanding of ancient Aksumite burial customs is greatly hampered by the fact that only two graves – the Tomb of the Brick Arches and one in the Gudit Stelae Field – have been found where robbing, although indicated, had left much of the original contents intact.[160] Both seem to date from the third century or shortly thereafter. There are signs of rich grave goods also having been present in the Mausoleum, for which a slightly later date is proposed. Although robbing had been total, leaving only the remains of a sarcophagus, the still later Tomb of the False Door gives the appearance of having been designed to accommodate a substantial quantity of grave goods; and the lengths to which the robbers went in order to gain access suggests their belief that these were of considerable value. Such is the evidence for the burial with the dead of large quantities of grave goods. It is incomplete; and the possibility that this practice progressively diminished after the adoption of Christianity can neither be proven or disproven since so few graves have been investigated that are demonstrably Christian. The only graves from which it appears that substantial accompaniments were absent are those attributed to less prosperous sections of the community.

Empty stone sarcophagi have been found in the Tomb of the False Door and the Tomb of Gebra Maskal: these may have been exceptional items as it is hard to imagine that similar sarcophagi have been removed without trace from other tombs. It could be that stone sarcophagi were restricted to the Christian period and were a royal prerogative, perhaps emphasising *Romanitas*.[161]

To what extent should grave goods be regarded as illustrative of artefacts in everyday use by the living? The paucity of detailed published accounts of excavations at occupation sites makes this a difficult question to answer. It cannot be demonstrated that objects buried in tombs were specially made for that purpose; indeed many appear to be utilitarian. Pottery from élite burials often seems to be poorly fired in comparison with that from settlements, and it is possible that it was made to a standard design but selected for burial use either before or after firing. We have little information about the arrangement of artefacts in tombs, although the presence of stone-built benches in two *loculi* at the Tomb of the Brick Arches suggests that care was sometimes taken over this.

The placement of metal scrap in a pit cut into the floor of the Tomb of the Brick Arches is difficult to interpret. Was it hidden during the tomb's construction and not recovered? Did bronze scrap have an enhanced value prior to the start of Aksum's own coinage, as perhaps implied in the *Periplus*?[162] Does the deposit represent objects intended for a funerary purpose and therefore placed in the tomb despite failed manufacture or subsequent damage? If, as suggested above, part of this deposit represents a failed casting of a plaque intended for mounting on top of a stela, this last possibility merits further investigation.

There are few indications of multiple burials or for retainers/sacrifices accompanying the élite deceased. The scattered human bones in the Tomb of the Brick Arches seem to represent not more than two individuals, despite the presence of multiple chambers and *loculi* there. The Mausoleum is an extraordinarily complex structure and its ten near-identical side chambers might suggest multiple interments: on the other hand, particular attention seems to have been paid to the north-westernmost side chamber which had a more massive roof than the others and to which the robbers seem to have taken particular trouble to gain access. Although vast, the Mausoleum is no greater in size or in investment of labour and material than Nefas Mawcha, which seems to have had only a single burial chamber. Only at the Tomb of Gabra Maskal, where three sarcophagi are present in the same chamber, does it seem that several individuals may for some reason have been buried together.

What can we learn from these observations about Aksumite beliefs and practices connected with the disposal of the dead? The regular use of grave-markers clearly shows the desire and intention that the deceased should be remembered. Furthermore, the colossal expenditure of effort on producing tombs and stelae shows that burial was used as a means of demonstrating the resources, power and authority of the ruling élite. Safeguarding the contents of tombs seems to have been a secondary consideration, depending (rarely successfully) on massiveness of construction rather than concealment.

Those élite tombs which are tentatively dated to the period after the adoption of Christianity appear to be less flamboyantly demonstrative of power, but nonetheless to retain many features rooted in the practice of earlier times. It has been argued above that, at least for the élite, use of large stelae as grave-markers was restricted to the pre-Christian period. The larger and more elaborate stelae were provided with base-plates,[163] on which the presence of carved bowls and runnels suggests that the placement of some sort of offering was an ongoing practice after death. The absence of base-plates in the case of smaller and simpler stelae does not, of course, mean that offerings were not made there also.

The Cathedral precinct has been used during the past few centuries for the burial of those with strong ecclesiastical connections. So far, there is no evidence for the presence of any ancient burials in this area. The position elsewhere, as at Yeha, however, suggests that such separation was not invariable. It seems nonetheless to have been general for burial to take place in circumscribed areas, often on the edge of a settlement.

Religion

Religion must have exerted a vital influence over Aksumite civilisation, as it has in all subsequent periods of Ethiopian history. These factors in themselves raise difficulties in interpreting the archaeological and historical evidence. Much foreign interest in Ethiopia during the past millennium and a half has centred on the fact that the place was seen as a bastion of Christianity in an area where traditional African belief-systems and, later, Islam predominated. This undoubtedly explains, in great part, the attention paid to the area by Byzantine interests and by the Portuguese. Much Ethiopian interest in the history of Aksum has derived from its status as the birthplace and holy city of the

Ethiopian Orthodox Church. This emphasis on Aksum's Christian past means that its earlier religion remains much less well understood.

Historical tradition recalls an early phase when serpent worship was practised in the Aksum region.[164] Although now entangled with legends relating both to the Queen of Sheba and to the establishment of the Cathedral of Maryam Tsion, this tradition may preserve a dim memory of a time when local animist beliefs had not yet been fully replaced by the broadly polytheistic religions of South Arabian origin which appear to have prevailed during the centuries immediately preceding the advent of Christianity. The latter religion is generally recalled in the extant traditions as Jewish – a misleading identification, as will be shown below. The fact that the traditions preserve so little detailed memory of the immediately pre-Christian religion/s of northern Ethiopia and Eritrea may be a reflection of the thoroughness with which the eventual conversion took place.

By contrast, traditions concerning the advent of Christianity to Aksum are detailed and explicit. Essentially the same narrative is recorded by Roman and Byzantine ecclesiastical historians:[165] it is uncertain whether the story came to Ethiopian tradition from the latter source or has been preserved independently. In summary, the accounts relate how a young Syrian Christian named Frumentius, captured with his brother on the Red Sea coast of what is now Eritrea, was brought to the court of the Aksumite King, where he gained great influence. The King, being persuaded of the merits of Christianity, dispatched Frumentius to Alexandria with the request that the Patriarch there, Athanasius, should nominate a bishop for Aksum. The Patriarch appointed to this position Frumentius himself, who then returned to Aksum and baptised both the King and the latter's brother or co-ruler. In the Ethiopian sources, Bishop Frumentius is recalled as Abba Salama and the rulers as Abraha and Atsbaha.[166]

The extant sources, written or traditional, preserve little information about subsequent developments until the event recalled as the arrival of 'nine saints' from the eastern Roman Empire. By contrast with Frumentius, the 'Nine Saints' are recalled as having taken Christianity to the countryside, founding churches and monasteries at several locations, including Abba Pantaleon near Aksum, Yeha and Debra Damo, all of which are still regarded as particularly holy establishments.[167] Links with other events support the view that these developments took place in the second half of the fifth century. By the fifth century, Adulis had its own bishop, one Moyses (Moses).[168]

By early in the sixth century, Aksum seems to have been recognised internationally as a thoroughly Christian state. Its King, Kaleb, was addressed as a brother Christian potentate by the Byzantine Emperor Justin who successfully enlisted the latter's support in avenging persecution of their mutual co-religionists in South Arabia. The diplomatic part of this episode is recounted in the writings of the Byzantine historian Procopius; inscriptions in South Arabia provide confirmatory information, while the reign of Kaleb himself is attested at Aksum both by coinage and inscriptions.[169] Kaleb's invasion of South Arabia led to that territory being incorporated within the Aksumite realm for some seven decades. It was ruled by a viceroy who developed considerable autonomy while imposing or encouraging Christianity.[170]

Later traditions relating to the period of Aksum's decline are expressed in terms of conflict with non-Christians, with particular reference to 'Jewish' elements which may indicate that, even by the late first millennium AD, the new religion was by no means ubiquitous in the highlands.[171]

The primary archaeological evidence for these processes is not as plentiful or as comprehensive as one might expect. As noted above, materials attributable to the period 100 BC – AD 250 are rare. Coins and inscriptions provide some indication that the religious beliefs and practices that had been established in earlier times, as at Yeha for example, continued through this period. The coming of Christianity is admirably demonstrated in the coinage which, suddenly and emphatically, halfway through Ezana's reign, replaced the crescent-and-disc symbol of the earlier religion with the Christian cross.[172] On the copper issues which were intended primarily for local use, but not on the internationally circulating gold, the cross became the major reverse type, often accompanied by inscriptions in Greek or, subsequently, Ge'ez, such as TOYTO APECH TH XⲰPA 'may this be pleasing in the countryside'.[173] Study of Ezana's inscriptions permits a broadly similar reconstruction.[174] The earlier ones include religious formulae and invocations which may be paralleled in older Aksumite and South Arabian texts. The Greek version of the bilingual inscriptions is informative, the name of the Sabaean deity Mahram being rendered as Ares, the Greek god of war. In contrast, other inscriptions of Ezana, generally presumed to be later in date, contain an invocation which may be translated 'to the Lord of Heaven'. Some uncertainty must surround the interpretation of this phrase: it probably (but not incontrovertibly) has monotheistic overtones, but these need not be specifically Christian.[175] Is this an indication that these supposedly Christian inscriptions date from a time before the new religion was publicly accepted? Only one of Ezana's inscriptions contains a specific mention of Christ,[176] and none bears the cross symbol.

It is pertinent here to quote brief excerpts from the relevant inscriptions of Ezana,[177] to emphasise the changes that took place:

– Ezana, king of the Aksumites, the Himyarites, Raeidan, the Ethiopians, the Sabaeans, ... king of kings, son of the unconquered God Ares ...
– By the might of the Lord of Heaven who in the sky and on earth holds power over all beings, Ezana, son of Ella Amida, ... king of Aksum, Himyar, Paydan, Saba, Salhin, ..., Beja and Kasu, king of kings ...
– In the faith of God and the power of the Father, Son and Holy Spirit who saved me for the kingdom by the faith of his Son Jesus Christ, who has helped me and will always help me, I, Ezana, king of the Aksumites and Himyarites ...

Subsequently, perhaps from the late fourth century, Christianity is more overtly represented in the archaeological record. Church buildings are discussed separately, below. The cross becomes a principal coinage design, particularly on denominations which circulated within the Aksumite realm itself. Elaborate crosses become part of pottery designs.[178] Cruciform metal pendants of late Aksumite date have been found at both Yeha and Matara.[179]

113

An attempt to pull together evidence relating to Aksumite pre-Christian religion must amalgamate data spread over the 800 – 1000 years from the Yeha period to the early fourth century AD. Where appropriate, the Ethiopian data may be supplemented with others from South Arabia. Although it is thus hoped to produce a comprehensive overview, it must be kept in mind that significant changes may well have taken place during this long period.

The pre-Christian religion was polytheistic, based largely but not exclusively on deification of the sun, moon and stars. Contrary to the practice in Graeco-Roman mythology, followed in western civilisations, the sun was regarded as female, the moon and the planet Venus as male. The crescent and disc symbol is clearly connected with these aspects of the pantheon.[180] In the South Arabian kingdoms there was a clear concept of national gods; divine kingship was not far removed. Ritual purity was important – presumably a widespread concept among Semitic-speaking peoples and one which has been retained in Ethiopian Christianity along with other features common to Islam and Judaism. Sacrifice and offering were widely practised, represented in Ethiopia and Eritrea by the numerous incense burners that have been recovered, and by the elaborate base plates of the Aksumite stelae. Ritual meals are attested, as are rain-making ceremonies linked to the maintenance of irrigation systems.[181]

Whereas in the Roman Empire, Christianity began as a popular religion and was eventually embraced by the Emperor Constantine, in Ethiopia the opposite process is indicated: it was the King (Ezana) in the capital (Aksum) who first adopted the new religion and subsequently sought its expansion. The numismatic evidence, cited above, emphasises the disparity which prevailed in the fourth to fifth centuries (although not necessarily in later times) between the centre and more peripheral regions of the Aksumite state. It was probably not until the late fifth century, with the activities of the 'Nine Saints', that Christianity became widely accepted in the countryside. Monasticism was introduced at this time.

It may be expected that the eventual widespread adoption of Christianity gave rise to a sizeable population of priests and monastics, but there is as yet no trace of this in the archaeological record.[182] Tradition confirms that ecclesiastical rule was separate from that of the state, and that the latter at least nominally derived its right to temporal rule from the former.[183] Strong links are implied by the traditions that Kaleb eventually abdicated the throne and became a monk at the monastery of Abba Pantaleon.[184]

Kingship in ancient Aksum was at least quasi-divine. The belief that the rulers were descended from Solomon probably already prevailed.[185] The kings of Aksum would thus have seen their lineage as collateral with that of Christ. Adoption of Christianity may thus have had political as well as religious overtones, as may the dedication of Aksum's Cathedral to Mary the mother of God.

The present Old Cathedral at Aksum stands on a massive podium, 66 m (215 ft) long, at least 41 m (135 ft) wide and 3.4 m (11 ft) high (fig. 50). Its western end comprises a flight of ten well-preserved stone steps, now 51.7 m (168 ft) in total width. The southern and eastern sides of the podium are near-vertical, recessed and rebated stone walls of typical Aksumite style, with large dressed blocks at the corners.[186] The flat top of the

Fig. 50 The Cathedral of Maryam Tsion at Aksum. Above: seen from the west, showing the steps to the Aksumite podium. Below: the south-east corner of the Aksumite podium on which the Cathedral stands.

podium, 52 x 36 m (170 x 117 ft), is only partly occupied by the present Cathedral which is generally regarded as a seventeenth-century construction replacing a building destroyed by Muslim invaders *c.* 1535. The latter church had been visited shortly before its destruction by a group of Portuguese including Fr. Francisco Alvares who described it as a five-aisled basilica.[187] There is doubt as to the antiquity of that building, and the extent to which it may have been rebuilt, extended or modified since its original construction.

115

The date of the original Maryam Tsion Cathedral at Aksum is firmly placed by Ethiopian tradition in the reign of Ezana (Abraha/Atsbaha), around the middle of the fourth century. Some recent writers have cast doubt on this, suggesting that construction may not have taken place until the reign of Kaleb early in the sixth century.[188] The fact that Christianity was adopted by the kings of Aksum at the earlier of these dates is, however, firmly established; and it seems almost inconceivable either that a major church would not have been built in the capital at that time, or that its site would subsequently have been moved. It is perfectly possible, however, that Kaleb may have enlarged, rebuilt or embellished an earlier structure. He was a renowned builder who, after his conquests in Yemen, is known to have established a great cathedral at Sana'a. Here is a description of the latter building:

> The cathedral was entered ... from the west end up a steep flight of alabaster steps, and the whole building was raised on a podium more than 5 m (16 ft) high. The doors were plated with gold studded with silver. Internally there was first a tripartite nave, nearly 50 m (160 ft) long and 25 m (80 ft) wide, supported on columns of precious wood, decorated with colour and gold and silver studs, then a vaulted transept 12 m (39 ft) wide extended across the church, its arches decorated with mosaic containing trees and shrubs with golden stars, and finally the domed martyrion nearly 20 m (65 ft) in diameter was reached, its walls covered with mosaic in a pattern of gold and silver crosses. At the centre of the dome was an alabaster panel admitting light which dazzled the eyes. The building was paved with coloured marble.[189]

Kaleb, being responsible for the erection of such a magnificent building in a captured territory, may well have arranged for a comparable edifice in his own capital, either through building or embellishment. An inscription of Kaleb, found at Aksum, refers briefly to his having built a church.[190]

Archaeological excavation adjacent to the Old Cathedral at Aksum has the potential to answer these questions, and also to ascertain whether the podium was originally erected to support a Christian church or was an earlier construction taken over for the latter purpose.[191] There are several examples of continuity in sacred sites from pre-Christian times, notably at Yeha and the rock pinnacle at Abba Pantaleon near Aksum. The presence of a reliable water source seems to have been a strong determinant for the location of a sacred site in both Christian and earlier times.

At Matara, three churches have been excavated, including a three-aisled, apsidal-ended basilica some 20 m (65 ft) in overall length, closely surrounded by additional buildings which may have formed part of the same religious complex. To the east, outside the basilica but on the same alignment, a deep baptistery was fed with water directed through a series of interlocking bodies of imported amphorae. The shape of the baptistery, a curved-sided pit approached by steps from two directions, may be paralleled at Yeha and elsewhere, as well as on Christian Nubian sites of somewhat later date. One of the smaller basilicas was built over a crypt.[192]

Fig. 51 Nineteenth-century views of Aksumite churches. Above: at Adulis, under excavation by members of the Napier expedition. Below: at Agula (after Acton 1868).

The somewhat piecemeal excavations that have taken place at Adulis (fig. 51) have also revealed a total of three basilicas, one of them being 38 m (123 ft) long and one having a baptismal tank.[193] At Agula, on the plateau north of Makelle, a similar ruin, now sadly robbed for building stone, has been known for many years (fig. 51). It appears to have been a rectangular structure on a massive plinth.[194] Such plinths were a not uncommon feature of Aksumite ecclesiastical buildings: several examples which appear to be of early date now support more recent churches.[195]

Aksumite churches thus show many features in common. They were rectangular structures, often forming basilicas with three or, exceptionally, five aisles. They varied considerably in size, the largest being at Aksum itself, although the cathedral at Sana'a, built in the reign of Kaleb, was even larger. It is known that, in the seventh century, the Cathedral at Aksum was decorated with paintings, but it is only for the Sana'a building that we have a reasonably detailed description which may in general terms apply to other major Aksumite churches. There is much continuity of site with churches of later periods; repeated rebuilding has generally left little trace of Aksumite churches other than their plinths. The question of ecclesiastical continuity between Aksumite and post-Aksumite Ethiopia is addressed in a later chapter.

Chapter 5

THE AKSUMITE SYSTEM

Town and countryside

Current research indicates that Aksumite Ethiopia and Eritrea operated a flourishing and well integrated system, both politically and economically. The overall impression is one of prosperity, although this undoubtedly reflects the biases of the investigations that have been conducted and the sources on which they are based. The precise area that was subject to Aksumite suzerainty is not easy to ascertain: research has been concentrated in the area extending from Adulis on the Red Sea coast in the north-east to Aksum on the Tigray plateau in the south-west. Away from this core area, the distribution of known sites peters out in northern and north-western Eritrea, in the Shire area of western Tigray and in the regions south of the Takkezze. It is recorded that, in the last-named area, the snowy peaks of the Simien Mountains (which can be seen from Aksum on a clear day) were used by the Aksumite rulers as a place of banishment for undesirables.[1]

The main archaeological study of the Aksumite landscape, incorporating town and country, was conducted by Joseph Michels in 1973-74. Full details are not yet published, but the results[2] clearly demonstrate that the countryside, at least in the area between Aksum and Yeha that was surveyed in detail, was intensively exploited. Areas of the greatest fertility were sought out and settled at least as densely as they are today. Approximately 250 sites were located within an area of 500 sq. km (200 sq. miles). A hierarchy of settlement types bound the countryside to the urban centres. Although Michels' methodology and the basis of his proposed chronology may be queried, his general results provide a vital insight into the workings and inter-relationships in one part of the Aksumite heartland. There is, however, no reason to suppose that these findings may necessarily be applicable in other areas.

Significant differences are in fact apparent between the eastern and western parts of Tigray in the Aksumite period.[3] There are more sites in the east, but they seem generally to be smaller and later in date. Perhaps linked with this chronological distinction is the fact that many eastern sites apparently represent the remains of churches in which monolithic pillars were a frequent feature. In the west, sites tend to be larger, more of them can be attributed to an early period, and stelae are more numerous.

It has been suggested that Aksum's westerly situation may be explained by the need to have access to, and control over, raw materials such as gold and ivory which were of

119

prime importance as exports.[4] The high fertility of the Hatsebo plain and (by local standards) its good water supply doubtless also contributed to the choice of site: then, as now, parts of western Tigray offered greater agricultural productivity than the more easterly regions. Water supplies and, where necessary, irrigation potential seem to have been important factors in determining the location of Aksumite settlements.[5]

It is noteworthy that the actual site of Aksum seems not to have been settled until around the first century AD. Local tradition states that the site on which the Cathedral of Maryam Tsion was built had formerly been a swamp.[6] It is significant in this connection that earlier settlements in the immediate vicinity were located on higher ground. Although there is controversy about the etymology of the name 'Aksum', there is some agreement that the syllable 'ak-' is derived from a Cushitic root signifying water.[7] It is striking how many printed maps of the sixteenth and seventeenth centuries show Aksum ('Cassumo' or variant) adjacent to a lake draining south-westwards to the Takkezze.[8]

Although more is known about the layout of Aksum than any other Aksumite settlement, understanding remains incomplete. The principal constituents – burial areas, cathedral, reservoir, élite structures, domestic/industrial occupation – have been noted above. The extent to which there was an overall formal plan remains unknown, as does the extent to which this changed during the six centuries or so of the site's florescence as a principal metropolis. Continuity in burial areas is indicated, and perhaps in the religious centre also. The known élite structures seem, with one peripheral exception, to be concentrated in the western part of Aksum (cf. fig. 18, above).

The other major sites that are known extend along the route from Aksum to the Red Sea port at Adulis. Aksumite sites away from this route seem mainly to represent isolated buildings or minor settlements. By far the largest, both in extent – some 20 hectares (50 acres) – and in the scale of research to which it has been subjected, is Matara (fig. 52) in southern Eritrea, some 140 km (90 miles) south of Asmara and 55 km (35 miles) north of Adigrat. It appears to have been settled in both the pre-Aksumite and Aksumite periods, from about the fifth century BC until the seventh century AD, with a long hiatus intervening. It is the only place where a substantial urban settlement of middle rank has been excavated and planned. Other features include churches, élite structures, a subterranean tomb of megalithic construction, and an inscribed stela. Although excavations were conducted over several seasons between 1959 and 1965, only preliminary reports have yet been published.[9] Although its buildings were on the whole less grand and ostentatious than those at Aksum, Matara was clearly a place of considerable wealth to judge from the artefacts that have been recovered. Tradition records its forcible conversion to Christianity in the reign of Kaleb.[10] The urban features are principally of late date, possibly subsequent to this event. Imported Mediterranean amphorae, often reused, were numerous: this suggests that Matara was a place where the commodity originally contained in these vessels was used in some quantity, not merely a transit point on the route from Adulis to Aksum. Anfray notes the presence in the countryside around Matara of numerous rural settlements, perhaps farmsteads, of

Fig. 52 Views of Aksumite sites. Above: Aksum from Mai Qoho hill. Below: Matara (after Anfray 1967).

apparent Aksumite date.[11] It is possible that Matara and other eastern sites remained prosperous for some time longer than Aksum, and that their final florescence took place at the time when the capital had been transferred from Aksum to the south-east.

Adulis is located some 50 km (30 miles) south of Massawa, a very short distance from the shore of the Gulf of Zula.[12] Being on the Red Sea coast it was the part of the Aksumite realm most frequently visited and recorded by outsiders. It first became the subject of antiquarian enquiry in the early sixth century, when Cosmas Indicopleustes was asked to copy ancient inscriptions there.[13] Some clearance of ruins was undertaken by the British force advancing on Magdala in 1867-68 (fig. 52).[14] Two separate excavations were carried out in 1907, by R. Sundstrom and R. Paribeni.[15] Lastly, Anfray conducted investigations at Adulis in 1961-62[16]. It is clear from the excavators' accounts and from the report of Sir Laurence Kirwan[17] who visited the site in 1969 that Aksumite coins occur there in exceptionally large numbers, as befits a place which was for centuries the main point of contact between the Aksumite economy and its foreign partners. The buildings that have been located include three basilicas and an area of low- or middle-rank rooms. Numerous fragments of finely carved architectural stonework have been collected: some are in the Museum at Asmara, others (collected by the Napier expedition) in the British Museum.[18]

Some 20 km (12 miles) north of Matara is the Aksumite site at Qohaito, close to the Haddas river which flows down the escarpment to the sea near Adulis. It is provisionally identified with the place called Koloe, mentioned by Claudius Ptolemy as the first staging post on the way from Adulis to Aksum.[19] There are at Qohaito extensive Aksumite ruins, including those of buildings with monolithic columns, which have not yet been investigated in detail. The place's main claim to fame is a dam of finely dressed masonry, 67 m (220 ft) long and over 3 m (10 ft) high.[20]

Located to the east-south-east of Adwa, the site of Hinzat preserves traces of a very extensive Aksumite site. Numerous fallen stelae are present; and tombs have been located there. Pottery suggests that some of the occupation may date to the fourth century AD or thereabouts. No archaeological excavations have been undertaken, nor have the remains been systematically recorded.

These towns have been cited as examples, chosen because research now provides at least some incomplete information about the age and status of the settlements and about the activities that were based there. The selection inevitably reflects the incomplete and inadequate coverage of research, as determined not least by twentieth-century accessibility.[21] Future investigations, especially in outlying areas, may reveal a markedly different picture.

In those areas for which data are available, it seems that the Aksumite countryside was occupied and, presumably, exploited at least as intensively as it is today. The centralised and specialist functions of the state would have required that those concerned with the production of food must have obtained an abundant surplus. This would have been supplemented by the exactions of tribute or the spoils of war which, to judge from the detail with which they were recorded in the royal inscriptions, were seen to have considerable economic importance and prestige.

It is only to be expected that the presence of major and prosperous urban centres like Aksum and Matara would have resulted in a more pronounced hierarchy among the rural sites in their vicinity. In the case of Aksum, this can be demonstrated archaeologically through, among others, the work of Joseph Michels.[22] Wuchate Golo, some 7 km (4 miles) north-west of Aksum may be taken as an example of a rural settlement with substantial stone architecture of the Aksumite period.[23] Lower down the scale, at least in terms of material prosperity, were numerous places now represented in the archaeological record by scatters of pottery and, on occasion, flaked stone artefacts, but no trace of dressed stonework. Without excavation it is not possible to estimate the extent to which buildings at these locations were of rough masonry or of less substantial wood and mud construction, although the near-ubiquity of stone as a building material today in Tigray and highland Eritrea lends support to the former.

Aksumite land tenure is a matter about which we remain wholly ignorant. Such indications as we have about the centralisation of economic activity may perhaps lend support to the view that ultimate rights over land were centrally held, albeit with usufruct exercised by individuals as has been the case in highland Ethiopia throughout the many centuries for which the relevant information is available. In the absence of documentary evidence, however, or of detailed archaeological investigation of such matters as land boundaries and the precise chronology of individual rural sites, such suggestions are little more than speculation. The extent of the territory over which such centralised control may have been exercised is likewise unknown: it could well be that local systems of land tenure were retained, subject to nominal suzerainty by the Aksumite ruler.

The Aksumite polity

The stage has been reached when an attempt can be made to present an overview of the Aksumite system. Like many other polities of the time, it was based on population rather than on territory. It may be significant that the earliest written references are to 'people called Aksumites' rather than to Aksum as a particular place. This may partly reflect the fact that Aksum was, for the first two centuries of its existence, a comparatively small place, far distant from its coastal entrepôt. Such usage did, however, also continue into later times, as evidenced by the coins and the stone inscriptions. From about the fifth century a significant change took place: internally the ruler continued to be termed 'king of the Aksumites'; externally he was increasingly known (usually anonymously) as the 'king of Ethiopia'.

The ruler was, so far as we know, autocratic. There is no mention of any advisory or power-sharing body or individual, other than the hints at co-regality noted above. On the other hand, there does seem to have been a system whereby governors or viceroys exercised authority in certain regions on behalf of the king. Abraha, viceroy over the Aksumite South Arabian territories, is one example, as is the governor of Adulis noted at the same time by Cosmas Indicopleustes.[24] This may have been an extension of the incorporation of tributary territories within the Aksumite empire, under their own

123

rulers. Inscriptions from Aksum support the suggestion that the Saizana addressed by Constantius II, apparently as co-ruler with Ezana, should be viewed in this light.

It is clear from the archaeological materials that there must have been a substantial and prosperous class of executive and/or administrative personnel not only in Aksum but also in the other principal centres of the realm. This class may have been distinct from, or have overlapped with, the large body of craft and technical specialists whose activities are clearly represented in the archaeological record. In some activities, notably those concerned with long-distance transport and with architecture and construction, these specialists must have had charge of large labour forces. It is clear from the archaeological provenances of luxury goods that some of these 'middle-class' personnel enjoyed considerable material prosperity.

It is perhaps almost inevitable, in the absence of archaeological research specifically designed to investigate the lower classes of Aksumite society, that these people – probably a majority of the total population – remain effectively invisible. Studies of the domestic economy and material culture, described above, provide an indication of the everyday tasks in which such commoners were engaged. It is possible that their numbers were significantly enhanced by slaves from conquered neighbouring populations, for whose presence there is considerable documentary evidence.

Other than as slaves, the position of subject peoples in the Aksumite polity can only be inferred from the laudatory royal inscriptions. Interest in the subjugation of neighbouring populations seems to have focused on the prestige which accrued to their conquerors and on the booty which could be extracted from them. One of Ezana's inscriptions may be cited as an example:

> When the Beja revolted, we sent our brothers Saiazana and Adefan to fight them. When they came back, having made them submit, they led them to us with their entire hoard and their animals, 3112 cattle, 6224 sheep and 677 beasts of burden, ... amounting to 4400 people. ... We established them in a part of our territory called Matlia ...[25]

There is no evidence that the territories of conquered peoples were incorporated within the Aksumite state in any formal sense: indeed, the way in which Aksumite rule over parts of South Arabia waxed and waned suggests that this was not the policy adopted. In the reign of Kaleb, a viceroy was appointed to rule in Arabia; he seems to have established his own dynasty with decreasing affiliation to the Aksumite homeland.[26]

After the adoption of Christianity, initially in Aksum and perhaps other major centres, but from the late fifth century in outlying regions also, ecclesiastics probably represented a significant and increasing element of the population. They may have played little role in the economic and administrative affairs of the state, for there is evidence that by the seventh century the spiritual and temporal hierarchies were effectively separated.[27]

There will always have been foreigners present in the Aksumite state. Indeed, the Head of the Ethiopian Church, the *Abuna*, would appear to have been one of their number throughout the period under discussion. The *Periplus of the Erythraean Sea* notes the presence of foreign traders at Adulis in the first century AD.[28] By the early fourth century there is evidence that such persons were resident at Aksum; it has even been hinted that they may have been adherents to Christianity before that religion was adopted by Ezana.[29] There is as yet no archaeological evidence for the presence of these foreigners; and the degree to which they were permanent or temporary residents, assimilated or not, cannot be assessed.

That such a foreign presence was always a slight or isolated element in Aksumite affairs may be inferred by the nature of diplomatic exchanges between the rulers of Aksum and distant potentates. These invariably suggest a respect for Aksumite power and influence, with relatively little knowledge of its actual working. Aksum seems to have been regarded as a distant but potentially influential element in international affairs from the first century AD until the onset of decline from the seventh century onwards.

The decline of Aksum

Previous researchers have paid little attention to the decline of the Aksumite polity, a process which has never attracted interest comparable with that devoted to its formation. The view was formerly held that Aksum gradually declined in prosperity and in the extent of its political influence. These processes were thought to be reflected in the coinage which finally petered out around the ninth century, the *coup de grâce* being administered by a non-Christian queen, Gudit (Judith), recalled in historical tradition as having sacked Aksum in about the tenth century.[30] Recent research permits a substantially different interpretation.

Stuart Munro-Hay argues that the coinage, rather than continuing into the ninth century, had ceased by the second quarter of the seventh.[31] As noted above, the end of the internationally circulating gold coinage seems to have been accompanied by a reform of the locally-used copper. The latter issues continued for a limited period before themselves ceasing, apparently quite suddenly. These final copper issues are among the commonest Aksumite coins: their size and quality of die-cutting and striking show some decline but no serious deterioration. They are often encountered in worn condition, which suggests that their use continued for some time after their issue had ceased.

Archaeological excavation at Aksum has revealed extensive areas of settlement, of both high and middle status, which may be dated to the sixth century.[32] Their abandonment appears to have been sudden. The final copper coins, those of increased size bearing the names of Gersem and Armah, are not as frequently represented on these sites as their overall commonness would lead one to anticipate, suggesting that the abandonment of these sites may shortly have preceded the end of the coinage. These observations are concordant with the tradition that the capital was at some time moved from Aksum to the south-east, to a place or succession of places not yet firmly identified.[33] Perhaps the change of capital coincided with the coinage reform. We shall be in a much better position to understand the processes involved when the successor capitals are identified and investigated.

The functions of church and state were, by this time, effectively separated. There is no indication that, when the capital was moved and Aksum declined into political obscurity, its ecclesiastical eminence was in any way reduced. Both internal and external reasons may be suggested for these changes. In the immediate area of Aksum, it is possible that environmental factors were primarily responsible, linked with over-exploitation by previous generations.[34] If this were the case, the onset must have been comparatively sudden, perhaps suggesting the relevance of climatic factors which would have affected a wider area. If local political changes, such as insurrection in formerly subject provinces, were also responsible, they have as yet no independent attestation.

Further afield, it is noteworthy that the decline of Aksum closely coincided with the initial Islamic expansion which led to Arab control of the Red Sea navigation.[35] As a result of this, Aksum was effectively cut off from its former trade links to the eastern Mediterranean. Amphorae and other imported materials effectively disappear from the Ethiopian archaeological record at this time. Subsequent contact between Christian Ethiopia on the one hand and Alexandria and Jerusalem on the other were overland, via Nubia where three Christian kingdoms had been established early in the sixth century.[36]

The long-term implications of these developments were profound. Christian Ethiopia had been a significant hub of international commerce and a recognised factor in ecclesiastical politics. Henceforth it became isolated and inward-looking, developing its traditions on Aksumite foundations and the foreign influences to which it had previously been exposed. Isolation was not, of course, total: the abunate continued to be filled on the nomination of the Alexandrian patriarch, and an Ethiopian monastic presence was maintained in Jerusalem. These factors nonetheless help to explain the long continuity of tradition, and the assiduity with which memories of ancient Aksum were maintained, as will be explained in the following chapter.

Chapter 6

CHRISTIAN ETHIOPIA AFTER AKSUM

Historical background

The history of the period after the decline of Aksum and prior to the thirteenth century remains exceptionally obscure. Such local writings as have survived from this time are almost exclusively liturgical. Documents which purport to relate to events between the seventh and the thirteenth centuries were nearly all compiled long subsequently and cannot be regarded as authoritative. References in foreign writings to events in Ethiopia are virtually nonexistent. No archaeological excavation has been undertaken in either Ethiopia or Eritrea on sites of this period. The monuments which survive are, almost without exception, churches; and they are extremely difficult to date, despite the traditions which relate to their foundation and development.

It seems that, with the abandonment of Aksum as a capital, the centre of political authority shifted in a general southward and eastward direction. This trend, at least in material prosperity, was already becoming apparent in late Aksumite times. By at least the early twelfth century, the monarchy was held by a dynasty known as Zagwe, centred in the mountainous region around the headwaters of the Takkezze some 250-300 km (150-180 miles) south-east of Aksum.[1] The origin of this dynasty and the manner in which it rose to power remain obscure. Its name is probably derived from that of the Agaw.[2] The Zagwe appear to have come to power shortly after widespread raiding and destruction attributed to a queen Gudit. Their advent seems also to have been accompanied by a hiatus of at least half a century in the provision of a bishop by the Alexandrian patriarch.[3] Although, as argued above, Aksum probably ceased to be a political capital in the seventh century, no great cultural break need be assumed. It is nonetheless possible that the Zagwe period began significantly earlier than has been assumed.

At Aksum, the only firm information about this period is that provided by an Ethiopic inscription carved on one of the throne bases near the foot of Mai Qoho hill. It records the military exploits of one *hatsani* (ruler) Danael, who appears to have protected Aksum from invasion from the south.[4] The inscription is dated on epigraphic and linguistic grounds to about the ninth century.[5] Clearly, by the time the inscription was carved, the throne base no longer fulfilled its original function. The lettering is crude and untidy. It may not be coincidental that the stones on which it is carved are located very close to the original position of the bilingual inscription of King Ezana, the phraseology and terminology of which it partly echoes:

> In the name of the Father and of the Son and of the Holy Spirit, I have written this, *hatsani* Danael ... When the people of Wolqayt devastated the land ... and came to Aksum, I expelled them and killed them and captured 102 foals and 802 cattle.[6]

The *hatsani* Danael inscription reflects a time when Aksum's importance had greatly declined, its monuments were in disarray but its former greatness was remembered.

One further glimmer of information which has survived from this mysterious period is a poorly preserved mural painting of the early eighth century at Qusayr Amra in Jordan.[7] Here, an Ethiopian king is portrayed (and labelled, in both Greek and Arabic) alongside the Byzantine emperor and the king of Persia.

Ecclesiastical developments are somewhat easier to discern, but only in outline. Although there must remain some doubt whether any extant church or monastery (other than the cathedral of Maryam Tsion) was founded during the Aksumite period, numerous establishments survive which date from at least the seventh to thirteenth centuries. The destruction traditionally attributed to the Agaw queen Gudit is independently dated to the tenth century but it does not necessarily follow that this destruction was complete and that no Christian buildings (especially those cut from rock or inaccessibly located) survive from earlier times. Material wealth seems to have been largely in church hands or devoted to ecclesiastical purposes. Links were maintained with Jerusalem, with Christian Nubia and, despite the conquest of Egypt by Muslim Arabs, with the Alexandrian patriarchate. It was through the Ethiopian presence in Jerusalem that Crusader Europe maintained its ill-defined knowledge of a distant Christian kingdom.

The monuments

The extant monuments of this period are almost exclusively ecclesiastical. Even at Lalibela, traditionally recalled as a Zagwe capital, the only structures that have survived are those with a religious significance or purpose.[8] The mobility that was maintained by the ruler and his entourage may mean that few non-ecclesiastical permanent features were constructed. The churches and related (primarily monastic) structures that have survived include a few built examples, but the majority are in caves or entirely or partly rock-cut.[9]

The finest and best recorded of the built structures belonging to this period comprise the church and monastic buildings at Debra Damo in northern Tigray (figs 53, 54). The monastery traces its origin to its foundation in the fifth to sixth century by Aregawi, one

Fig. 53 Debra Damo. Above: the *amba* and the ascent. Below: water tanks and monks' houses.

of the 'Nine Saints', and the building of its church to the reign of Gabra Masqal, successor to Kaleb. It is located on the flat summit of an *amba* which dominates a very extensive tract of plateau country at an altitude approaching 2800 m (9100 ft) above sea level. The mountain top covers an area some 600 m (650 yds) long and between 180 and 300 m (200 and 320 yds) wide, surrounded on all sides by vertical cliffs. The only practicable means of access for people, livestock or goods is near the north–eastern

Fig. 54 The monastery church at Debra Damo. Above left: the exterior from the west.
Above right: wooden window tracery. Below left: wooden ceiling panel, carved with the figure
of a camel. Below right: capital of monolithic column.

extremity where a rope is provided to assist the 17 m (55 ft) ascent. For many centuries
no female creature has been allowed access. The first informative eyewitness description
accessible to outsiders was prepared by the Deutsche Aksum-Expedition in 1906.[10]

In 1948, the monastery's principal church, which had fallen into serious disrepair,
was comprehensively restored under the supervision of Derek Matthews, who has also
published details of the other buildings.[11] There are two churches located, perhaps
symbolically, at the easternmost extremity of the *amba*. The larger one displays many
Aksumite architectural and structural features; it has, indeed, been used as a model to
help interpret earlier archaeological traces. The walls, of overall rectangular plan, show
the repeated recesses and rebates that have been recognised in the excavated remains of
Aksumite structures back to at least the fifth century AD. They have massive carefully-
dressed corner blocks, between which the walls are built of smaller roughly-trimmed
stones set in mud within a framework of wooden beams. The horizontal beams parallel
to the line of the wall, and the domed ends (monkey heads) of those set at right angles,

130

are virtually identical to those represented on the carved stelae at Aksum. The western entrance to the church is by means of a portico, aligned with the outer wall, comprising three monolithic pillars: there is evidence for comparable features, albeit more elaborate and finely finished, in the élite structures at Aksum. The other doorways, like the windows, are of wood with projecting square beam-ends, remarkably similar to those portrayed at Aksum. One window retains wooden tracery virtually identical to that shown in stone on the upper storeys of the largest of the Aksum stelae.

Inside the church several important architectural features are preserved.[12] The roof is supported by square-sectioned monolithic pillars connected by flat lintels. Above them is a good example of the so-called Aksumite frieze: a band of false window apertures constructed entirely of wood. The horizontal wooden ceiling is divided into square coffers, each containing a relief geometric or zoomorphic carving; the species depicted include lions, camels and antelope.

The question of the age of the main Debra Damo church is almost endlessly debatable. Almost certainly, the building has been repeatedly renewed over many centuries. Its inaccessibility and sanctity will have contributed to its escape from destruction or abandonment. There can be no reasonable doubt that the architecture preserves numerous features which may be traced back to an Aksumite ancestry. Whether any of the surviving structure is coeval with the traditional foundation of Debra Damo by Aregawi or the subsequent works under Gebra Maskal cannot be ascertained.[13] Derek Matthews considered that much of the existing structure dated from the eleventh century or thereabouts. This is plausible but cannot be proven; in the present writer's opinion, it may be an underestimate. The paintings attached to the interior walls are all recent.

Close to the main church, at the eastern end of the Debra Damo *amba*, is another, much smaller, church the construction of which has not been studied in great detail. There is also a series of rock-cut tombs and hermitages, some decorated with carvings which appear to be of considerable antiquity. Elsewhere on the flat top of the amba are deep, rectangular, rock-cut open cisterns for rain, being the mountain's sole source of water, and stone-built houses and communal facilities for the monks. The cisterns cannot be dated and the stone buildings are probably of no great antiquity.

Debra Damo has been cited as the best known and most informative of the ancient built churches of northern Ethiopia and Eritrea. There are other examples which would clearly repay comparative study. These include Debra Libanos near Ham in southernmost Eritrea, not far from Debra Damo, a fine example in Asmara (now destroyed) and Imraha Kristos near Lalibela.[14]

Some of the built churches noted above, such as Imraha Kristos, are constructed in caves. There are numerous other instances where a cave has itself been adapted for use as a church, being sometimes walled across its entrance and/or subdivided by the construction of internal walls, or extended by hollowing out supplementary chambers (fig. 55). From this it is a logical progression to the development of the fully rock-cut church, entirely hewn both internally and externally from the solid rock. Such rock-cut churches are widespread in the northern highlands, extending from the vicinity of Addis

Fig. 55 Cave- and rock-cut churches.
Above: interior and exterior of a cave-church
near Shire. Below: Rock-cut church at
Wukro.

Ababa northwards into Eritrea.[15] Because of their very nature it is not surprising that
they have survived in greater numbers than have their built counterparts. Their
inaccessibility and lack of prominence also serve to explain why these churches remained
comparatively unknown to the outside world until quite recently. Although Lalibela was
visited by Francisco Alvares in the early sixteenth century, no further account was
prepared by a foreigner for more than three centuries. The fact that Lalibela, although
representing the pinnacle of achievement of Ethiopian rock-church carving, was not a

wholly unique phenomenon was not widely recognised by outsiders until the mid-twentieth century.

The architectural features of the rock-cut churches vary greatly in complexity and sophistication. Almost without exception, however, the underlying idiom is Aksumite. The chronology remains very imperfectly understood. Gire and Schneider have argued that rock churches near Dengelat and Edaga Hamus between Adigrat and Makelle may date back as far as the fifth century.[16] The Lalibela group as a whole is traditionally attributed to the reign of the eponymous king in the early thirteenth century although, as will be argued below, there are reasons to believe that at least some of the Lalibela churches may be significantly older. Rebuilding and modification have continued up to the present.

The finest rock-cut churches are those at Lalibela (figs 56, 57). It is recalled in tradition that this remote place in the mountains of Wollo was formerly known as Roha, and that it was the capital of the Zagwe dynasty under their King Lalibela, who reigned in the early thirteenth century and after whom it was renamed. Lalibela is remembered as a ruler of great piety who sought to create in his native mountains a symbolic counterpart of Jerusalem. There are twelve individual churches at Lalibela, together with complex and extensive associated works: their attribution to a single reign is based entirely upon historical tradition. In fact, the churches display so much variation in architecture, workmanship and preservation that a much longer period of construction seems highly probable. It has even been suggested that two of the churches may originally have had a different function, being subsequently converted at a time when Lalibela's overall symbolism was being imposed. If this view is accepted, it would presumably mean that the carving of the Lalibela churches extended over a long period – perhaps several centuries – and that the complex took its final form and symbolism during the thirteenth-century reign of King Lalibela.

With one exception, the Lalibela churches fall into two close-knit groups, located on either side of a canalised watercourse known, as part of the site's biblical symbolism, as the Jordan. Underground passages which formerly connected them are now blocked. Several detailed descriptions of the churches are available;[17] here enough detail and illustration will be provided to give an indication of their range and variety, as well as to emphasise the connections between their architectural features and those of ancient Aksum.

The largest and in many ways the most impressive church, part of the northern group, is Medhane Alem (the Saviour of the World). It measures 33.5 x 23.5 m (109 x 76 ft) and is 11 m (36 ft) high, standing in a great vertical-sided pit with its roof roughly level with the adjacent hillside. It was originally surrounded on all four sides by a row of slender rectangular columns.[18] The pitched roof is carved to represent an arcade. The dark interior is divided by massive, plain square columns into a vaulted nave and five flat-roofed aisles, all virtually devoid of decoration. It has been suggested that this church may replicate features of the original cathedral at Aksum.[19]

In an adjacent courtyard stands the rock-cut church of Mary, notable both for its comparatively small size and for the detail and colour of its decoration. Three elaborate

Fig. 56 Exteriors of Lalibela churches. Above: church of Mary. Below: Emmanuel church.

Fig. 57 Interiors of Lalibela churches. Left: Medhane Alem.
Right: Mary, showing 'Aksumite frieze'.

porches lead to the three-aisled interior with columns, arches and ceilings finely carved and painted (pl. 9). It is possible, but cannot be demonstrated, that the painting is contemporary with the carving of the church. The nave is higher than the aisles, having a typical 'Aksumite frieze' of false window-apertures above the arcade. At the east end of the nave is a tall pillar, kept permanently wrapped, on which 'the past and future of the world' are said to be inscribed.

The interconnecting churches of St Michael, Golgotha and the Trinity are carved in the wall of the pit surrounding the church of Mary. Golgotha is decorated with a series of life-size relief carvings which are without parallel in Ethiopian art (fig. 59). It also contains two highly venerated tombs, traditionally recalled as those of Lalibela and of Christ.

The eastern group of churches includes that of Emmanuel, cut into a cliff to which it is joined at the roof but separated on all four sides. Its exterior clearly displays many features derived from Aksumite architecture, with wooden features such as beams and doorways represented in stone, as on the stelae at Aksum. Here, also, are the features now known as the churches of Merkurios (pl. 11) and Gabriel which may have been converted from older structures of different function.

135

The isolated church of St George displays many features not seen elsewhere at Lalibela. It is a cruciform structure, set in a deep pit. It is exceptionally well preserved and tradition regards it as the most recent of the Lalibela churches. It nonetheless retains many Aksumite architectural features, clearly seen in the accompanying illustration (pl. 10).

Ethiopian tradition attributes the carving of the Lalibela churches to external intervention, variously that of angels or of foreign artisans. These claims serve to emphasise the wonder with which the monuments have always been regarded. There can be no doubt, however, that their designs are firmly rooted in the Aksumite tradition, and that stone-working expertise had itself been widespread in earlier times. The view that there is little need to invoke external influence to explain Lalibela is strengthened when we recall that, as noted above, these churches are not strictly unique but represent the finest achievement of a longstanding tradition.

The arts

Architectural decoration, where integral to the structures described, has been noted in the previous section. By far the largest category of non-integral decoration comprises mural painting (cf. pl. 8). This is exceptionally difficult to date, being often applied on cloth stuck to the walls of both built and rock-cut churches. It is particularly susceptible to damage by damp. There is a long tradition of repainting or replacing damaged paintings and internal evidence as to date is exceptionally rare. It is probable that none of the extant examples belongs to the Zagwe period, although it is known that the practice of decorating churches with paintings extends back to Aksumite times.[20]

Tens of thousands of manuscripts have been preserved from past centuries in the custody of churches and monasteries in Ethiopia and Eritrea. A comparatively small number have been removed to museums, libraries and private collections overseas, while others are preserved in local non-ecclesiastical institutions notably the Institute of Ethiopian Studies at Addis Ababa University. Those that remain in ecclesiastical hands constitute a large majority and are at risk through poor storage, careless handling, wholly inadequate protection from fire and flood, and – increasingly – pillage, theft or unauthorised sale. Only a small proportion of the Church-held manuscripts has been recorded, although a programme of microfilming is in progress.[21]

The vicissitudes described above, together with the widespread destruction of ecclesiastical property which took place in the tenth and sixteenth centuries, combine to explain why very few manuscripts have survived which can confidently be attributed to a period before the thirteenth to fourteenth centuries. Known examples of this early period probably number less than a score, and their precise dating is controversial.[22] Like most of their successors, they are largely religious in content; even when they are concerned with historical or economic matters such as grants of land, the context or viewpoint is almost invariably ecclesiastical.[23]

Manuscripts of this early period are comprise bound books of vellum or parchment leaves, written in Ge'ez (fig. 58). The script employed is bold, angular and monumental, as if still reflecting a time when writing was carved in stone as often as penned on pages.

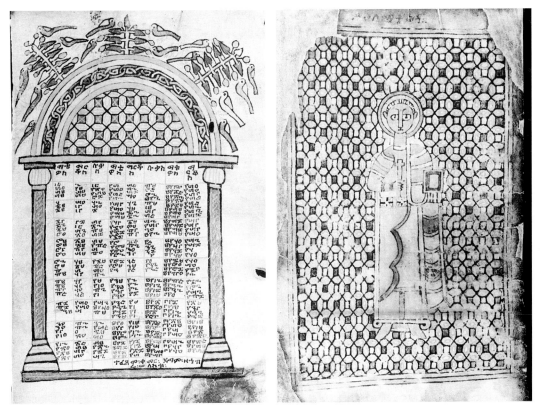

Fig. 58 Fourteenth-century manuscripts on parchment in the museum of the Institute of Ethiopian Studies, Addis Ababa University. Left: Canon table (5023a).
Right: St Matthew (3475b).

The indication of vowel sounds as well as consonants is general but not invariable. Among the oldest extant manuscripts, possibly as early as the tenth century, are three Gospels at the monastery of Abba Garima near Adwa.[24] Cogent arguments have, however, been presented for tracing the Ethiopian manuscript tradition back to about the sixth century. Techniques of book production established in Ethiopia preserve the traditions of the Byzantine world at that time, as do some of the most popular works and their presentation, most notably the canon tables devised by Eusebius of Caesarea in the fourth century.[25] Decorative paintings in these early manuscripts are very rare. The canon tables in the Abba Garima Gospels are contained within elaborate frames in a late classical tradition, and one version contains also a poorly preserved portrait of an evangelist. A clearer view of early Ethiopian figurative painting is provided by a manuscript of the Four Gospels at Debra Maar in Tigray,[26] and by other fragments in the Institute of Ethiopian Studies and the National Museum, Stockholm, all of which may date from the early fourteenth century.[27] Buxton illustrates further examples of this period from a Gospel book at Debra Maryam in Eritrea, arguing that they are inspired by sixth-century Syriac originals.[28] The same is true of the oldest known Ethiopian

137

manuscript to record its own date: the book of the Four Gospels of Abbot Iyasus Moa, produced in 1280-81 for the monastery of Debra Hayq Estifanos, where it is still kept.[29]

As with the manuscripts, virtually all metalwork surviving from this period is ecclesiastical. This situation may change significantly if archaeological excavation is conducted on domestic sites or those of political significance. As with other portable antiquities which have remained in use and have not been incorporated in archaeological contexts, dating is difficult and uncertain.

The principal artefacts relevant to the present discussion are metal crosses. In the Ethiopian context (if we ignore rare examples used as architectural embellishments) these fall into three categories: pectorals which are worn by Christians from all walks of life, hand crosses carried by priests, and long-handled processional crosses which are often extremely elaborate.[30] The first two types are owned by individuals and it is hardly surprising, in the absence of archaeological investigation on appropriate sites, that no examples have survived which may confidently be attributed to the period with which this chapter is concerned. Processional crosses are, however, owned by individual churches and have a much greater likelihood of long-term preservation. Examples are depicted on Aksumite coins of the seventh century.[31] The oldest extant specimens are the so-called 'Lalibela' crosses, tentatively dated to the twelfth and thirteenth centuries (fig. 59). They are carefully made, of flowing symmetrical design, generally significantly longer than they are broad. Their bold simplicity contrasts with the complex elaborations which later came into vogue. A fine example of a 'Lalibela' processional cross in silver is kept at the church of Maryam Dengelat, some 15 km (10 miles) south of Adigrat.[32] Further examples, in copper and iron, are recorded from Lalibela, Debra Libanos in Eritrea, and at Abba Yohani and Abba Salama in Tigray.[33]

The absence of archaeological investigation of sites dating from the period between the decline of Aksum as a political capital and the restoration of the Solomonic dynasty in AD 1270 means that we have effectively no knowledge of the domestic artefacts of this time. From the sixteenth century onwards mural decorations in churches and illustrations in manuscripts provide some insights on everyday life,[34] but this source is not available for earlier periods. One can but extrapolate both from Aksumite archaeology and from knowledge of the last four hundred years.

Continuity

Although the Zagwe period is peripheral to the main theme of this book, a brief outline has been included in order to emphasise the way in which the traditions of ancient Aksum have continued into much more recent periods of the Ethiopian and Eritrean past. Although our knowledge is effectively limited to ecclesiastical monuments and art, there can be little doubt that, when the domestic lifestyles and material culture of post-Aksumite Ethiopia come to be investigated, further evidence will be forthcoming to demonstrate the debt which Ethiopia owes to its Aksumite past (pl. 10). Such a debt is not restricted to material matters, but is also reflected in the historical traditions which provide a context for much of the heritage here described.

Fig. 59 Processional crosses at Lalibela. Above: shown in relief carving in the Golgotha chapel. Below: at the church of St George.

Chapter 7

THE MEANING OF
TRADITION

A recurring theme in this book has been the interplay of sources about the Ethiopian and Eritrean past. The framework which has been presented is primarily archaeological, based on the results of excavations as well as the study of extant monuments and artefacts. This is, however, only part of the story. The modern peoples of this region, like their predecessors, are deeply conscious of their history. Past happenings have been discussed, interpreted and recorded over many centuries, resulting in a complex web of tradition which augments, explains and, in some cases, contradicts the evidence of archaeology. This chapter seeks to improve understanding of this inter-relationship of sources in the context of the last three thousand years in the Ethiopian highlands.

Many Ethiopian historical documents were written long after the period to which they primarily relate. They incorporate material which may have been transmitted orally from earlier times, preserved in older documents no longer extant, or compiled at the time by way of reconstruction in the light of contemporary circumstances or to meet needs currently perceived. They should thus be interpreted in terms both of their sources of information and of the conditions under which they were compiled.

An excellent example of these factors is presented by the *Kebra Negast*, 'the Book of the Glory of Kings', which presents an account of the early history of Ethiopia from the time of the Queen of Sheba to the rise of the Zagwe dynasty.[1] Although composition of the *Kebra Negast* in its current form appears to date from the early decades of the Solomonic dynasty's restoration at the end of the thirteenth century, there is internal evidence which suggests that primary sources dating back to the sixth century are incorporated.[2] As it survives today, the book is in essence a confirmation of the rights of the Solomonic dynasty, which is hardly surprising in view of the date and circumstances of its compilation. This does not of course mean that the whole work should be written off as thirteenth-century political propaganda, although the historical information which it contains must be considered in that light.

In view of the foregoing, it is less surprising than might at first sight appear that traditional sources which, in their present form, do not predate the thirteenth century, seem to contain memories of events which took place over a thousand years earlier. For example, there is recollection (confirmed by archaeology) that Aksum was established in a place previously uninhabited. There are memories of serpent-worship which, as argued above, may reflect a dim memory of belief systems which prevailed in pre-Christian times. Although these sources do not themselves carry implications relating to the ancient connections between Ethiopia/Eritrea and South Arabia, such connections do permit a useful re-evaluation of the place of the Queen of Sheba in Ethiopian tradition.

The traditional Ethiopian king-lists, although differing in detail, conform in tracing the rulers of Aksum back to Menelik I, the son of King Solomon and the Queen of Sheba. The *Kebra Negast* includes a detailed account of Makeda (The Queen of Sheba)'s journey to Jerusalem, her impregnation by Solomon and subsequent return to Ethiopia where she gave birth to Menelik. The latter, having grown up, travelled to the court of his father, by whom he was acknowledged. He subsequently returned to Ethiopia, bringing with him the Ark of the Covenant and accompanied by the first-born son of each of the principal families of Israel. It is instructive to examine this tradition in the historical context of its transmission and the circumstances under which it was committed to writing.

This account has two principal achievements. It provides a context and explanation for the belief, still implicitly held by the Ethiopian Orthodox Church, that the Ark of the Covenant has long been at Aksum, symbolising Christian Ethiopia's view of itself as a direct successor to Israel as a nation chosen by God. It also directly links the Aksumite royal dynasty (and, by implication, the post-Zagwe Solomonic dynasty) with the remote past and with this manifestation of divine favour. The *Kebra Negast* appears to have been first written, in essentially its present form, around the time when the post-Zagwe rulers were establishing their Solomonic credentials and their right to rule.[3] In these circumstances, it is only to be expected that emphasis should be given to traditions which would consolidate the new rulers' position. In so doing, it seems coincidentally to have perpetuated traditions whose origins lay at least as far back as the sixth century.

The antiquity of these traditions is confirmed by the numerous variations that have become incorporated in related and derivative sources, both oral and written. Among their most recent manifestations are a book entitled *Ethiopian Civilisation*, widely available at Aksum in both Amharic and English, and the 1955 Ethiopian Constitution.[4] Independently, the link between Makeda and Aksum may be traced back at least to the early sixteenth century, when it was recorded by Alvares, and the seventeenth century, when it was related to Ludolf by Gregory.[5]

What are the historical implications of these traditions? The Queen of Sheba features not only in the traditional history of Ethiopia, but in that of Yemen[6] and in that of Israel.[7] This wide distribution of analogous and interlocking traditions may be understood by reference to the close cultural connection noted above between Ethiopia/Eritrea and South Arabia, as well as by reference to the centrality of the Solomonic link in sanctioning the political and ecclesiastical establishments of post-Zagwe Ethiopia.

In this context, it is easy to see how ancient sites at Aksum and elsewhere have become specifically attributed to the Queen of Sheba.[8] Sites on the western side of the modern town seem to be principally involved, although the Mai Shum reservoir has long been known popularly as 'the Queen of Sheba's bath'. To the west, the largest stela in the Gudit Stelae Field is pointed out as marking the Queen of Sheba's grave; and the nearby Dungur building has entered local tradition, notably among the tourist guides, as the Queen of Sheba's palace. It is noteworthy that the sites traditionally identified as the Graves of Menelik I and of Etiopis are in the same general area on the western side of Aksum. Some of these attributions date back at least as far as the visit of the Deutsche Aksum-Expedition in 1906, others must be more recent: Dungur, for example, was not revealed until the 1960s. The development of tradition within the established framework is thus an ongoing process.[9] It is by no means an exclusively Ethiopian practice for historical traditions to postulate links between visible monuments or other features and events which are independently recalled.[10]

There are major inconsistencies between these traditional attributions and the evidence which is currently revealed by archaeology. The chronological problems are particularly acute. The Queen of Sheba is clearly recalled as a contemporary of King Solomon, whose reign must be placed around the tenth century BC. There is no archaeological evidence that the site of Aksum was settled until approximately one thousand years after this date. Dungur appears to have been constructed in about the sixth century AD; and the Gudit Stelae Field was in use during the first half of the first millennium AD. An attribution to the Queen of Sheba is thus contradicted by the chronological evidence revealed by archaeology. It must be recalled, however, that the Queen of Sheba traditionally occupies a central position in Ethiopian (and, specifically, Aksumite) history which has been reinforced by many centuries of political and ecclesiastical manipulation.[11]

Not all such attributions are to be dismissed as subsequent rationalisations. Some, notably that of the Tombs of Kaleb and Gabra Masqal, appear concordant with archaeological evidence and may represent continuity of memory.

With these considerations in mind, it is instructive to turn to the traditions relating to the adoption of Christianity at Aksum. In its basics, the traditional account reveals no fundamental discrepancies with that revealed by non-Ethiopian documentary sources, by contemporary inscriptions, and by archaeology. The essential difference is that the traditions preserve the names of numerous individuals, and these are often difficult to correlate with the other sources.[12] Most crucially, the ruler of Aksum at the time of the initial conversion is given in inscriptions, coins and the letter of Constantius II as Ezana (sometimes linked with that of his 'brother' Saizana). In traditional accounts of the adoption of Christianity, the rulers of Aksum are named as Abraha and Atsbaha. There is evidence that, in ancient Aksum as in many other contexts, the same individual could be known by more than one name and that a ruler might change his name on assuming power. There is no indication, however, that Ezana ever bore either name.

The second stage in the development of Aksumite Christianity took place in the late fifth and early sixth centuries. This stage, sometimes designated a 'second conversion' is traditionally recalled as having been precipitated by the arrival of the 'Nine Saints' from the eastern Roman Empire; it was continued and consolidated under King Kaleb. It has even been suggested that the erection of the basilican cathedral at Aksum may have been undertaken under Kaleb rather than under Ezana.[13] Certainly, the Aksumite viceroy under Kaleb or his successor was responsible for the erection of a magnificent cathedral at Sana'a in Yemen, which land was at that time under Aksumite suzerainty. One of Kaleb's names was Ella Atsbaha; the viceroy in Yemen was Abraha. It is perhaps not excessively fanciful, and is fully in accord with the arguments here presented about the role and development of tradition, to suggest that the names of Abraha and Atsbaha, venerated as prime instigators of Aksumite Christianity, may over the centuries of oral transmission have become transferred from the sixth to the fourth century and linked with events which took place during the reign of Ezana.

The situations noted above are by no means restricted to Aksumite history and sites: they can apply equally to later periods and to individual artefacts as well as sites. Lalibela provides clear examples. The traditional view is that all eleven churches were completed during a single reign as part of a unified plan to create a new Jerusalem in the mountains of Lasta. It has been argued above that the extant churches in fact represent diverse architectural styles and were probably executed over a considerable period of time. The complex took its final form and symbolism in the reign of King Lalibela to whom was subsequently attributed its total creation. This is confirmed by the presence in several of the churches of wooden arks or *tabots* bearing Ge'ez inscriptions attributing their establishment to Lalibela;[14] it is by no means certain, however, that these *tabots* are contemporary with the events which they purportedly commemorate.

It is only to be expected that many churches, like those at Lalibela, will preserve traditions relating to their foundation. Debra Damo is a further example. It must be recalled that it is the foundation which is important in this respect, not the origin of the present building: modifications or replacements often feature little if at all in the extant traditions. It is also reasonable that ancient and revered artefacts held at such churches will be traditionally linked with the founder, as in the case of a metal cross at Lalibela. While such attributions can rarely be confirmed by independent means, in many, but not all, cases the implied chronology is not implausible. The same cannot be said for some of the elaborations which have been woven around these traditions. The Abba Garima gospels, for example, are attributed to one of the 'Nine Saints'. It is conceivable, if unlikely, that they are of such antiquity.[15] Tradition also recalls that the saint completed his work on the manuscript in a single day, and that the setting of the sun was delayed by divine intervention in order that the task might be finished.

Finally, we may note that tradition is a powerful ally in the task of preserving the heritage of the past. The ancient monuments of Aksum suffered virtually no damage during the upheavals of 1974-91. Not far away, in a country church, is a shrine containing an imported amphora of the fifth-sixth centuries AD (fig. 60). It is preserved as the cup from which God drank beer while overseeing the activities of the early Christian residents of the site. There could be no better example of the way in which the Ethiopian past lives on.

143

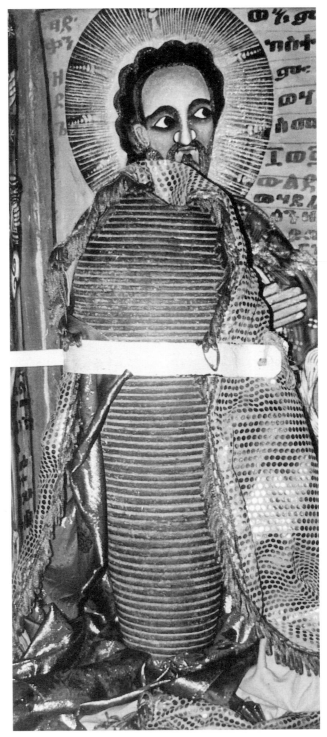

Fig. 60 An amphora preserved in a shrine
at a village church near Aksum.

NOTES AND REFERENCES

Introduction

1 With the sole exception of Armenia (Arpee 1946; Der Nersessian 1969), Ethiopia can claim to have been the first country in the world to adopt Christianity as its official religion.

2 To avoid excessive repetition, this book sometimes uses the word 'Ethiopia' in a sense which subsumes the present Eritrea. Such usage reflects the shared traditions of the region, and implies no disrespect for or disapproval of Eritrean nationhood.

3 The late Dr Neville Chittick, in a lecture to the British Academy in 1974.

4 The traditional version of early Ethiopian history has been committed to writing in the work known as *Kebra Negast* (The Glory of Kings), most accessibly published by Bezold 1905, and Budge 1922. The translation by Hausman 1997 is of questionable reliability. See also pp. 111-18, 123-5 and 140-43, below.

5 The most accessible general accounts which are reasonably up to date are those by Buxton 1970 and Anfray 1990. More specialised works include that of Munro-Hay 1991a.

6 The recent history and traditional lifestyles of the region are discussed by Ullendorff 1960, Simoons 1960, Bahru 1991, Marcus 1994, Parker 1995 and Van der Stappen 1996.

7 Only preliminary reports have yet been published: D. Phillipson 1994, 1995; D. Phillipson, Reynolds *et al.* 1996; D. Phillipson and Phillips in press.

8 An exception to this generalisation was provided, until recently, by the appointment of the head of the Ethiopian Church by the Patriarch of Alexandria.

9 For example, the recent account of African archaeology by Cornevin 1993 makes no mention whatsoever of post-palaeolithic Ethiopia. In *The Cambridge History of Africa*, Aksum and its immediate predecessors are accorded less than 1 per cent of the volume on the period 500 BC – AD 1000 (Fage 1978).

10 See pp. 33-5, below.

11 Mani, cited in Monneret de Villard 1948. See also Sergew 1972: 81-2; Munro-Hay 1991a: 17. The other three kingdoms mentioned by Mani were Rome, Persia and (probably) China.

Chapter 1 Background

1 The physiography of Eritrea and parts of northernmost Ethiopia is described by Abul-Haggag 1961.

2 Ullendorff 1960: 26-7; Buxton 1970: 20.

3 Abul-Haggag 1961; Mohr 1971; Getaneh and Russo 1994.

4 von Breitenbach 1963; Wilson 1977; Hedberg and Edwards 1989ff.

5 Bonnefille and Ummer 1994; Bard 1994. It appears that the rainfall pattern in the sixth century, both on the plateau and near the coast, was similar to that which prevails today (Nonnosus, in Photius' *Bibliotheca*, cited by Sergew 1972: 139-40).

6 Nonnosus, cited by Sergew 1972: 139.

7 DiBlasi 1994; Dramis and Fattovich 1994; McCann 1994.

8 Butzer 1981.

9 Cf. B. Davidson 1992.

10 For a widely accepted classification of African languages, see Greenberg 1963. A good account of Ethiopian and Eritrean languages is by Bender *et al.* 1976. See also Ullendorff 1955; Hezron 1972.

11 Ge'ez is now used exclusively for liturgical purposes, fulfilling a role in the Ethiopian Orthodox Church in some ways analogous to that taken until recently by Latin in the Roman Catholic Church. Tigrinya is significantly closer to Ge'ez than is Amharic, the latter displaying a greater quantity of foreign influences and loanwords.

12 R. Pankhurst 1979, 1982a.

13 See pp. 119-23, below.

14 Excellent up-to-date surveys are provided by contributors to a volume prepared under the auspices of the Musée royale de l'Afrique Centrale, Tervuren (Van der Stappen 1996).

15 See pp. 35-7 and 58-63, below.

16 Camels were not seen in highland Tigray during the 1960s and 1970s, but were re-introduced as transport animals during the subsequent war and have remained in use. They do not, however, breed at this altitude.

17 For an account of the salt trade, including 'trans-shipment' from lowland camel to highland donkey, see O'Mahoney 1970.

18 The history of coinage and currency in Ethiopia and Eritrea is discussed by Gill 1991 and Belai 1987.

19 See below, pp. 63-70.

20 Tapeworm infestation is consequently widespread. It is traditionally treated by an infusion prepared from the bark of the *kosso* tree, *Hagenia abyssinica* (Buxton 1970: 22).

21 Simoons 1960; R. Pankhurst 1961, 1968.

22 The old systems are conveniently if uncritically summarised by Ullendorff 1960: 187-9.

23 The most recent demonstration of this, with the connivance both of many Falasha and of the then Ethiopian government, was in the years 1985-91 when almost the whole Falasha population of Ethiopia was transferred to Israel. The moral, political and religious controversies surrounding this transfer need not be considered here.

24 Kaplan 1994.

25 Ullendorff 1956. Such features include a prohibition on eating pork and circumcision on the eighth day after birth.

26 There are comparatively few adherents to Roman Catholicism and to western protestant denominations, although a Swedish protestant mission has been particularly active in twentieth-century Eritrea.

27 For general accounts of the Ethiopian Orthodox Church, see Hyatt 1928; Aymro and Motovu 1970; Zanetti 1996a.

28 Grierson 1993; Girma 1996.

29 For a comprehensive, if dated, account of Ethiopian and Eritrean Islam, see Trimingham 1952.

30 A general and up-to-date account is provided by Dubois 1996.

31 Descriptions and illustrations of Tigray architecture and house-contents have been published by the Deutsche Aksum-Expedition (Littmann *et al.* 1913, III). See also Gebremedhin 1976.

32 See pp 83-95, below.

33 Lime cement had been known in Aksumite times (see pp. 92-3, below) and, from the seventeenth century, around Gondar where it was probably owed to Portuguese influences.

34 See the drawings, photographs and descriptions of Littmann *et al.* 1913 and, for a brief commentary on more recent developments, D. Phillipson 1997: chapter 2.

35 Ullendorff 1960: 1-2, 1968. The name (whence is derived the linguistic term 'Cushitic') came subsequently to be applied particularly to inhabitants of Nubia, the part of the Nile Valley immediately to the south of Egypt, who were the non-Egyptian Africans with whom the outside world was most familiar.

36 Ethiopians have nonetheless long taken these biblical references as support for their status as a divinely chosen people. Verse 31 in Psalm 68 is frequently cited in this connection and was quoted on the edge-inscription of Ethiopia's first modern coinage (Gill 1991).

37 The term 'Erythraean Sea' applied both to the Red Sea and the Indian Ocean (as well as the Persian Gulf). Early accounts of its navigation are conveniently summarised by Burstein 1989.

38 The Land of Punt is discussed in greater detail below (p. 38).

39 For a comprehensive survey, see J. Phillips 1995. A remarkable exception is the *cippus* (fig. 8), said to be from Aksum, which was presented to James Bruce in the eighteenth century and is now in the Royal Museum of Scotland, Edinburgh (Bruce 1790, I:417-8, III: 496; Sternberg-el Hotabi 1994).

40 The best rendition of the *Periplus* is that by Casson 1989, which has replaced Hunt-ingford 1980. The commentary by Schoff 1912 is still useful. For a succinct summary of the dating, see Casson 1989: 6-7.

41 Page 1930.

42 These matters are discussed in greater detail on pp. 111-18 below, with supporting references.

43 For Cosmas, see McCrindle 1897; Winstedt 1909; or the superior rendition of Wolska-

146

Conus 1968-73. The writings of Nonnosus are partially preserved in Photius' *Bibliotheca*.

44 The inscriptions from Ethiopia and Eritrea are detailed by Bernand *et al.* 1991. References to those from South Arabia are more scattered; see, however, Jamme 1962 and Beeston 1988.

45 See pp. 50-4 and 123-5, below.

46 Kobishchanov 1979: 111-2.

47 van Donzel 1986.

48 Kobishchanov 1969.

49 Mordini 1960; Juel-Jensen 1994; Hahn 1995.

50 'Pseudo-Callisthenes', cited by Kobishchanov 1979: 75. See also Priaulx 1862-3; R. Pankhurst 1974.

51 See below, pp. 67-8.

52 If they have been so studied, the results are not available to the present writer.

53 Needham 1986: 132-9.

54 van Donzel 1979.

55 Pedersen 1986, 1993.

56 E.g. the map of Fra Mauro, c. 1460 (de la Roncière 1925: plate xxxvi).

57 For general surveys, the works of Rey 1929 and Caraman 1985 may be recommended. Translations of the principal primary sources are provided by Beckingham and Huntingford 1954, 1961; Crawford 1958. A particularly informative seventeenth-century account by M. Barradas was published in English translation in 1996.

58 For a detailed account of Gran's exploits, see Basset 1897-1909.

59 Bruce 1790.

60 E.g. Salt 1814; Pearce 1831; Rüppell 1838-40; Isenberg and Krapf 1843; W. Harris 1844; Parkyns 1853; d'Abbadie 1868; Johnston 1868.

61 There are numerous published accounts of the Magdala operation, notably Markham 1869; Holland and Hozier 1870. A more dispassionate modern account is by Rubenson 1966.

62 The history of the twentieth century is here summarised very briefly, to provide a context for the research described below. For more detail, the reader is referred to the works of Bahru 1991 and Marcus 1994a.

63 Beckingham and Huntingford 1961.

64 Ludolf 1661, 1681, 1691, 1698. For an evaluation of Ludolf's work, see Haberland 1969.

65 Bruce 1790. For the life of Bruce and an evaluation of his work, see Ullendorff 1953a; Reid 1968.

66 These are published in Valentia 1809; Salt 1809, 1814.

67 Bernand *et al.* 1991: inscription 185/270. The subsequent history of Aksumite archaeological research is surveyed by Brandt and Fattovich 1990.

68 Monneret de Villard (1938) has published an invaluable anthology of early accounts of Aksum.

69 Rüppell 1838-40; Lefebvre 1845-8.

70 Acton 1868 is an invaluable and profusely illustrated compendium. Blanford 1870 records geological and zoological observations. Henry Stanley obtained his first taste of African travel as a journalist accompanying the expedition; his account (Stanley 1874: 320-4) provides a mention and illustration of an Aksumite ruin at Agula, north of Makelle. For accounts of manuscripts taken from Magdala, see especially Wright 1877; Ullendorff 1953b.

71 Dillmann 1878, 1880.

72 Bent 1893a. Bent secured the collaboration of H.D. Müller in the study of the inscriptions which he recorded.

73 Bent 1893b.

74 Littmann *et al.* 1913. A comprehensively illustrated English translation of the D.A.E. account of Aksumite monuments is in course of publication (D. Phillipson 1997).

75 Sundström 1907; Paribeni 1907.

76 It appears that the Italian administration of Eritrea sought to prohibit such investigations (Duncanson 1947).

77 Kammerer 1926, 1929.

78 E.g. Guida 1938.

79 Matthews 1949; Matthews and Mordini 1959.

80 E.g. de Contenson 1959, 1961a, 1961b, 1963a, 1963b; Anfray 1963, 1967, 1968, 1972b, 1974.

81 This institution has been known successively as Addis Ababa University College, Haile Sellassie I University, and Addis Ababa University.

82 Ricci and Fattovich 1987.

83 Michels 1994.

84 A preliminary report was promptly published (Chittick 1974), followed by a detailed one (Munro-Hay 1989a) prepared after Dr Chittick's death.

85 Bard and Fattovich 1993, 1995; Fattovich 1995; Fattovich and Bard 1993, 1995.

Chapter 2 **Ethiopia before Aksum**

1 For a general account of early African prehistory, and explanations of terminology, see the relevant chapters in D. Phillipson 1993a. Greater detail is provided by Klein 1989.

2 Johanson and White 1979; Leakey and Harris 1987.

3 This skeleton is preserved at the National Museum in Addis Ababa. It was nicknamed 'Lucy' by the American team responsible for its discovery (Johanson and Edey 1981). Many Ethiopians prefer the name 'Dinqanesh'.

4 Roche and Tiercelin 1980; J. Harris 1983. New discoveries are being made but have so far received only preliminary publication.

5 D. Phillipson 1993a: chapter 3; also see Klein 1989.

6 Bailloud 1965; Chavaillon 1976.

7 Klein 1989.

8 Clark 1988. Sparse archaeological remains from this period have recently been recognised in highland Tigray.

9 Much controversy surrounds the time when human speech developed. This is partly due to lack of appreciation of the diversity which the concept encompasses. For an African perspective, see Tobias 1991; for more general surveys, see I. Davidson 1991; also the papers edited by K. Gibson and Ingold 1993.

10 Much basic data and evaluation is provided in the papers edited by Mellars and Stringer 1989. A more popular overview is that by Fagan 1990.

11 Rightmire 1989 and references.

12 D. Phillipson 1977.

13 D. Phillipson 1993b.

14 See the papers edited by Manning and Serpell 1994 and by D. Harris 1996.

15 Huffnagel 1961.

16 D. Phillipson 1993b.

17 Such studies date back to Vavilov 1931. For a recent survey see Engels *et al.* 1991.

18 BOSTID 1996: chapter 12.

19 BOSTID 1996: 239-48.

20 BOSTID 1996: chapter 2.

21 S. Edwards 1991.

22 D. Phillipson 1993b; Maes 1996.

23 Ehret 1979.

24 For a summary, see D. Phillipson 1993b.

25 Sheep and goats appear to have been first domesticated in the Near East. There is increasingly convincing evidence that cattle were separately domesticated in at least two areas, one in the eastern Sahara and one in western Asia (Clutton-Brock 1987; Blench and MacDonald 1998).

26 D. Phillipson 1977.

27 Clark and Williams 1978.

28 Clutton-Brock 1993.

29 Rowley-Conwy 1988.

30 Bulliet 1975; D. Phillipson 1984.

31 West and Zhou 1988; MacDonald 1992.

32 Fattovich *et al.* 1984; Fattovich 1990.

33 Fattovich 1996a, 1996b.

34 The Nile Valley sequence is well surveyed by Welsby 1996; for South Arabia the reader is referred to the works of Van Beek 1969, Doe 1971, de Bayle 1976, Tosi 1986 and Daum 1988a.

35 Kitchen 1971, 1993; Fattovich 1993; J. Phillips in press.

36 Tringali 1965; Tringali and Munro-Hay 1991.

37 Fattovich 1990; Tosi 1986; see also Tringali 1965.

38 *Pace* Fattovich 1990.

39 The term 'art' is employed for convenience, but does not carry any implication for the original motivation of the rock paintings and petroglyphs here described.

40 Bender 1971; Hudson 1978; Zanetti 1996b.

41 For a general descriptive account of African rock art, see Willcox 1984. The Eritrean and north-Ethiopian material is illustrated and discussed by Graziosi 1964 and by Joussaume 1981.

42 A possible exception is the group of petroglyphs west of Asmara, described by Cervicek 1976.

43 Lewis-Williams 1981, 1983.

44 The most accessible reproductions are those published by Graziosi 1964.

45 Brandt 1984.

46 Brandt and Carder 1987.

47 Drew 1954. The painting is also reproduced here, in fig. 12.

48 Lewis-Williams 1981, 1983. This does not mean that specific insights provided by South African research are necessarily applicable in other parts of the continent (cf. Garlake 1995).

49 See, especially, Irvine 1965; Ricci 1984; and the papers edited by Daum 1988a.

50 Early evidence for *teff* at Hajar bin Humeid is noted by Van Beek 1969; for a more general discussion see Mehra 1991; Haaland 1996.

51 Tosi 1986; de Maigret 1988, 1990; Fedele 1988. For a concise summary, see Glanzman 1996. For affinities of pottery, see Tringali 1965, Fattovich 1989, 1990 and Munro-Hay 1993a. For a linguistic perspective, see Korotayev 1996.

52 But see Kitchen 1994.

53 W. Phillips 1955; Bowen and Albright 1958; Doe 1971; Daum 1988a.

54 Bowen and Albright 1958; J. Schmidt 1988a.

55 Such contacts are reflected in the biblical accounts of the visit of the Queen of Sheba to King Solomon in Jerusalem.

56 Dembski 1988; Munro-Hay 1994, 1996.

57 Burstein 1989.

58 Bowersock 1983.

59 Breton 1991.

60 For a masterly summary, see Sutton 1989; also Raunig 1988. For archaeological sites of the Isamic period in Yemen, see King and Tongleni 1996.

61 Copper and its alloys, notably bronze, had probably been known long before this period. The oldest datable iron artefacts from Ethiopia or Eritrea were found at Yeha. For discussions of early Ethiopian metallurgy, see Todd and Charles 1978; Mapunda 1997.

62 For the earliest Ethiopian inscriptions, see Drewes 1962; R. Schneider 1973, 1976; Avanzini 1989.

63 Michels 1994.

64 Anfray 1990; Munro-Hay 1991a, 1993a. The inscriptions are detailed in the work of Bernand *et al.* 1991, where full bibliographic references are cited.

65 The best account of the building is still that prepared by the Deutsche Aksum-Expedition in 1906 (Littmann *et al.* 1913, II: 79-87). At that time much of the later encumbrances were still visible. They have since been demolished, although the baptistry constructed inside the south-west corner of the temple may still be seen today.

66 A remarkably close parallel, from Marib, is illustrated by J. Schmidt 1988b: 88.

67 This building is traditionally known as Mahram Bilqis (W. Phillips 1955; Bowen and Albright 1958).

68 Littmann *et al.* 1913, II: 87-9; Anfray 1972a, 1972b, 1973, 1990.

69 Fattovich 1990. See also Anfray 1990.

70 Fattovich 1977.

71 de Contenson 1961a, 1963a. The throne and other sculptures, now in the National Museum at Addis Ababa, are described and illustrated by de Contenson 1962. For South Arabian parallels, see Daum 1988a.

72 For discussions, see de Contenson 1981; Anfray, 1990: 62-3; Fattovich 1990; Munro-Hay 1991a: 33-44, 1993a. The sparse archaeological material has not been well recorded (cf. Caquot and Drewes 1955).

Chapter 3 **Aksumite Civilisation**

1 For an evaluation of this problem, see pp. 140-4, below.

2 Useful compendia, not always critical, are by Sergew 1972 and Kobishchanov 1979.

3 See fig. 27 (p. 72), below.

4 For discussions, see Munro-Hay 1989a: 19-26, 1990; Michels 1990. The decline of Aksum is further considered on pp. 125-6, below.

5 But see Michels 1979, 1994; also continuing research by K. Bard and R. Fattovich.

6 Anfray 1974; Munro-Hay 1989a: 150-6, 329-32. Earlier material occurs in the vicinity of Aksum at Hawelti-Melazzo (de Contenson 1961a, 1963a), Seglamen (Ricci and Fattovich 1987), Abba Pantaleon (Littmann *et al.* 1913, II: 90-4), Beta Giyorghis (Bard and Fattovich 1995; Fattovich and Bard 1995) and a recently investigated area of domestic occupation a short distance to the north of Aksum (D. Phillipson, Reynolds *et al.* 1996; D. Phillipson and Phillips in press).

7 The relevant inscriptions from Aksum are those of King Ezana (Bernand *et al.* 1991: nos. 185/270 and 185*bis*/270*bis*; for English translations, see Kirwan 1960; Sergew 1972: 93-4, 103, 105-6; Munro-Hay 1991a: 224-6). Although its date is uncertain, the inscription of an un-named Aksumite king at Adulis, the so-called 'Monumentum Adulitanum' (Wolska-Conus 1968-73), may also be relevant to this discussion.

8 S. Smith 1954; Sergew 1972: 123-58 and references.

9 Kirwan 1960; Shinnie 1978; Burstein 1981; Hägg 1984, 1994 and references.

10 Munro-Hay 1991a: 95-9. The decline of Aksum is discussed in greater detail on pp. 125-6, below.

11 Sutton 1989. Climatic and environmental factors have also been emphasised (Butzer 1981).

12 See pp. 86-90 and 95-111, below.

13 See the gazetteer in Munro-Hay 1989a: 340-6.

14 I.e. at Ta'akha Maryam, Enda Semon, Enda Mikael, Dungur and a recently excavated site to the north of Aksum, discussed on p. 86, below.

15 Szymusiak 1958. King Ezana is known from coins and inscriptions as well as from other documentary sources; Saizana was apparently his 'brother' or military commander.

16 Belaynesh *et al.* 1975. The identification is further discussed – and queried – on pp. 123-5 and 140-3, below.

17 For a discussion of the numismatic evidence, see pp. 71-4, below.

18 Munro-Hay 1993b.

19 See, for example, the following types listed by Munro-Hay and Juel-Jensen 1995: 36/7 (gold, Ezana, fourth century, depicting sceptre and fly-whisk); 59 (gold, Eon, early fifth century, showing fly-whisk); 147 (silver, Gersem), 151 (silver, Armah), and 153 (copper, Armah) all of the early seventh century and showing crosses.

20 S. Smith 1954; Sergew 1972: 138. For the primary source, by John Malalas, see Migne 1860; Spinka 1940. The mention of linen is specific: it is known from archaeobotanical investigations (discussed on p. 59, below) that *Linum* was grown at Aksum at this time, although there is no other indication that it was used for textile production rather than for oil. It is possible that a Byzantine visitor may have mistaken cotton cloth for linen, although the latter was reaching Ethiopia from Egyptian sources by at least the ninth century, as indicated by materials preserved at Debra Damo (Matthews and Mordini 1959). Likewise it is uncertain whether pearls or beads were meant. For the domestication of elephants, see also p. 25, above.

21 These monuments are described in detail and illustrated by Littmann *et al.* 1913, II: 45-67; D. Phillipson 1997: chapter 6.

22 For an illustration, see D. Phillipson 1995: fig. 40.

23 Littmann *et al.* 1913, II: 49-54.

24 Beckingham and Huntingford 1954: 92-6.

25 Littmann *et al.* 1913, II: 60.

26 Wolska-Conus 1968-73. It is not always noted that, according to Cosmas, the Adulis throne was adorned with relief carvings of Hercules and Mercury.

27 Kirwan 1960.

28 Beckingham and Huntingford 1961: 227.

29 See below; also pp. 112-14 and 123-8.

30 Photographs of the inscription in its original position were taken by the Deutsche Aksum-Expedition (see D. Phillipson 1997: figs 208, 209) and by Cheesman 1936: 376.

31 Bernand *et al.* 1991: no. 185/270; for English translations, see Kirwan 1960; Sergew 1972: 93-4; Munro-Hay 1991a: 224-6.

32 Bernand 1982; Bernand *et al.* 1991: no. 185*bis*/270*bis*.

33 Wolska-Conus 1968-73.

34 Munro-Hay 1991a: 222.

35 It is noteworthy that urban settlements of this and earlier times in South Arabia did have mural defences (Audouin *et al.* 1988).

36 See the translations provided by Sergew 1972: 93-4, 103, 105-6, 123-4 and by Munro-Hay 1991a: 221-32.

37 The presence of slaves is confirmed by several ancient accounts: for a discussion, see Kobishchanov 1979: 150-9; also pp. 54 and 119-23 below.

38 For Matara and Adulis, see Anfray 1974. For Aksum see D. Phillipson, Reynolds *et al.* 1996.

39 Models from Hawelti-Melazzo are described by de Contenson 1963a, one from Aksum by Chittick 1974 (fig. 39 here).

40 Anfray 1963: pls lxi, lxxxi-ii.

41 Matthews and Mordini 1959. The church at Debra Damo is discussed in greater detail on pp. 128-31, below.

42 Buxton and Matthews 1974.

43 The most comprehensive assemblage comes from the third-century Tomb of the Brick Arches at Aksum, see D. Phillipson 1995 and pp. 98-100, below.

44 The imports concerned were 'African red-slip ware', of North African origin, cf. p. 65, below.

45 There is nonetheless much overall similarity between the locally produced pottery wares in different parts of the Aksumite realm, cf. Anfray 1966; Wilding 1989; Dr J. S. Phillips *pers. comm.*; personal observations. Study of Aksumite pottery fabrics and clay sources is ongoing by Dr J. S. Phillips and others.

46 E.g. de Roux 1976.

47 Casson 1989. See also Mapunda 1997.

48 Cf. Chapter IVb, below.

49 For examples, see D. Phillipson 1995: figs. 18, 20.

50 For examples, see D. Phillipson 1995: 28.

51 Munro-Hay 1989a; Anfray 1990: 111.

52 Littmann *et al.* 1913; D. Phillipson 1997: 164-7.

53 It is unfortunate that archaeological research has not yet revealed smelting sites, forges, workshops or the mint.

54 See p. 80, below.

55 D. Phillipson 1990; L. Phillipson 1997.

56 L. Phillipson 1997. Research continues.

57 Cotton is now mostly grown at significantly lower altitudes. Different varieties have distinct altitude tolerances (Huffnagel 1961). It is not yet known which variety/varieties were represented at Aksum.

58 For the possibility that linen may also have been used, see p. 52, above.

59 The existence of a substantial ecclesiastical population is indicated in several sources cited by Sergew 1972.

60 The only archaeological attestation for painting at this period (other than on pottery) comes from an Aksumite-type site at Shabwa in Yemen (Audouin 1991).

61 L. Phillipson 1997.

62 Michels 1994; see also pp. 119-23, below.

63 Bard and Fattovich 1995; D. Phillipson, Reynolds *et al.* 1996. Research continues.

64 Kobishchanov 1979. Contemporary inscriptions in South Arabia make specific mention of camels. For the chronology of the introduction of camels to Ethiopia/Eritrea, see D. Phillipson 1993b and references.

65 For such trade in recent times, see O'Mahoney 1970.

66 Some occurrences are marked in the National Atlas of Ethiopia (1988). No ancient mines have been located in the Aksumite heartland. The fanciful account of a possible ancient mine in western Ethiopia by Bartleet 1934: 113-5 is not easy to evaluate.

67 Wolska-Conus 1968-73; see also Wainwright 1942.

68 Obsidian, chert, chalcedony, breccia, soapstone and fine-grained siltstones were all utilised in Aksumite times.

69 This is the journey-time recorded by Procopius in the sixth century. Other ancient estimates which have been recorded vary between eight and fifteen days.

70 Cf. Bent 1893b.

71 D. Phillipson 1990.

72 D. Phillipson 1977.

73 D. Phillipson 1990, 1993b. This case should be taken as a salutary warning of the danger of jumping to conclusions about the age of specimens whose stratigraphic associations are less than certain.

74 Casson 1989: 52-5; see also D. Phillipson 1993b and references.

75 Bard and Fattovich 1995; Fattovich and Bard 1995.

76 D. Phillipson, Reynolds *et al.* 1996; S. Boardman *pers. comm.* Ms Boardman's research continues.

77 Illustrations of both are provided by Littmann *et al.* 1913. A comparable stone from Adulis, now in the Museum at Asmara, is regarded as a Byzantine import (Heldman 1994).

78 Littmann *et al.* 1913, II: 74-7; D. Phillipson 1997. A similar installation at Ham, in south-easternmost Eritrea not far from Adigrat, has been recorded by Anfray 1965.

79 Significant numbers of amphorae, imported from the eastern Mediterranean, occur at Aksum and several related sites at approximately the same date. They were presumably imported for their contents rather than as pots *per se*. Such vessels were most commonly used in the *circum-*Mediterranean region for the transport of wine or olive oil, but they also held other commodities and were reused as empty receptacles (Peacock and Williams 1986). Their presence at Aksumite sites does not therefore necessarily mean that wine was imported as well as being produced locally.

80 Munro-Hay 1989a: 33-149.

81 D. Phillipson 1977.

82 A clay figurine from a probable sixth-century context at Aksum (D. Phillipson, Reynolds *et al.* 1996: fig. 33) may represent a camel.

83 Bard and Fattovich 1995; Fattovich and Bard 1995.

84 *Pers. comm.* from Mr C. Cain, whose research continues.

85 Wilding 1989: 261; D. Phillipson 1995: fig. 16.

86 Mordini 1953; de Contenson 1961a, 1963a.

87 Anfray 1990: 46; Ricci 1959, 1960. Although not precisely datable, the Eritrean rock paintings (see pp. 39-41) support a similar conclusion.

88 de Contenson 1963a; Anfray 1990: 47.

89 Anfray 1966; Wilding 1989.

90 For a discussion, see D. Phillipson 1993b and references.

91 Munro-Hay 1984c.

92 Casson 1989: 52-3; Munro-Hay 1991b.

93 D. Phillipson 1990.

94 Research on methods of ascertaining the source of ancient ivory is in progress.

95 For a similar criticism relating to Nubia, see D. Edwards 1996.

96 Despite the clear link with contemporary Roman coinage there are other aspects which display strong affinities with slightly earlier South Arabian issues, as discussed on pp. 71-4, below.

97 Zoscales, king of the Aksumites, was described in the *Periplus of the Erythraean Sea* (Casson 1989: 52-3) as well acquainted with reading and writing Greek. For the coinage, see Munro-Hay and Juel-Jensen

1995; for the inscriptions, see Bernand *et al.* 1991.

98 Conti Rossini 1904, 1928; Sergew 1972: 115-21; see also pp. 111-18, below. For arguments that the Syrian connection has been exaggerated, see Marrassini 1990.

99 Casson 1989.

100 Kobishchanov 1969; Begley and Puma 1991; the specifically African aspects are considered by Desanges 1978; Chittick 1979; Stern 1987; M. Smith and Wright 1988; Juma 1996.

101 Caquot and Drewes 1955; Anfray 1990: 63; J. Phillips 1995.

102 Anfray 1972c.

103 Identified by Dr P. Rose *pers. comm.* Such flasks were usually used for carrying oil.

104 Morrison 1989a; Bard 1995.

105 These are the Tomb of the Brick Arches (D. Phillipson 1995) and a tomb in the Gudit Stelae Field excavated by Chittick (Munro-Hay 1989a: 142-9).

106 Wilding 1989; Hayes 1972; Peacock and Williams 1986.

107 O. Hoogzaad *pers. comm.* Further studies are in progress by Professor D. Peacock and colleagues.

108 cf. Peacock and Williams 1986.

109 Anfray and Annequin 1965.

110 See note 103, above.

111 Kindly identified by staff of the Departments of Western Asiatic Antiquities and of Scientific Research at the British Museum.

112 Morrison 1989b; Bard 1995.

113 de Contenson 1963a.

114 Craddock 1995: 234-83.

115 A Roman embassy is reported to have reached China, via India and presumably via Adulis, before the end of the second century, and the Chinese at this period had knowledge of eastern Africa (Needham 1986: 104, 132-52; Snow 1988: 1-4).

116 D. Phillipson 1990; for the presence of large numbers of elephants on the Tigray plateau in the sixth century, see p. 25, above.

117 Local working would have reduced weight prior to transport, and would have ensured that at least some carving was done while the ivory was fresh and comparatively easy to work. An unworked tusk has, however, been excavated at Adulis (Anfray 1981).

118 E.g. Cutler 1985; M. Gibson 1994; Ross 1992; Scullard 1974.

119 The relevant research is in progress.

120 Miller 1969.

121 Shinnie 1978; Munro-Hay 1991b and references.

122 Meshorer and Spaer 1966; Barkay 1981; Kindler 1988; Whitcomb 1994. The Aksumite bronze coin discovered as a chance find near Hastings in southern England (Juel-Jensen and Munro-Hay 1994) probably resulted from recent loss rather than ancient trade.

123 For an overview of the Adulis trade, drawn largely from documentary sources, see Munro-Hay 1982.

Chapter 4 **Aksumite Material Culture and Beliefs**

1 Munro-Hay and Juel-Jensen 1995. Few of the base-metal coins have been analysed and all are, for convenience, noted as 'copper' in the following discussion.

2 Munro-Hay 1989b.

3 Munro-Hay 1979, 1980, 1984a, 1993b; Barrandon *et al.* 1990.

4 Munro-Hay and Juel-Jensen 1995 number their types 1-153, but nos. 45, 64, 65 and 68 are dismissed as modern forgeries. There seems to have been a tendency for gold coins (which are usually well preserved) to be classified in rather greater detail than the far commoner issues in copper. See also Hahn 1983; Munro-Hay 1984b.

5 The earliest Aksumite gold coins appear to be based on a standard weight of 2.70 grammes, being half the weight of the Roman aureus of the late third century.

6 Munro-Hay 1988.

7 Casson 1989: 52-3; see also pp. 25 and 64-5, above.

8 E.g. Munro-Hay 1991b; Anfray and Annequin 1965.

9 A possible correlation with a ruler Hendor, named in some traditional king-lists, has been noted by Belaynesh *et al.* 1975.

10 This feature may have been inspired by some earlier South Arabian issues (Dembski 1988; Munro-Hay 1994, 1996).

11 There has been controversy over the identity of the cereal represented which could be either barley or emmer wheat, both of which were grown in ancient Aksum; opinion now tends to favour the latter (D. Phillipson 1993b).

12 For a unique exception, see Munro-Hay 1995.

13 This symbol is discussed on p. 113, below.

14 Munro-Hay and Juel-Jensen 1995.

15 Russo and Russo 1989. The term 'inlay', often used in this connection, is inappropriate.

16 The next coinage in sub-Saharan Africa was that of the cities on the East African coast (H. Brown in Horton 1996: 368-77).

17 It is noteworthy that the Aksumite coinage began at a time when the monetary affairs of the Roman Empire were in a particularly sorry state. From the mid-fourth century the weight of Aksumite gold coins seems to have been based on one-third of the contemporary Roman solidus, introduced in 324. The weight-adjustments of successive Roman reforms were followed at Aksum, albeit sometimes belatedly, until c. 383.

18 E.g. D. Phillipson, Reynolds *et al.* 1996. For the significance of the reverse legends used for propaganda purposes, see p. 111, below.

19 Juel-Jensen and Atkins 1996.

20 Munro-Hay and Juel-Jensen 1995.

21 As noted elsewhere (pp. 125-6), this change in policy may have been connected with the move of the capital away from Aksum.

22 The most detailed studies are those by Anfray 1966 and Wilding 1989.

23 Dr J. S. Phillips *pers. comm.*

24 A contrary view has been expressed by Wilding 1989: 312 but is not supported by more recent research.

25 de Roux 1976.

26 This is the 'Red Aksumite' ware of Wilding 1989: 236-90.

27 It need not be assumed that these shapes necessarily had any religious significance.

28 These are Wilding's (1989: 301-11) 'Grey/Black Aksumite' wares.

29 Wilding 1989; J. S. Phillips *pers comm.*

30 *Gebeta* (R. Pankhurst 1982b) is a board game which, in variant forms, is widespread in Africa. Comparative descriptions are provided by Natsoulas 1994; de Voogt 1997.

31 Casson 1989.

32 All were produced by forging.

33 See p. 56, above.

34 See p. 98, below.

35 John Malalas' description of King Kaleb (p. 52, above) may refer to such a textile.

36 E.g. Munro-Hay 1989a; D. Phillipson, Reynolds *et al.* 1996.

37 Munro-Hay 1989a.

38 This was first observed by Puglisi 1941, 1946.

39 Flaked stone tools are still used in parts of Ethiopia for the processing of hides (Brandt 1996).

40 Munro-Hay 1982; Casson 1989: 54-5.

41 D. Phillipson 1995. For the working of ivory in a broadly contemporary and culturally-related South Arabian context, see Beal 1991.

42 Noted by Dr L. Phillipson, *pers. comm.*

43 For an Aksumite throne, albeit later in date, see the copper coins of Armah (Munro-Hay and Juel-Jensen 1995: type 153). The famous sixth-century ivory throne of Maximian in the Archiepiscopal Museum at Ravenna (Rodley 1994 and references) incorporates rectangular panels with analogous decoration which are thought to be of Alexandrian origin.

44 Munro-Hay 1989a: 143-6, 347-8; Morrison 1989a.

45 Cf. D. Phillipson 1995: figs. 32, 18.

46 Cf. D. Phillipson 1995: fig. 10.

47 Studies are being undertaken by Ms S. Boardman in an attempt to ascertain the kinds of wood that were used.

48 Wilding 1989: 313; D. Phillipson, Reynolds *et al.* 1996.

49 Munro-Hay 1991a: 176.

50 Munro-Hay 1989a: 211-21; Wilding 1989: 278.

51 Casson 1989: 52-5.

52 Munro-Hay 1989a: 211-21.

53 Van Endt 1977, 1978.

54 Wilding 1989: 313.

55 Sergew 1972: 186; Munro-Hay 1989a: 210.

56 Traces of mural painting are, however, present at an Aksumite-period building at Shabwa in Yemen (Audouin 1991).

57 Uhlig 1993; see pp. 136-8, below.

58 Taddesse 1985.

59 Cf. pp. 86-90 and 95-111, below.

60 Littmann *et al.* 1913, II: 107-21; see also

D. Phillipson 1997.

61 Chittick 1974; Munro-Hay 1989a: 121-42.

62 Anfray 1990.

63 D. Phillipson, Reynolds *et al.* 1996.

64 This feature is often compared with the description by Cosmas Indicopleustes of the 'four-towered palace of the king of Ethiopia' (Wolska-Conus 1968-73).

65 Littmann *et al.* 1913, II: fig. 251. The illustration cited has been reproduced on several occasions, notably by Buxton 1970 and Michels 1979.

66 Littmann *et al.* 1913, II: 107-12; D. Phillipson 1997: 96-104.

67 Chittick 1974, 1976; Munro-Hay 1989a: 158.

68 Anfray 1990: 120-1.

69 A comparable structure has, however, been investigated at Shabwa in Yemen (Seigne 1991). For non-élite buildings at the same site, see Darles 1991.

70 Anfray 1963, 1967, 1974; Anfray and Annequin 1965.

71 Anfray 1974.

72 D. Phillipson, Reynolds *et al.* 1996; D. Phillipson and Phillips in press.

73 D. Phillipson 1994.

74 It was erected in the Piazza di Porta Capena. Arrangements for its return to Ethiopia are under discussion.

75 Littmann *et al.* 1913, II: 6.

76 D. Phillipson 1995.

77 E.g. Sergew 1972.

78 If the stela is to be returned to Aksum, it is essential that the whole area be thoroughly investigated archaeologically before any attempt is made at re-erection.

79 A detailed illustrated account of these stelae is presented by Littmann *et al.* 1913, II: 10-27; cf. also the English translation (with additional illustrations) provided by D. Phillipson 1997: chapter 3.

80 A discussion, with references, is provided by Schoff 1912: 61-6.

81 The church at Debra Damo is discussed in greater detail below, on pp. 128-31, below.

82 Daum 1988b: 11-12; Lewcock 1988.

83 For the tracery on the Aksum stela, see D. Phillipson 1994: fig. 15. For Debra Damo, see Mathews and Mordini 1959: fig. 11; also pp. 128-31, below.

84 None of these plaques remains *in situ*. For

their fixings, see D. Phillipson 1997: fig. 39. Artefacts which may represent the remains of such a plaque are described on p. 98, below.

85 D. Phillipson 1994.
86 Chittick 1974.
87 de Contenson 1963a.
88 Buxton and Matthews 1974; Munro-Hay 1989a: 159-65.
89 Examples are illustrated by Littmann *et al.* 1913, II: 101-6; D. Phillipson 1997: figs 249, 250.
90 J. Phillips 1995; D. Phillipson 1994; further research is in progress.
91 D. Phillipson 1994.
92 Munro-Hay 1989a: 116-20, 165-6; D. Phillipson 1994; see also pp. 101-102, below.
93 See pp. 107-9, below.
94 See pp. 101-5, below.
95 Littmann *et al.* 1913, II: 94-6, 112-21.
96 Munro-Hay 1989a: pl. 6.35; see also fig. 48 here.
97 Littmann *et al.* 1913, II: 112-21.
98 Anfray 1967.
99 Munro-Hay 1989a: 113, 156-7.
100 Examples may most easily be seen at the Old Cathedral of Maryam Tsion at Aksum, and in churches at Lalibela.
101 Buxton and Matthews 1974.
102 Munro-Hay 1989a: 158.
103 See pp. 132-6, below.
104 For a brief critique, see D. Phillipson 1990.
105 That the word was already applied to stelae in pre-Christian Aksumite times is shown by the inscribed stelae at Matara and elsewhere (e.g. Ullendorff 1951; Bernand *et al.* 1991).
106 Fattovich 1987; Joussaume 1996; see also pp. 37-8, above. The practice has continued into recent times.
107 E.g. S. Pankhurst 1955: 62-3.
108 Littmann *et al.* 1913, II: 33 and fig. 5; D. Phillipson 1997: 60-1; Valentia 1809, III: map at p. 82.
109 Bazen is recorded in traditional king-lists as ruler of Aksum at the time of the birth of Christ (Belaynesh *et al.* 1975). There is no evidence that the area was linked with Bazen prior to the tomb's discovery in the 1950s. It should not be assumed that the attribution has any chronological significance.
110 Kebbede and Leclant 1955. The human

bones that were recovered may or may not have belonged to a primary deposit.
111 Cf. Littmann *et al.* 1913, II: fig. 5. The stela now standing in the grounds of the Touring Hotel may have been moved from this area.
112 A plan has been published by Munro-Hay 1989a: 34-40. Despite the small break opposite Mai Shum, it seems best to regard the whole area as comprising a single stelae field.
113 Chittick 1974; Munro-Hay 1989a: 60-104, 152-6. See also Leclant 1959; de Contenson 1959.
114 Munro-Hay 1989a: 28-9 and references.
115 Stelae were likewise set on platforms at the pre-Aksumite burial ground of Ona Enda Aboi Zague on Beta Giyorghis hill near Aksum (Fattovich and Bard 1993, 1995).
116 Chittick 1974.
117 The work was instigated by Ras Mengesha Seyoum, then Governor of Tigray, at the time the new Cathedral in Aksum was built. The author and his colleagues have learned about this operation in the course of discussions with several residents of Aksum, whose interest and courtesy is gratefully acknowledged.
118 Munro-Hay 1989a: especially pp. 340-6.
119 The term 'granite', often applied, is not strictly correct. Some of the smaller stelae are of fine-grained trachyte.
120 D. Phillipson 1994. This and other technological matters relating to the quarrying, transport, finishing and erection of the stelae are described above on pp. 86-90.
121 For detailed descriptions and illustrations, see Littmann *et al.* 1913, II: 7-30, pls ii-x (D. Phillipson 1997: 11-43). See also Buxton and Matthews 1974.
122 D. Phillipson, Reynolds *et al.* 1996; Fattovich *pers. comm.*
123 In the case of the largest stela, this was undoubtedly the case, as is described below.
124 Chittick 1974; Munro-Hay 1989a: 78-100.
125 After preliminary exploration by Doresse in 1954, the area was further investigated by Chittick in 1973-74, when the tomb itself was located (Munro-Hay 1989a: 55-60). A preliminary account of more recent excavations is provided by D. Phillipson 1995.

126 These artefacts are described on pp. 74-83, above.

127 This cannot yet be read, reconstruction of the fragments not having been finalised. Dr Roger Schneider (*pers. comm.*) has, however, suggested that the letters are of a type which dates from the late third or early fourth century AD.

128 D. Phillipson 1994.

129 The name 'Nefas Mawcha' means, in Tigrinya, 'the place whence the winds blow'. The monument has been investigated on several occasions. See, in particular, Littmann *et al.* 1913, II: 94-6, pl. xvi (D. Phillipson 1997: 68-71) and Munro-Hay 1989a: 116-20.

130 Chittick 1974; Munro-Hay 1989a: 75, 100-102, 154.

131 D. Phillipson 1994, 1995; D. Phillipson, Reynolds *et al.* 1996.

132 The letter is the 'A' or glottal stop. Dr Roger Schneider of Addis Ababa University has kindly examined photographs and tentatively suggested, on epigraphic grounds, that the inscription may date to about the time of King Ezana, i.e. the mid-fourth century AD.

133 The complex arguments, based on architectural and stratigraphic observations, will be discussed elsewhere. It would clearly be wholly inappropriate for any effort to be made to re-erect (or, more correctly, to erect) the stela, as recently proposed by Francaviglia *et al.* 1990.

134 One might even go so far as to speculate whether the erection of the great stela could have been deliberately sabotaged with the intent of encouraging conversion.

135 Kobishchanov 1981: 394.

136 Chittick 1974; Munro-Hay 1989a: 104-13.

137 Within days of the discovery of this previously unknown tomb, local people were suggesting that it was the burial place of Frumentius, first Bishop of Aksum. By 1993, this attribution had been replaced by another: to Ramhai, an early ruler of Aksum recalled in the traditional king-lists but not elsewhere. This attribution, the chronological implication of which is contradicted by the archaeological evidence, provides an insight into the development of popular tradition at Aksum, discussed at greater length on pp. 140-4.

138 For a plan and reconstruction, see Munro-Hay 1989a: 116-20, 165-6. Note the basic similarity of the substructure plan to that of Nefas Mawcha. Similar metal clamps were also used in the construction of the two monuments; the Tomb of the False Door is the only place at Aksum where such a clamp has been preserved *in situ*.

139 Although the substructure was largely supported by the basal slab, the superstructure extended beyond it, had inadequate foundations and has been badly affected by subsequent subsidence.

140 Munro-Hay 1989a: 157. A more detailed evaluation is in preparation.

141 See pp. 84-6, above.

142 Sergew 1972: 225-32; Belaynesh *et al.* 1975; see also p. 125-7, below.

143 Littmann *et al.* 1913, II: pl. xxvii.

144 The plan published by Littmann *et al.* 1913, II: 34 and reproduced with minor modification by Munro-Hay 1989a: 142 is very incomplete and is currently being resurveyed.

145 The 1994-96 excavations were supervised by Ato Ayele Tarekegn.

146 Morrison 1989a. The glass is preserved at the museum in Aksum.

147 Munro-Hay 1989a: 42-7.

148 Kaleb was king of Aksum in the early sixth century, being known from the coinage and documentary sources. Gabra Maskal is traditionally recalled as his successor.

149 The superstructure itself has never been subjected to thorough archaeological investigation and has been disfigured by inaccurate restoration. Several architectural elements were removed *c.* 1938 to the park known as the 'Ezana Garden' in Aksum town (see fig. 18, above). Anfray (1990: 97) has suggested that the superstructure may be significantly later than the tombs themselves.

150 Beckingham and Huntingford 1961: 158-9. Ethiopian sources indicate that the tombs' existence was remembered locally in earlier times: Conti Rossini 1910.

151 Littmann *et al.* 1913, II: 127-34; D. Phillipson 1997: 73-88.

152 Bernand *et al.* 1991.

153 Cf. Buxton 1971: fig. 36.
154 Anfray 1967.
155 Menelik (I) is recalled as the son of Solomon and the Queen of Sheba, who brought the Ark of the Covenant to Ethiopia (Budge 1922; Belaynesh *et al.* 1975).
156 Littmann *et al.* 1913, II: 134.
157 Bard and Fattovich 1995; Anfray 1963, 1967.
158 Anfray 1963; Anfray and Annequin 1965.
159 Anfray and Annequin 1965.
160 The tombs at Yeha were likewise little disturbed: most seem to belong to the pre-Aksumite period or earlier.
161 The possible provision for a sarcophagus in the Tomb of Bazen has been noted above. This observation has chronological implications.
162 Casson 1989: 52-3.
163 Littmann *et al.* 1913, II: pls ii-iv, vi; D. Phillipson 1997: 11-43.
164 Littmann 1947; see also Sergew 1972: 95.
165 E.g. Rufinus, writing in the late fourth century: for an English translation of the relevant passage, see Jones and Monroe 1935: 26-7.
166 E.g. Sergew 1972: 92-3. For Abraha and Atsbaha, see also pp. 140-3, below.
167 Conti-Rossini 1928: 156-63; Sergew 1972: 115-21; Taddesse 1972: 23-5.
168 Monneret de Villard 1947.
169 For Procopius, see Dewing 1961; for the coins, see Munro-Hay and Juel-Jensen 1995; for the inscriptions see Bernand *et al.* 1991 and Munro-Hay 1991a: 221-32.
170 Kobishchanov 1979: 91-108.
171 See pp. 20-21, above.
172 Munro-Hay and Juel-Jensen 1995. There is also a series of Ezana's coins bearing no religious symbol. It is not known whether these were issued between the pagan and Christian series.
173 For this meaning of XWPA, see Liddell and Scott 1883: 1749.
174 For translations, see Munro-Hay 1991a: 223-9.
175 It could be that these usages were deliberately ambiguous, or that the conversion was primarily a hastening and formalisation of a process already widespread. Literary records and historical tradition may have exaggerated the contrast between old and new, as is the case with the earliest stages of Palestinian Christianity.
176 Anfray *et al.* 1970.
177 Munro-Hay 1991a: 224-9.
178 E.g. Wilding 1989: fig. 16.394.
179 Doresse 1957; Anfray and Annequin 1965.
180 The continuity of symbolism may be noted.
181 Daum 1988b; see also Gentelle 1991.
182 This would be expected if Aksumite ecclesiastics, like their modern counterparts, engaged in secular activities and had few material possessions specific to their religious activities.
183 Taddesse 1972: 21-68.
184 Sergew 1972: 143.
185 Budge 1922; Shahid 1976.
186 Littmann *et al.* 1913, II: 136-40; D. Phillipson 1995, 1997: chapter 8.
187 Alvares' description, translated by Beckingham and Huntingford 1961: 145-53, is not easy to understand. A detailed reconstruction, based on the account of Alvares, has been proposed by Buxton and Matthews 1974.
188 Heldman 1995; see also pp. 140-3, below.
189 Quoted from Lewcock 1988: 204-5, where sources are cited. It is noteworthy that the account makes no mention that people were depicted, contrary to the general practice of Christian decoration at that time.
190 R. Schneider 1974.
191 Excavations by de Contenson (1959, 1963b) and Anfray (1965) immediately north of the Cathedral podium indicated the presence of substantial structures of pre-fourth-century date, but no clear indication of their function.
192 Anfray 1967, 1990.
193 Anfray 1974.
194 Acton 1868: 12-13 and personal observation.
195 Examples are cited by Godet 1977, 1982.

Chapter 5 **The Aksumite System**

1 McCrindle 1897: 67; Wolska-Conus 1968-73.
2 Michels 1994. For a courageous attempt to compare the chronologies of Aksum and Matara, based in part on Michel's work, see Negussie 1993.
3 Anfray 1974.
4 D. Phillipson 1990.

5 For a similar situation in Yemen, see Gentelle 1991.

6 Conti Rossini 1910.

7 R. Schneider *pers. comm.*

8 E.g. Ortelius 1573.

9 Anfray 1963, 1967, 1974;

10 Sergew 1972: 126; Anfray 1963: 90.

11 Anfray 1974: 760. Unlike the Aksum/Yeha region, there is no evidence for the density of rural settlement around Matara.

12 Casson 1981 argues that Adulis moved from near the modern Massawa to this inland location sometime after the first century AD.

13 Wolska-Conus 1968-73.

14 Munro-Hay 1989c.

15 Sundström 1907; Paribeni 1907.

16 Anfray 1974.

17 Kirwan 1972.

18 Heldman 1994; Munro-Hay 1989c.

19 Stevenson 1932.

20 Littmann *et al.* 1913, II: 148-52; S. Pankhurst 1955: pl. v.

21 Invaluable gazetteers of known sites have been published by Godet 1977, 1982.

22 Michels 1994.

23 de Contenson 1961b.

24 Kobishchanov 1979: 99-108; Wolska-Conus 1968-73.

25 Munro-Hay 1991a: 224-5.

26 Kobishchanov 1979: 99-108.

27 Aksum's ecclesiastical prominence survived the removal of the political capital. The traditionally recorded lists of kings and *abunas* are completely distinct. See also Sergew 1969.

28 Casson 1989: 52-3.

29 Guidi 1922; Frend 1989.

30 Sergew 1972: 225-32; el Chennafi 1976.

31 Munro-Hay 1984b. This dating is concordant with the possibility (noted above on p. 72) that Armah, the last Aksumite king to issue coins according to the sequence proposed by Munro-Hay and Juel-Jensen (1995), may have been a contemporary of the prophet Mohammed.

32 D. Phillipson, Reynolds *et al.* 1996.

33 al Masudi: cf. Barbier de Meynard and de Courteille 1864-77; Sergew 1972: 223.

34 Cf. Butzer 1981.

35 Sutton 1989.

36 de Contenson 1969; Zurawski 1993.

Chapter 6 **Christian Ethiopia after Aksum**

1 The traditional date for the inception of Zagwe rule is AD 1137. The period immediately before this remains exceptionally poorly known and there is no agreement whether or not it should be subsumed within the Aksumite period.

2 For this and alternative derivations, see Sergew 1972: 239.

3 Known mainly through ecclesiastical tradition (e.g. Budge 1928), this hiatus seems to have been marked by the activities of several pretenders or impostors. It is tempting to suggest that it represents a time when the Christian credentials of the Ethiopian rulers were questioned by the Patriarch in Alexandria. Muslim settlement in Tigray was also taking place at this time, as is shown by a series of Arabic-inscribed tombstones from Makelle (Pansera 1945; M. Schneider 1967). Whether or not the early Zagwe rulers were nominally or sincerely Christian, it seems to have been through the intervention of the Nubian King George that the Patriarch was persuaded to resume nomination of an *abuna* for Ethiopia (Budge 1928; Sergew 1972: 223).

4 R. Schneider 1984; Munro-Hay 1991a: 232.

5 Littmann *et al.* 1913, IV; Sergew 1972; R. Schneider 1984. The dating should be regarded as approximate.

6 Munro-Hay 1991a: 232.

7 Almagro *et al.* 1975.

8 There are clear surface traces at Lalibela of substantial ancient buildings apparently unconnected with the rock-cut churches, but they have received no scholarly attention.

9 See Plant 1985 for a useful and comprehensively illustrated survey which does not, unfortunately, cover Eritrea. The pioneering work of Beatrice Playne 1954 should also be noted.

10 Littmann *et al.* 1913, II: 168-95.

11 Matthews and Mordini 1959.

12 Mordini 1947.

13 Coins and textiles have been recorded at Debra Damo which confirm use of the site by late in the first millennium (Matthews and Mordini 1959).

14 Buxton 1947 (Debra Libanos and Imraha

Kristos); Littmann *et al.* 1913, II: 195-8 (Asmara).

15 For good general accounts, with distribution maps, see Buxton 1971; Plant 1985.

16 Gire and Schneider 1970.

17 E.g. Monti della Corte 1940; Bidder 1959; Gerster 1970; see also Buxton 1971.

18 Many of these columns have collapsed and have been replaced by replicas built with stone blocks.

19 Cf. Buxton and Matthews 1974; Heldman 1995.

20 A possibly early example is shown in pl. 11.

21 Getatchew 1993: 55; Getatchew and Macomber 1975-87.

22 Leroy *et al.* 1961; Uhlig 1993.

23 Cerulli 1968; for a masterly summary, see Getatchew 1993.

24 Leroy 1960, 1968; Uhlig 1990; Heldman 1993: 129-30.

25 Heldman 1993.

26 Lepage 1987.

27 Heldman 1993: 130-32.

28 Buxton 1970: 138-41, pls 68-75.

29 Heldman 1983, 1993: 176.

30 For a general discussion, see Buxton 1970: 164-76; Korabiewicz 1973. Hand crosses are discussed in greater detail by Hecht *et al.* 1990, and processional crosses by Moore 1971. See also Perczel 1986; Juel-Jensen 1993.

31 E.g. on copper coins of Armah (type 153 of Munro-Hay and Juel-Jensen 1995).

32 Juel-Jensen and Rowell 1975: 24, pls 62, 63.

33 Buxton 1970: 172-4, pls 120-22.

34 E.g. R. Pankhurst 1961.

Chapter 7 **The Meaning of Tradition**

1 Budge 1922; see also Littmann 1904; Shahid 1976.

2 The importance of this work is brought out by the request from Yohannes IV for the return of the copy removed from Magdala by British forces (Budge 1922: xv; Ullendorff 1960: 64-5).

3 A counterbalance to this tradition may be detected in the version which traces the Zagwe dynasty to a union earlier the same night between Solomon and a servant of Makeda.

4 Belai 1992; The 1955 constitution is summarised by Ullendorff 1960: 194-6.

5 Beckingham and Huntingford 1961: 145-8; Ludolf 1681.

6 Cf. Pritchard 1974; Philby 1981. The name 'Bilqis', by which she is recalled in Yemeni tradition, carries the implication 'concubine'.

7 1 Kings ch. x, vv. 1-13.

8 This book is concerned with instances of such attribution in Ethiopia and Eritrea. It should be noted, however, that similar attributions occur in Yemen (Daum 1988c). See also Spencer 1979.

9 For a comparable attribution of the Tomb of the False Door, see pp. 105-7 and note 137, above.

10 Examples include Stonehenge in England (Chippindale 1983) as well as sites in Buhaya, Tanzania (P. Schmidt 1978).

11 Within recent decades the growth of tourism, both Ethiopian and foreign, has added its own pressures.

12 This discrepancy is not unusual. As noted above, few of the Aksumite kings named on the coinage inscriptions may be convincingly identified in the traditional king-lists.

13 Heldman 1995.

14 Gigar 1984, 1987.

15 Heldman 1993: 129.

BIBLIOGRAPHY

Y. Abul-Haggag 1961. *A Contribution to the Physiography of Northern Ethiopia*. London: Athlone Press.

A. d'Abbadie 1868. *Douze ans de séjour dans la Haute Ethiopie (Abyssinie)*. Paris: Hachette.

R. Acton 1868. *The Abyssinian Expedition and the Life and Reign of King Theodore*. London: Illustrated London News.

M. Almagro *et al.* 1975. *Qusayr Amra: residencia y baños omeyas en el deserto de Jordania*. Madrid: Instituto Hispano-Arabe de Cultura.

F. Anfray 1963. La première campagne de fouilles à Matara (Nov. 1959 – Janv. 1960). *Annales d'Ethiopie* 5: 87- 166.

F. Anfray 1965. Chronique archéologique 1960-64. *Annales d'Ethiopie* 6: 3-48.

F. Anfray 1966. La poterie de Matara. *Rassegna di Studi Etiopici* 22: 5-74.

F. Anfray 1967. Matara. *Annales d'Ethiopie* 7: 33-88.

F. Anfray 1968. Aspects de l'archéologie éthiopienne. *Journal of African History* 9: 345-66.

F. Anfray 1972a. Les fouilles de Yeha, Mai-Juin 1972. *Documents pour servir à l'histoire des civilisations éthiopiennes* 3: 57-63.

F. Anfray 1972b. Les fouilles de Yeha. *Annales d'Ethiopie* 9: 45-56.

F. Anfray 1972c. L'archéologie d'Axoum en 1972. *Paideuma* 18: 60-78.

F. Anfray 1973. Les fouilles de Yeha, Mai-Juin 1973. *Documents pour servir à l'histoire des civilisations éthiopiennes* 4: 35-8.

F. Anfray 1974. Deux villes axoumites: Adoulis et Matara. pp. 745-65 in *Atti IV Congresso Internationale di Studi Etiopici*. Rome: Accademia Nazionale dei Lincei.

F. Anfray 1981. The civilisation of Aksum from the first to the seventh century. Mokhtar 1981: 362-78.

F. Anfray 1990. *Les anciens Ethiopiens: siècles d'histoire*. Paris: Armand Colin.

F. Anfray and G. Annequin 1965. Matara: deuxième, troisième et quatrième campagnes de fouilles. *Annales d'Ethiopie* 6: 49-92.

F. Anfray *et al.* 1970. Une nouvelle inscription grecque d'Ezana, roi d'Axoum. *Journal des Savants* (1970): 260-73.

L. Arpee 1946. *A History of Armenian Christianity from the Beginning to our own Time*. New York: Armenian Missionary Association of America.

R. Audouin 1991. Sculptures et peintures du château royal de Shabwa. *Syria* 68: 165-81.

R. Audouin *et al.* 1988. Towns and temples – the emergence of South Arabian civilisation. Daum 1988a: 63-77.

A. Avanzini 1989. Un exemple de langues en contact: les inscriptions sudarabes d'Ethiopie. pp. 469-78 in T. Fahd (ed.) *L'Arabie préislamique et son environnement historique et culturelle*. Leiden: Brill.

Aymro Wondmagegnehu and J. Motovu 1970. *The Ethiopian Orthodox Church*. Addis Ababa: Ethiopian Orthodox Mission.

Bahru Zewde 1991. *History of Modern Ethiopia*. London: Currey.

G. Bailloud 1965. *Les gisements paléolithiques de Melka-Kontouré*. Addis Ababa: Cahiers de l'Institut Ethiopien d'Archéologie.

C. Barbier de Meynard and P. de Courteille (trans.) 1965. *al Masudi: Les prairies d'or*. Paris: Société Asiatique.

K. Bard 1994. Environmental history of early Aksum. Marcus 1994b: 2-5.

K. Bard 1995. New excavations in Ethiopia. *Context* 12: 13-15.

K. Bard and R. Fattovich 1993. The 1993 excavations at Ona Enda Aboi Zague (Aksum, Tigray). *Nyame Akuma* 40: 14-17.

K. Bard and R. Fattovich 1995. The I.O.U./B.U. excavation at Bieta Giyorgis (Aksum): an interim report. *Nyame Akuma* 45: 25-7.

R. Barkay 1981. An Axumite coin from Jerusalem. *Israel Numismatic Journal* 5: 57-9.

M. Barradas 1996. *Tractatus Tres Historico-Geographici (1634): a seventeenth-century historical and geographical account of Tigray,*

Ethiopia, trans. E. Filleul, ed. R. Pankhurst. Wiesbaden: Harrassowitz.

J. N. Barrandon *et al.* 1990. Le monnayage d'or axoumite: une altération particulière. *Revue numismatique* 32: 186-211.

E. J. Bartleet 1934. *In the Land of Sheba*. Birmingham: Cornish.

R. Basset (ed.) 1897-1909. *Ahmad ibn 'Abd al-Kadir: Histoire de la conquête de l'Abyssinie (xvi siècle)*. Algiers: Ecole Supérieur des Lettres d'Alger.

de Bayle des Hermens 1976. Première mission de recherches préhistoriques en République Arabe du Yémen. *L'Anthropologie* 80: 5-38.

J-C. Beal 1991. Le coffret (?) d'ivoire du 'château royal' de Shabwa. *Syria* 68: 187-208.

C. F. Beckingham and G. W. B. Huntingford 1954. *Some Records of Ethiopia 1593–1646*. London: Hakluyt Society.

C. F. Beckingham and G. W. B. Huntingford 1961. *The Prester John of the Indies: a true relation of the lands of the Prester John, being the narrative of the Portuguese Embassy to Ethiopia in 1520 written by Father Francisco Alvares*. London: Hakluyt Society.

A. F. L. Beeston 1988. Pre-Islamic Yemeni inscriptions. Daum 1988a: 99-103.

V. Begley and R. D. de Puma (eds) 1991. *Rome and India: the ancient sea trade*. Madison: University of Wisconsin Press.

Belai Giday 1987. *Currency and Banking, Ethiopia*. Addis Ababa: the author.

Belai Giday 1992. *Ethiopian Civilization*. Addis Ababa: the author.

Belaynesh Michael *et al.* 1975. *Dictionary of Ethiopian Biography, I*. Addis Ababa: Institute of Ethiopian Studies.

M. L. Bender 1971. The languages of Ethiopia. *Anthropological Linguistics* 13: 165-288.

M. L. Bender *et al.* (eds) 1976. *Language in Ethiopia*. London: Oxford University Press.

J. T. Bent 1893a. *The Sacred City of the Ethiopians*. London: Longman.

J. T. Bent 1893b. The ancient trade route across Ethiopia. *Geographical Journal* 2: 140-6.

E. Bernand 1982. Nouvelles versions de la campagne du roi Ezana contre les Bedja. *Zeitschrift für Papyrologie und Epigraphik* 45: 105-14.

E. Bernand *et al.* 1991. *Receuil des Inscriptions de l'Ethiopie des périodes pré-Axoumite et Axoumite*. Paris: Académie des Inscriptions et Belles-Lettres.

C. Bezold 1905. *Kebra Negast*. Munich: Königliche Akademie der Wissenschaften.

I. Bidder 1959. *Lalibela: the monolithic churches of Ethiopia*. Cologne: DuMont.

W. T. Blanford 1870. *Observations on the Geology and Zoology of Abyssinia made during the Progress of the British Expedition to that Country in 1867-68*. London: Macmillan.

R. M. Blench and K.C. MacDonald (eds) 1998. *The Origins and Development of African Livestock*. London: U.C.L. Press.

R. Bonnefille and Ummer Mohammed 1994. Pollen-inferred climatic fluctuations in Ethiopia during the last 3000 years. *Palaeogeography, Palaeoclimatology, Palaeoecology* 109: 331-43.

BOSTID 1996. *Lost Crops of Africa, I: grains.* (Board on Science and Technology for International Development, National Research Council). Washington DC: National Academy Press.

F. Le B. Bowen and F. P. Albright 1958. *Archaeological Discoveries in South Arabia*. Baltimore: Johns Hopkins Press.

G. W. Bowersock 1983. *Roman Arabia*. Cambridge MA: Harvard University Press.

S. A. Brandt 1984. New perspectives on the origins of food production in Ethiopia. pp. 173-90 in J. D. Clark and S. A. Brandt (eds) *From Hunters to Farmers: the causes and consequences of food production in Africa*. Berkeley: University of California Press.

S. A. Brandt 1996. The ethnoarchaeology of flaked stone tool use in southern Ethiopia. Pwiti and Soper 1996: 733-8.

S. A. Brandt and N. Carder 1987. Pastoral rock art in the Horn of Africa: making sense of udder chaos. *World Archaeology* 19: 194-213.

S. A. Brandt and R. Fattovich 1990. Late Quaternary archaeological research in the Horn of Africa. pp. 95-108 in P. Robertshaw (ed.) *A History of African Archaeology*. London: Currey.

J-F. Breton 1991. Le site et la ville de Shabwa. *Syria* 68: 59-75.

F. von Brietenbach 1963. *The Indigenous Trees of Ethiopia*. Addis Ababa: Ethiopian Forestry Association.

J. Bruce 1790. *Travels to Discover the Source of the*

Nile in the Years 1768, 1769, 1770, 1771, 1772 and 1773. Edinburgh: Robinson.

E. A. W. Budge 1922. *The Queen of Sheba and her only son Menyelek, being the Book of the Glory of Kings.* London: Medici Society.

E. A. W. Budge 1928. *The Book of the Saints of the Ethiopian Church.* Cambridge: Cambridge University Press.

R. W. Bulliet 1975. *The Camel and the Wheel.* Cambridge MA: Harvard University Press.

S. Burstein 1981. Axum and the fall of Meroe. *Journal of the American Research Center in Egypt* 18: 47-9.

S. M. Burstein 1989. *Agatharchides of Cnidus on the Erythraean Sea.* London: Hakluyt Society.

K. W. Butzer 1981. The rise and fall of Axum, Ethiopia: a geoarchaeological interpretation. *American Antiquity* 40: 471-95.

D. R. Buxton 1947. The Christian antiquities of northern Ethiopia. *Archaeologia* 92: 1-42.

D. R. Buxton 1970. *The Abyssinians.* London: Thames and Hudson.

D. R. Buxton 1971. The rock-hewn and other medieval churches of Tigre province, Ethiopia. *Archaeologia* 103: 33-100.

D. R. Buxton and D. Matthews 1974. The reconstruction of vanished Aksumite buildings. *Rassegna di Studi Etiopici* 25: 53-76.

A. Caquot and A. J. Drewes 1955. Les monuments receuillis à Maqalle. *Annales d'Ethiopie* 1: 17-51.

P. Caraman 1985. *The Lost Empire: the story of the Jesuits in Ethiopia.* London: Sidgwick and Jackson.

L. Casson 1981. The location of Adulis. pp. 113-22 in L. Casson and M. Price (eds) *Coins, Culture and History in the Ancient World: numismatic and other studies in honour of Bluma L. Trell.* Detroit: Wayne State University Press.

L. Casson 1989. *The Periplus Maris Erythaei.* Princeton: Princeton University Press.

E. Cerulli 1968. *La letteratura etiopica.* Florence: Sansoni.

P. Cervicek 1976. Rock engravings from the Hamasen region, Eritrea. *Paideuma* 22: 237-56.

J. Chavaillon 1976. Mission archéologique franco-éthiopienne de Melka Kontouré. *L'Ethiopie avant l'histoire* 1: 1-11.

R. E. Cheesman 1936. *Lake Tana and the Blue Nile.* London: Macmillan.

M. el Chennafi 1976. Mention nouvelle d'une 'reine éthiopienne' au IVè siècle de Hégire / Xè siècle après J.-C. *Annales d'Ethiopie* 10: 119-21.

C. R. Chippindale 1983. *Stonehenge Complete.* London: Thames and Hudson.

H. N. Chittick 1974. Excavations at Aksum 1973-74: a preliminary report. *Azania* 9: 159-205.

H. N. Chittick 1976. Radiocarbon dates from Aksum. *Azania* 11: 179-81.

H. N. Chittick 1979. Early ports in the Horn of Africa. *International Journal of Nautical Archaeology* 8: 274-5.

J. D. Clark 1988. The Middle Stone Age of East Africa and the beginnings of regional identity. *Journal of World Prehistory* 2: 235-305.

J. D. Clark and M. A. J. Williams 1978. Recent archaeological research in south-eastern Ethiopia (1974-5): some preliminary results. *Annales d'Ethiopie* 11: 19-44.

J. Clutton-Brock 1987. *A Natural History of Domesticated Mammals.* Cambridge: Cambridge University Press.

J. Clutton-Brock 1993. The spread of domestic animals in Africa. Shaw *et al.* 1993: 61-70.

H. de Contenson 1959. Les fouilles à Axoum en 1957: rapport préliminaire. *Annales d'Ethiopie* 3: 25-42.

H. de Contenson 1961a. Les fouilles à Haoulti-Melazo en 1958. *Annales d'Ethiopie* 4: 39-60.

H. de Contenson 1961b. Les fouilles à Ouchatei Golo près d'Axoum en 1958. *Annales d'Ethiopie* 4: 3-16.

H. de Contenson 1962. Les monuments d'art sud-arabes découverts sur le site de Haoulti (Ethiopie) en 1959. *Syria* 39: 68-83.

H. de Contenson 1963a. Les fouilles à Haoulti en 1959 – rapport préliminaire. *Annales d'Ethiopie* 5: 41-86.

H. de Contenson 1963b. Les fouilles à Axoum en 1958: rapport préliminaire. *Annales d'Ethiopie* 5: 1-40.

H. de Contenson 1969. Relations entre la Nubie chrétienne et l'Ethiopie axoumite. pp. 17-18 in *Proceedings of the Third International Conference of Ethiopian Studies,* I. Addis Ababa: Institute of Ethiopian Studies.

H. de Contenson 1981. Pre-Axumite culture. Mokhtar 1981: 341-61.

C. Conti Rossini 1904. *Acta Yared et Pantaleon (Corpus Scriptorum Christianorum Orientalium, Scriptores Aethiopici II, 17)*. Rome: de Luigi.

C. Conti Rossini 1910. *Liber Axumae (Corpus Scriptorum Christianorum Orientalium, Scriptores Aethiopici II, 8)*. Paris: e typographeo reipublicae.

C. Conti Rossini 1928. *Storia d'Etiopia*. Bergamo: Istituto Italiano d'Arti Grafiche.

M. Cornevin 1993. *Archéologie africaine*. Paris: Maisonneuve et Larose.

P. Craddock 1995. *Early Metal Mining and Production*. Edinburgh: Edinburgh University Press.

O. G. S. Crawford 1958. *Ethiopian Itineraries c. 1400–1524*. London: Hakluyt Society.

A. Cutler 1985. *The Craft of Ivory: sources, techniques and uses in the Mediterranean world AD 200–1400*. Washington DC: Dumbarton Oaks.

C. Darles 1991. L'architecture civile à Shabwa. *Syria* 68: 77–110.

W. Daum (ed.) 1988a. *Yemen: 3000 years of art and civilisation in Arabia Felix*. Innsbruck: Pinguin.

W. Daum 1988b. From the Queen of Saba to a modern state: 3,000 years of civilisation in southern Arabia. Daum 1988a: 9–31.

W. Daum (ed.) 1988c. *Die Konigin von Saba: Kunst, Legende und Archäologie zwischen Morgenland und Abendland*. Stuttgart: Belser.

B. Davidson 1992. *The Black Man's Burden: Africa and the curse of the nation-state*. London: Currey.

I. Davidson 1991. The archaeology of language origins: a review. *Antiquity* 65: 39–48.

G. Dembski 1988. The coins of Arabia Felix. Daum 1988a: 125-8.

S. Der Nersessian 1969. *The Armenians*. London: Thames and Hudson.

J. Desanges 1978. *Recherches sur l'activité des Méditerranéens aux confins de l'Afrique*. Rome: Ecole française de Rome.

H. B. Dewing (ed. and trans.) 1961. *Procopius' History of the Wars*. London: Loeb.

M. DiBlasi 1994. An agenda for palynological research on the late Holocene environmental history and human ecology in northern Ethiopia. Marcus 1994b: 675-87.

A. Dillmann 1878. Uber die Anfänge des Axumitischen Reiches. *Abhandlungen der Koniglichen Akademie der Wissenschaften zu Berlin*.

A. Dillmann 1880. Zur Geschichte des Axumitischen Reiches im vierten bis sechsten Jahrhundert. *Abhandlungen der Koniglichen Akademie der Wissenschaften zu Berlin*.

B. Doe 1971. *Southern Arabia*. London: Thames and Hudson.

E. J. van Donzel 1979. *Foreign Relations of Ethiopia 1642- 1700: documents relating to the journeys of Khodja Murâd*. Istanbul: Nederlands Instituut voor het Nabije Oosten.

E. J. van Donzel 1986. *A Yemenite Embassy to Ethiopia 1647-49*. Stuttgart: Steiner.

J. Doresse 1957. *L'empire du Pretre Jean*. Paris: Plon.

F. Dramis and R. Fattovich 1994. From past to present: research perspectives in environmental archaeology on the Ethiopian plateau. pp. 9-14 in Bahru Zewde *et al.* (eds) *Proceedings of the Eleventh International Conference of Ethiopian Studies, vol. I*. Addis Ababa: Institute of Ethiopian Studies.

S. F. Drew 1954. Notes from the Red Sea hills. *South African Archaeological Bulletin* 9: 101-02.

A. J. Drewes 1962. *Inscriptions de l'Ethiopie antique*. Leiden: Brill.

J. Dubois 1996. L'artisanat traditionnel des hauts plateaux. Van der Stappen 1996: 343-54.

D. J. Duncanson 1947. Girmaten: a new archaeological site in Eritrea. *Antiquity* 21: 158-63.

D. N. Edwards 1996. *The Archaeology of the Meroitic State: new perspectives on its social and political organisation*. Oxford: Tempus Reparatum.

S. B. Edwards 1991. Crops with wild relatives found in Ethiopia. Engels *et al.* 1991: 42-74.

C. Ehret 1979. On the antiquity of agriculture in Ethiopia. *Journal of African History* 20: 161-77.

J. M. M. Engels *et al.* (eds) 1991. *Plant Genetic Resources of Ethiopia*. Cambridge: Cambridge University Press.

B. M. Fagan 1990. *The Journey from Eden: the peopling of our world*. London: Thames and Hudson.

J. D. Fage (ed.) 1978. *The Cambridge History of Africa, vol. II: 500 BC – AD 1500*. Cambridge: Cambridge University Press.

R. Fattovich 1977. Some data for the study of

cultural history in ancient northern Ethiopia. *Nyame Akuma* 10: 6-18.

R. Fattovich 1987. Some remarks on the origins of the Aksumite stelae. *Annales d'Ethiopie* 14: 43-69.

R. Fattovich 1989. Remarks on the later prehistory and early history of northern Ethiopia. *Proceedings of the Eighth International Conference of Ethiopian Studies*, pp. 85-104. Addis Ababa: Institute of Ethiopian Studies.

R. Fattovich 1990. Remarks on the pre-Aksumite period in northern Ethiopia. *Journal of Ethiopian Studies* 23: 1-33.

R. Fattovich 1993. Punt: the archaeological perspective. pp. 399-405 in G. M. Zaccone and T. R. di Netro (eds) *Atti Sesto Congresso Internazionale di Egittologia, vol. II*. Turin.

R. Fattovich 1995. Archaeological excavations at Bieta Giyorgis (Aksum, Tigray), 1994 field season: a preliminary report. *Nyame Akuma* 43: 34-7.

R. Fattovich 1996a. The origins of the kingdom of Kush: views from the African hinterland. *Archéologie du Nil Moyen* 7: 69-78.

R. Fattovich 1996b. The Afro-Arabian circuit: contacts between the Horn of Africa and southern Arabia in the third – second millennia BC. pp. 395-402 in L. Krzyzaniak *et al.* (eds) *Inter-regional Contacts in the Later Prehistory of North-eastern Africa*. Poznan: Poznan Archaeological Museum.

R. Fattovich and K. Bard 1993. Scavi archeologici nella zona di Aksum: C – Ona Enda Aboi Zague (Bieta Giyorgis). *Rassegna di Studi Etiopici* 35: 41-71.

R. Fattovich and K. Bard 1995. Scavi archeologici nella zona di Aksum: E – Ona Enda Aboi Zague e Ona Nagast (Bieta Giyorgis). *Rassegna di Studi Etiopici* 37: 5- 35.

R. Fattovich *et al.* 1984. The archaeology of the eastern sahel, Sudan: preliminary results. *African Archaeological Review* 2: 173-88.

F. G. Fedele 1988. North Yemen: the neolithic. Daum 1988a: 34-7.

V. Francaviglia *et al.* 1990. Preliminary considerations for the restoration of the great obelisk at Aksum. *Journal of Ethiopian Studies* 23: 67-78.

W. H. C. Frend 1989. The Church in the reign of Constantius II (337-361): mission, monasticism, worship. pp. 73- 111 in *L'église et l'empire au IVè siècle*. Geneva: Fondation Hardt.

P. Garlake 1995. *The Hunter's Vision: the prehistoric art of Zimbabwe*. London: British Museum Press.

N. Gebremedhin 1976. Some traditional types of housing in Ethiopia. pp. 106-23 in P. Oliver (ed.) *Shelter in Africa*. London: Barrie and Jenkins.

P. Gentelle 1991. Les irrigations antiques à Shabwa. *Syria* 68: 5-54.

G. Gerster 1970. *Churches in Rock*. London: Phaidon.

Getaneh Assefa and A. Russo 1994. Stratigraphy and age of rock sequence in Aksum and its surrounding regions. Marcus 1994b: 36-44.

Getatchew Haile 1993. Ethiopic literature. Grierson 1993: 47-55.

Getatchew Haile and W. F. Macomber 1975-87. A *Catalogue of Ethiopian Manuscripts Microfilmed for the Ethiopian Manuscript Microfilm Library, Addis Ababa, and for the Hill Monastic Manuscript Library, Collegeville*. Collegeville, Minnesota: Hill Library.

K. R. Gibson and T. Ingold (eds) 1993. *Tools, Language and Cognition in Human Evolution*. Cambridge: Cambridge University Press.

M. Gibson 1994. *The Liverpool Ivories: late antique and medieval ivory and bone carving in Liverpool Museum and the Walker Art Gallery*. London: H.M.S.O.

Gigar Tesfaye 1984. Inscriptions sur bois de trois églises de Lalibela. *Journal of Ethiopian Studies* 17: 107-26.

Gigar Tesfaye 1987. Découverte d'inscriptions guèzes a Lalibela. *Annales d'Ethiopie* 14: 75-80.

D. Gill 1991. *The Coinage of Ethiopia, Eritrea and Italian Somalia*. New York: the author.

J. Gire and R. Schneider 1970. Etudes des églises rupestres du Tigre. *Documents pour servir à l'histoire des civilisations éthiopiennes* 1: 73-9.

Girma Fisseha 1996. Architecture et trésors de l'église éthiopienne. Van der Stappen 1996: 181-93.

W. D. Glanzman 1996. Arabia and the Persian / Arabian Gulf. pp. 39-42 in B. M. Fagan (ed.) *The Oxford Companion to Archaeology*. New York: Oxford University Press.

E. Godet 1977. Répertoire des sites pré-

Axoumites et Axoumites du Tigre, Ethiopie. *Abbay* 8: 19-58.

E. Godet 1982. Répertoire de sites pré-Axoumites et Axoumites d'Ethiopie du Nord, IIè partie: Erythrée. *Abbay* 11: 73-113.

G. Goldenberg (ed.) 1986. *Ethiopian Studies: Proceedings of the Sixth International Conference, Tel Aviv, 1980.* Rotterdam: Balkema.

P. Graziosi 1964. New discoveries of rock paintings in Ethiopia. *Antiquity* 38: 91-8, 187-90.

J. Greenberg 1963. *Languages of Africa.* The Hague: Mouton.

R. Grierson (ed.) 1993. *African Zion: the sacred art of Ethiopia.* New Haven: Yale University Press.

Guida 1938. *Guida dell' Africa Orientale Italiana.* Milan.

I. Guidi 1922. La chiesa abissina. *Oriente moderno* 2: 123-8, 186-90, 252-6.

R. Haaland 1996. A socio-economic perspective on the transition from gathering to cultivation and domestication: a case study of sorghum in the middle Nile region. Pwiti and Soper 1996: 391-400.

E. Haberland 1969. Hiob Ludolf, father of Ethiopian studies in Europe. pp. 131-6 in *Proceedings of the Third International Conference of Ethiopian Studies, vol. I.* Addis Ababa: Institute of Ethiopian Studies.

T. Hägg 1984. A new Axumite inscription in Greek from Meroe. *Meroitica* 7: 436-41.

T. Hägg 1994. Sayce's Axumite inscription from Meroe: again. *Meroitic Newsletter* 25: 45-8.

W. R. O. Hahn 1983. Die Münzprägung des Aksumitisches Reiches. *Litterae Numismaticae Vindobonenses* 2: 113- 80.

W. R. O. Hahn 1995. Letter to the Editor. *Spink Numismatic Circular* 103: 92.

D. R. Harris (ed.) 1996. *The Origins and Spread of Agriculture and Pastoralism in Eurasia.* London: U.C.L. Press.

J. W. K. Harris 1983. Cultural beginnings: Plio/Pleistocene archaeological occurrences from the Afar, Ethiopia. *African Archaeological Review* 1: 3-31.

W. C. Harris 1844. *The Highlands of Aethiopia.* London: Longman.

G. Hausman 1997. *The Kebra Negast: the book of Rastafarian wisdom and faith from Ethiopia and Jamaica.* New York: St Martin's Press.

J. W. Hayes 1972. *Late Roman Pottery.* London: British School at Rome.

D. Hecht *et al.* 1990. *The Hand Crosses of the I. E. S. Collection.* Addis Ababa: Institute of Ethiopian Studies.

I. Hedberg and S. Edwards 1989ff. *Flora of Ethiopia.* Addis Ababa: National Herbarium.

M. Heldman 1983. An Ethiopian miniature of the head of St Mark: Egyptian influence at the Monastery of Saint Stephen, Hayq. pp. 554-68 in S. Segert and A. J. E. Bodrogligeti (eds) *Ethiopian Studies Dedicated to Wolf Leslau on the Occasion of his Seventy-fifth Birthday.* Wiesbaden: Harrassowitz.

M. Heldman 1993. The heritage of Late Antiquity. Grierson 1993: 117-32.

M. Heldman 1994. Early Byzantine sculptural fragments from Adulis. *Etudes éthiopiennes* 1: 239-52.

M. Heldman 1995. Legends of Lalibala: the development of an Ethiopian pilgrimage site. *Res* 27: 25-38.

P. Henze (ed.) 1993. *Aspects of Ethiopian Art from Ancient Axum to the Twentieth Century.* London: Jed Press.

R. Hezron 1972. *Ethiopic Semitic.* Manchester: Manchester University Press.

T. J. Holland and H. M. Hozier 1870. *Record of the Expedition to Abyssinia, compiled by Order of the Secretary for War.* London: H.M.S.O.

M. Horton, 1996. *Shanga: the archaeology of a Muslim trading community on the coast of East Africa.* London: British Institute in Eastern Africa.

G. Hudson 1978. Geolinguistic evidence for Ethiopian Semitic prehistory. *Abbay* 9: 71-85.

G. W. B. Huntingford (ed.) 1980. *The Periplus of the Erythraean Sea.* London: Hakluyt Society.

H. P. Huffnagel 1961. *Agriculture in Ethiopia.* Rome: Food and Agriculture Organisation of UNESCO.

H. M. Hyatt 1928. *The Church of Abyssinia.* London: Luzac.

A. Irvine 1965. On the identity of Habashat in the South Arabian inscriptions. *Journal of Semitic Studies* 10: 178-96.

C. W. Isenberg and J. L. Krapf 1843. *Journals of the Rev. Messrs. Isenberg and Krapf, Missionaries of the Church Missionary Society, Detailing their Proceedings in the Kingdom of*

Shoa and Journeys in Other Parts of Abyssinia in the Years 1839, 1840, 1941 and 1842. London: Seeley.

A. Jamme 1962. *Sabaean Inscriptions from Mahram Bilqis (Marib).* Baltimore: Johns Hopkins Press.

D. C. Johanson and M. A. Edey 1981. *Lucy: the beginnings of humankind.* Saint Albans: Granada.

D. C. Johanson and T. White 1979. A systematic assessment of early African hominids. *Science* 203: 321-30.

C. Johnston 1868. *Travels in Southern Abyssinia, through the Country of Adal to the Kingdom of Shoa.* London: Madden.

A. H. M. Jones and E. Monroe 1935. *A History of Abyssinia.* Oxford: Clarendon Press.

R. Joussaume 1981. L'art rupestre de l'Ethiopie. pp. 159-75 in C. Roubet *et al.* (eds) *Préhistoire africaine.* Paris: Editions A.P.D.F.

R. Joussaume 1996. Les cultures mégalithiques de l'Ethiopie. Van der Stappen 1996: 58-75.

B. Juel-Jensen 1993. The evolution of the Ethiopian cross. Henze 1993: 17-27.

B. Juel-Jensen 1994. A gold coin of Aksum struck from hitherto unpublished dies. *Spink Numismatic Circular* 102: 212.

B. Juel-Jensen and B. Atkins, 1996. The gold coinage of Aksum: new analyses. *Spink Numismatic Circular* 104: 124-5.

B. Juel-Jensen and S. C. Munro-Hay 1994. Further examples of coins of Offa inspired by Aksumite designs. *Spink Numismatic Circular* 102: 256-7.

B. Juel-Jensen and G. Rowell (eds) 1975. *Rock-Hewn Churches of Eastern Tigray: an account of the Oxford University Expedition to Ethiopia, 1974.* Oxford: Oxford University Exploration Club.

A. M. Juma 1996. The Swahili and the Mediterranean world: pottery of the late Roman period from Zanzibar. *Antiquity* 70: 147-54.

A. Kammerer 1926. *Essai sur l'histoire antique d'Abyssinie: le royaume d'Aksum et ses voisins d'Arabie et de Meroe.* Paris: Geuthner.

A. Kammerer 1929. *Le mer rouge, l'Abyssinie et l'Arabie depuis l'antiquité: essai d'histoire et de géographie historique.* Cairo: Société royale de géographie d'Egypte.

S. Kaplan 1994. Beta Israel (Falasha) religion:

ancient Judaism or evolving Ethiopian tradition? *Etudes éthiopiennes* 1: 107-14.

Kebbede Mikael and J. Leclant 1955. La section d'archéologie (1952-55). *Annales d'Ethiopie* 1: 1-6.

A. Kindler 1988. Relations between Israel and Ethiopia in late Roman and Byzantine times according to numismatic discoveries. pp. 106-11 in T. Matouk (ed.) *Jews and Samaritans in Byzantine Israel.* Jerusalem.

G. King and C. Tonghini 1996. A Survey of the Islamic *Sites near Aden and in the Abyan District of Yemen.* London: School of Oriental and African Studies.

L. P. Kirwan 1960. The decline and fall of Meroe. *Kush* 8: 163-73.

L. P. Kirwan 1972. The *Christian Topography* and the Kingdom of Axum. *Geographical Journal* 138: 166-77.

K. A. Kitchen 1971. Punt and how to get there. *Orientalia* 40: 184-207.

K. A. Kitchen 1993. The land of Punt. Shaw *et al.* 1993: 587-608.

K. A. Kitchen. 1994. *Documentation for Ancient Arabia.* Liverpool: Liverpool University Press.

R. G. Klein 1989. *The Human Career: human bioloical and cultural origins.* Chicago: University of Chicago Press.

Y. Kobishchanov 1969. The sea voyages of ancient Ethiopians in the Indian Ocean. pp. 19-24 in *Proceedings of the Third International Conference of Ethiopian Studies, vol. I.* Addis Ababa: Institute of Ethiopian Studies.

Y. Kobishchanov 1979. *Axum* (ed. J. Michels). University Park: Pennsylvania State University Press.

Y. M. Kobishchanov 1981. Aksum: political system, economics and culture, first to fourth century. Mokhtar 1981: 381-400.

W. Korabiewicz 1973. *The Ethiopian Cross.* Addis Ababa: Holy Trinity Cathedral.

A. Korotayev 1996. *Ancient Yemen: some general trends of evolution of the Sabaic language and Sabaean culture.* Oxford: Oxford University Press for the University of Manchester.

M. D. Leakey and J. M. Harris (eds) 1987. *Laetoli: a Pliocene site in northern Tanzania.* Oxford: Clarendon Press.

J. Leclant 1959. Les fouilles à Axoum en 1955-56: rapport préliminaire. *Annales d'Ethiopie* 3: 3-24.

166

Bibliography

T. Lefebvre 1845-8. *Voyage en Abyssinie*. Paris: Bertrand.

C. Lepage 1987. Les monuments chrétiens rupestres de Degum en Ethiopie (rapport préliminaire). *Cahiers archéologiques* 27: 167-200.

J. Leroy 1960. L'évangeliaire éthiopien du couvent d'Abba Garima et ses attaches avec l'ancien art chrétien de Syrie. *Cahiers archéologiques* 11: 131-43.

J. Leroy *et al.* 1961. *Ethiopia: illuminated manuscripts*. Greenwich, Connecticut: UNESCO World Art Series.

J. Leroy 1968. Un nouvel évangeliaire éthiopien illustré du monastère d'Abba Garima. *Synthronon: Bibliothèque des Cahiers archéologiques* 2: 75-87.

R. Lewcock 1988. The medieval architecture of Yemen. Daum 1988a: 204-11.

J. D. Lewis-Williams 1981. *Believing and Seeing*. London: Academic Press.

J. D. Lewis-Williams 1983. *The Rock Art of Southern Africa*. Cambridge: Cambridge University Press.

H. G. Liddell and R. Scott 1883. *A Greek-English Lexicon*. Oxford: Clarendon Press.

E. Littmann 1904. *The Legend of the Queen of Sheba in the Tradition of Axum (Bibliotheca Abessinica I)*. Leiden: Brill.

E. Littmann 1947. La leggenda del dragone del Aksum in lingua Tigrai. *Rassegna di Studi Etiopici* 6: 42-5.

E. Littmann *et al.* 1913. *Deutsche Aksum-Expedition*. Berlin: Reimer.

J. Ludolf 1661. *Grammatica Aethiopica*. London: Roycroft.

J. Ludolf 1681. *Historia Aethiopica*. Frankfurt: Zunner.

J. Ludolf 1691. *Commentarius ad suam Historiam Aethiopicam*. Frankfurt: Zunner.

J. Ludolf 1698. *Grammatica Linguae Amharicae*. Frankfurt: Zunner.

J. C. McCann 1994. Historical methods toward a landscape history of the Aksum region, 1500 – 1900. Marcus 1994b: 846-56.

J. W. McCrindle (ed.) 1897. *The Christian Topography of Cosmas Indicopleustes*. London: Hakluyt Society.

K. C. MacDonald 1992. The domestic chicken (*Gallus gallus*) in sub-Saharan Africa. *Journal of Archaeological Science* 19: 303-18.

F. Maes 1996. Production agricole des hauts plateaux. Van der Stappen 1996: 36-52.

A. de Maigret 1988. The Yemeni Bronze Age. Daum 1988a: 38-40.

A. de Maigret (ed.) 1990. *The Bronze Age Cultures of Hawlan At-Tyial and Al-Hada*. Rome: Ismeo.

A. Manning and J. Serpell (eds) 1994. *Animals and Human Society: changing perspectives*. London: Routledge.

B. B. B. Mapunda 1997. Patching up evidence for ironworking in the Horn. *African Archaeological Review* 14: 107-24.

H. C. Marcus 1994a. *A History of Ethiopia*. Berkeley: University of California Press.

H. G. Marcus (ed.) 1994b. *New Trends in Ethiopian Studies*. Lawrenceville: Red Sea Press.

C. R. Markham 1869. *A History of the Abyssinian Expedition*. London: Macmillan.

P. Marrassini 1990. Some considerations on the problem of the 'Syriac influences' on Aksumite Ethiopia. *Journal of Ethiopian Studies* 23: 35-46.

D. H. Matthews 1949. The restoration of the monastery church of Debra Damo, Ethiopia. *Antiquity* 23: 188-200.

D. H. Matthews and A. Mordini 1959. The monastery of Debra Damo, Ethiopia. *Archaeologia* 97: 1-58.

K. L. Mehra 1991. Prehistoric Ethiopia and India: contacts through sorghum and millet genetic resources. Engels *et al.* 1991: 160-8.

P. Mellars and C. Stringer (eds) 1989. *The Human Revolution: behavioural and biological perspectives on the origins of modern humans*. Edinburgh: Edinburgh University Press.

Y. Meshorer and A. Spaer 1966. An Axumite coin from Caesarea. *Israel Numismatic Journal* 3: 76.

J. W. Michels 1979. Axumite archaeology: an introductory essay. Kobishchanov 1979: 1-34.

J. W. Michels 1990. Review article: excavations at Aksum. *African Archaeological Review* 8: 177-87.

J. W. Michels 1994. Regional political organisation in the Axum-Yeha area during the pre-Axumite and Axumite eras. *Etudes éthiopiennes* 1: 61-80.

J-P. Migne 1860. *Ioannes Malalas Chronographica*. Paris: Migne.

J. Miller 1969. *The Spice Trade of the Roman*

Empire. Oxford: Oxford University Press.

P. Mohr 1971. *The Geology of Ethiopia*. Addis Ababa: Haile Sellassie I University Press.

G. Mokhtar (ed.) 1981. *General History of Africa, vol. II*. Paris: UNESCO.

U. Monneret de Villard 1938. *Aksum: ricerche di topografia generale*. Rome: Pontificium Institutum Biblicum.

U. Monneret de Villard 1947. Mose, vescovo di Adulis. *Orientalia Cristiana Periodica* 13: 613-23.

U. Monneret de Villard 1948. Aksum e i quattro re del mondo. *Annali Lateranensi* 12: 125-80.

A. A. Monti della Corte 1940. *Lalibela: le chiese ipogee e monolitiche e gli alti monumenti medievali del Lasta*. Rome: Societa Italiana Arti Grafice.

E. Moore 1971. *Ethiopian Processional Crosses*. Addis Ababa.

A. Mordini 1947. Il soffito del secondo vestibolo dell'Enda Abuna Aragawi in Dabra Damo. *Rassegna di Studi Etiopici* 6: 29-35.

A. Mordini 1953. Un vasetto con figurazioni votive proveniente de Baroca (Tigrai). *Il Bolletino* 1: 17-20.

A. Mordini 1960. Gli aurei Kushana del convento di Dabra Dammo. pp. 249-54 in *Atti del Convegno di Studi Etiopici*. Rome.

H. M. Morrison 1989a. The glass. Munro-Hay 1989a: 188-209.

H. M. Morrison 1989b. The beads. Munro-Hay 1989a: 168-78.

S. C. Munro-Hay 1979. MHDYS and Ebana, kings of Aksum: some problems of dating and identity. *Azania* 14: 21-30.

S. C. Munro-Hay 1980. Ezana (Ezana and Ezanas): some numismatic comments. *Azania* 15: 109-19.

S. C. Munro-Hay 1982. The foreign trade of the Aksumite port of Adulis. *Azania* 17: 105-25.

S. C. Munro-Hay 1984a. The Ge'ez and Greek palaeography of the coinage of Aksum. *Azania* 19: 134-44.

S. C. Munro-Hay 1984b. *The Coinage of Aksum*. New Delhi: Manohar.

S. C. Munro-Hay 1984c. An African monetarised economy in ancient times. *Proceedings of the Second International Conference on Indian Ocean Studies*. Perth.

S. C. Munro-Hay 1988. The dating of Ezana(s)

and Frumentius. *Rassegna di Studi Etiopici* 33: 111-27.

S. C. Munro-Hay 1989a. *Excavations at Aksum: an account of research at the ancient Ethiopian capital directed in 1972-74 by the late Dr Neville Chittick*. London: British Institute in Eastern Africa.

S. C. Munro-Hay 1989b. The al-Madhariba hoard of gold Aksumite and late Roman coins. *Numismatic Chronicle* 149: 83-100.

S. C. Munro-Hay 1989c. The British Museum excavations at Adulis, 1868. *Antiquaries Journal* 69: 43-52.

S. C. Munro-Hay 1990. The rise and fall of Aksum: chronological considerations. *Journal of Ethiopian Studies* 23: 47-53.

S. C. Munro-Hay 1991a. *Aksum: an African Civilisation of Late Antiquity*. Edinburgh: Edinburgh University Press.

S. C. Munro-Hay 1991b. The coinage of Shabwa (Hadhramawt) and other ancient South Arabian coinage in the National Museum, Aden. *Syria* 68: 393-418.

S. C. Munro-Hay 1993a. State development and urbanism in northern Ethiopia. Shaw *et al.* 1993: 609-21.

S. C. Munro-Hay 1993b. The iconography of Aksumite coinage. Henze 1993: 28-32.

S. C. Munro-Hay 1994. Coins of ancient South Arabia. *Numismatic Chronicle* 154: 191-203.

S. C. Munro-Hay 1995. A new gold coin of King MHDYS of Aksum. *Numismatic Chronicle* 155: 275-7.

S. C. Munro-Hay 1996. Coins of ancient South Arabia, II. *Numismatic Chronicle* 156: 33-47.

S. C. Munro-Hay and B. Juel-Jensen 1995. *Aksumite Coinage*. London: Spink.

S. C. Munro-Hay and G. Tringali 1993. The Ona sites of Asmara and Hamasien. *Rassegna di Studi Etiopici* 35: 135-70.

National Atlas 1988. *National Atlas of Ethiopia*. Addis Ababa: National Mapping Agency.

A. Natsoulas 1994. The game of *mancala* with reference to commonalities among the peoples of Ethiopia and in comparison to other African peoples: rules and strategies. pp. 653-63 in Bahru Zewde *et al.* (eds.) *Proceedings of the Eleventh International Conference of Ethiopian Studies, vol. II*. Addis Ababa: Institute of Ethiopian Studies.

J. Needham 1986. *The Shorter Science and*

Civilisation in China, vol. III (ed. C. A. Ronan). Cambridge: Cambridge University Press.

C. Negussie 1993. *Aksum and Matara: a stratigraphic comparison of two Aksumite towns.* Uppsala: Uppsala University.

K. O'Mahoney 1970. The salt trail. *Journal of Ethiopian Studies* 8, 2: 147-54.

A. Ortelius 1573. *Additamentum ad Theatrum Orbis Terrarum.* Antwerp: the cartographer.

T. E. Page (ed. and trans.) 1930. *The Geography of Strabo.* London: Loeb.

R. K. Pankhurst 1961. *An Introduction to the Economic History of Ethiopia from Early Times to 1800.* London: Lalibela House.

R. K. Pankhurst 1968. *Economic History of Ethiopia 1800–1935.* Addis Ababa: Haile Sellassie I University Press.

R. K. Pankhurst 1974. The history of Ethiopia's relations with India prior to the nineteenth century. pp. 205- 22 in *IV Congresso Internazionale di Studi Etiopici.* Rome: Accademia Nazionale dei Lincei.

R. K. Pankhurst 1979. Ethiopian medieval and post- medieval capitals: their development and physical features. *Azania* 14: 1-19.

R. K. Pankhurst 1982a. *History of Ethiopian Towns from the Middle Ages to the Early Nineteenth Century.* Wiesbaden: Steiner.

R. K. Pankhurst 1982b. *Gabata* and other board games in Ethiopia and the Horn of Africa. *Azania* 17: 27-42.

S. Pankhurst 1955. *Ethiopia: a cultural history.* London: Lalibela House.

C. Pansera 1945. Quattro stele musulmane presso Uogher Hariba nell' Enderta. *Studi Etiopici raccolti da C. Conti Rossini*: 3-6 (cited in M. Schneider 1967).

R. Paribeni 1907. Richerche nel luogo dell'antica Adulis. *Monumenti Antichi, Reale Accademia dei Lincei* 18: 437-572.

B. Parker 1995. *Ethiopia: breaking new ground.* Oxford: Oxfam.

M. Parkyns 1853. *Life in Abyssinia.* London: Murray.

D. P. S. Peacock and D. F. Williams 1986. *Amphorae and the Roman Economy: an introductory guide.* London: Longman.

N. Pearce 1831. *The Life and Adventures of Nathaniel Pearce, written by himself during a residence in Abyssinia from the year 1810 to 1819.* London: Colburn and Bentley.

K. S. Pedersen 1986. The historiography of the Ethiopian monastery in Jerusalem. Goldenberg 1986: 419-26.

K. S. Pedersen 1993. Ethiopian iconography in Jerusalem. Henze 1993: 141-4.

C. F. Perczel 1986. Ethiopian crosses: Christianized symbols of a pagan cosmology. Goldenberg 1986: 427- 46.

H. St J. Philby 1981. *The Queen of Sheba.* London: Quartet.

J. S. Phillips 1995. Egyptian and Nubian material from Ethiopia and Eritrea. *Sudan Archaeological Research Society Newsletter* 9: 2-10.

J. S. Phillips in press. Punt and Aksum: Egypt and the Horn of Africa. *Journal of African History.*

W. Phillips 1955. *Qataban and Sheba.* London: Gollancz.

D. W. Phillipson 1977. The excavation of Gobedra rockshelter, Axum. *Azania* 12: 53-82.

D. W. Phillipson 1984. Aspects of early food production in northern Kenya. pp. 489-95 in L. Krzyzaniak and M. Kobusiewicz (eds) *Origin and Early Development of Food-Producing Cultures in North-East Africa.* Poznan: Polish Academy of Sciences.

D. W. Phillipson 1990. Aksum in Africa. *Journal of Ethiopian Studies* 23: 55-65.

D. W. Phillipson 1993a. *African Archaeology (second edition).* Cambridge: Cambridge University Press.

D. W. Phillipson 1993b. The antiquity of cultivation and herding in Ethiopia. Shaw *et al.* 1993: 344-57.

D. W. Phillipson 1994. The significance and symbolism of Aksumite stelae. *Cambridge Archaeological Journal* 4: 189-210.

D. W. Phillipson 1995. Excavations at Aksum, Ethiopia, 1993-4. *Antiquaries Journal* 75: 1-41.

D. W. Phillipson 1997. *The Monuments of Aksum.* Addis Ababa: Addis Ababa University Press.

D. W. Phillipson and J. S. Phillips in press. Excavations at Aksum, 1993-96: a preliminary report. *Journal of Ethiopian Studies.*

D. W. Phillipson, A. Reynolds *et al.* 1996. The B.I.E.A. excavations at Aksum, northern Ethiopia, 1993-95. *Azania* 31: 99-147.

L. Phillipson 1997. A functional consideration of Gudit scrapers from Aksum, Ethiopia. Paper presented at a conference on the Stone Age of north-eastern Africa, Poznan, Poland, August 1997.

R. Plant 1985. *The Architecture of the Tigre, Ethiopia.* Worcester: Raven Press.

B. Playne 1954. *Saint George for Ethiopia.* London: Constable.

O. de B. Priaulx 1862-3. On the Indian embassies to Rome from the reign of Claudius to the death of Justinian. *Journal of the Royal Asiatic Society* 19: 274-98, 20: 269-312.

J. B. Pritchard (ed.) 1974. *Solomon and Sheba.* London: Phaidon.

S. Puglisi 1941. Primi risultati delle indagini compiute dalla missione archeologica di Aksum. *Africa Italiana* 8: 95-153.

S. Puglisi 1946. Industria litica di Aksum nel Tigrai occidentale. *Rivista di Studi Preistoriche* 1: 284- 90.

G. Pwiti and R. Soper (eds) 1996. *Aspects of African Archaeology.* Harare: University of Zimbabwe Publications.

W. Raunig 1988. Yemen and Ethiopia – ancient cultural links between two neighbouring countries on the Red Sea. Daum 1988a: 409-18.

J. M. Reid 1968. *Traveller Extraordinary: the life of James Bruce of Kinnaird.* London: Eyre and Spottiswoode.

C. F. Rey 1929. *The Romance of the Portuguese in Abyssinia.* London: Witherby.

L. Ricci 1959. Ritrovamenti archeologici in Eritrea. *Rassegna di Studi Etiopici* 14: 48-68.

L. Ricci 1960. La statuetta di bovino in bronzo da Keban Kutur. *Rassegna di Studi Etiopici* 15: 112-13.

L. Ricci 1984. L'expansion de l'Arabie méridionale. pp. 249-57 in S. Chélod (ed.) *L'Arabie du sud: histoire et civilisation.* Paris.

L. Ricci and R. Fattovich 1987. Scavi archeologici nella zona di Aksum: A – Seglamien. *Rassegna di Studi Etiopici* 30: 117-69.

G. P. Rightmire 1989. Middle Stone Age humans from eastern and southern Africa. Mellars and Stringer 1989: 109-22.

M. Ripinski 1985. The camel in dynastic Egypt. *Journal of Egyptian Archaeology* 71: 134-41.

H. Roche and J. J. Tiercelin 1980. Industries lithiques de la formation plio-pléistocene d'Hadar, Ethiopie. pp. 194-9 in R. E. Leakey and B. A. Ogot (eds) *Proceedings of the Eighth Panafrican Congress of Prehistory.* Nairobi: Louis Leakey Memorial Institute.

L. Rodley 1994. *Byzantine Art and Architecture: an introduction.* Cambridge: Cambridge University Press.

C. de la Roncière 1925. *La découverte de l'Afrique au moyen age, vol. II.* Cairo: Société royale de géographie d'Egypte.

D. H. Ross (ed.) 1992. *Elephant: the animal and its ivory in African culture.* Los Angeles Fowler Museum of Cultural History.

H. de Roux 1976. Aperçu sur la fabrication de la poterie à Yeha, Tigre. *Annales d'Ethiopie* 10: 305-20.

P. Rowley-Conwy 1988. The camel in the Nile Valley: new radiocarbon accelerator (AMS) dates for Qasr Ibrim. *Journal of Egyptian Archaeology* 74: 245-8.

S. Rubenson 1966. *King of Kings, Tewodros of Ethiopia.* Addis Ababa: Oxford University Press.

E. Rüppell 1838-40. *Reise in Abessinien.* Frankfurt: Schmerber.

F. Russo and G. Russo 1989. Sugli intarsi in oro nella monetazione aksumite. *Bolletino di Numismatica* 13: 144-60.

H. Salt 1809. *Twenty-four views in Saint Helena, the Cape, India, Ceylon, the Red Sea, Abyssinia and Egypt.* London: Miller.

H. Salt 1814. *A Voyage to Abyssinia and Travels into the Interior of that Country executed under the Orders of the British Government in the years 1809 and 1810.* London: Rivington.

J. Schmidt 1988a. The Sabaean irrigation economy of Marib. Daum 1988a: 55-62.

J. Schmidt 1988b. Ancient South Arabian sacred buildings. Daum 1988a: 78-98.

P. R. Schmidt 1978. *Historical Archaeology.* Westport, Connecticut: Greenwood Press.

M. Schneider 1967. Stèles funéraires arabes de Quiha. *Annales d'Ethiopie* 7: 107-18.

R. Schneider 1973. Deux inscriptions sudarabiques du Tigre. *Bibliotheca Orientalis* 30: 385-9.

R. Schneider 1974. Trois nouvelles inscriptions royales d'Axoum. pp. 767-86 in *Atti IV Congresso Internationale di Studi Etiopici.* Rome: Accademia Nazionale dei Lincei.

R. Schneider 1976. Les débuts de l'histoire éthiopienne. *Documents pour servir à l'histoire des civilisations éthiopiennes* 7: 47-54.

R. Schneider 1984. Review article on

Kobishchanov 1979. *Journal of Ethiopian Studies* 17: 148-74.

W. H. Schoff (ed.) 1912. *The Periplus of the Eryhraean Sea*. New York: Longman.

H. H. Scullard 1974. *The Elephant in the Greek and Roman World*. London: Thames and Hudson.

J. Seigne 1991. Le château royal de Shabwa: architecture, techniques de construction et restitutions. *Syria* 68: 111-64.

Sergew Hable Selassie 1969. Church and state in the Aksumite period. pp. 5-8 in *Proceedings of the Third International Conference of Ethiopian Studies, vol. I*. Addis Ababa: Institute of Ethiopian Studies.

Sergew Hable Sellassie 1972. *Ancient and Medieval Ethiopian History to 1270*. Addis Ababa: United Printers.

I. Shahid 1976. The *Kebra Negast* in the light of recent research. *Le Muséon* 89: 133-78.

T. Shaw *et al.* (eds) *The Archaeology of Africa: food, metals and towns*. London: Routledge.

P. L. Shinnie 1978. The Nilotic Sudan and Ethiopia *c.* 660 BC to *c.* AD 600. Fage 1978: 210-71.

F. Simoons 1960. *Northwest Ethiopia: peoples and economy*. Madison: University of Wisconsin Press.

M. C. Smith and H. T. Wright 1988. The ceramics from Ras Hafun in Somalia: notes on a classical maritime site. *Azania* 23: 115-41.

S. Smith 1954. Events in Arabia in the sixth century AD. *Bulletin of the School of Oriental and African Studies* (University of London) 16: 425-68.

P. Snow 1988. *The Star Raft: China's encounter with Africa*. London: Weidenfeld and Nicolson.

M. Spencer 1979. Structural analysis and the Queen of Sheba. pp. 343-58 in R. L. Hess (ed.) *Proceedings of the Fifth International Conference on Ethiopian Studies (Session B, Chicago, 1978)*. Chicago: University of Illinois.

M. S. Spinka (ed.) 1940. *The Chronicle of John Malalas, books viii – xviii*. Chicago: University of Chicago Press.

H. M. Stanley 1874. *Coomassie and Magdala: the story of two British campaigns in Africa*. London: Sampson Low.

E. M. Stern 1987. Early Roman glass from Heis on the north Somali coast. pp. 23-26 in *Annales du X Congrès International pour l'Histoire du Verre*. Amsterdam.

H. Sternberg-el Hotabi 1994. Die verschollene Horusstele aus Aksum. pp. 189-91 in H. Behlmer (ed.) *Quaerentes Scientiam: Festgabe fur Wolfhart Westendorf zu seinen 70*. Göttingen.

E. L. Stevenson 1932. *The Geography of Claudius Ptolemy*. New York: New York Public Library.

R. Sundström 1907. Report on Adulis in E. Littmann, Preliminary report of the Princeton expedition to Abyssinia. *Zeitschrift für Assyriologie* 20: 171-82.

J. E. G. Sutton 1989. Aksum, the Erythraean Sea, and the world of late antiquity: a foreword. Munro-Hay 1989a: 1-6.

J. M. Szymusiak 1958. *Athanasius: Apologia ad Constantium Imperatorem (Sources Chrétiennes 56)*. Paris: Editions du Cerf.

Taddesse Tamrat 1972. *Church and State in Ethiopia, 1270–1527*. Oxford: Clarendon Press.

Taddesse Tamrat 1985. A short note on Ethiopian church music. *Annales d'Ethiopie* 13: 137-43.

P. V. Tobias 1991. The emergence of spoken language in hominid evolution. pp. 67-78 in J. D. Clark (ed.) *Cultural Beginnings: approaches to understanding early hominid life-ways in the African savanna*. Bonn: Habelt.

J. A. Todd and J. A. Charles 1978. Metallurgy as a contribution to archaeology in Ethiopia. *Abbay* 9: 31-42.

M. Tosi 1986. The emerging picture of prehistoric Arabia. *Annual Review of Anthropology* 15: 461-90.

J. S. Trimingham 1952. *Islam in Ethiopia*. London: Oxford University Press.

G. Tringali 1965. Cenni sulle 'Ona' di Asmara e dintorni. *Annales d'Ethiopie* 6: 143-52.

G. Tringali and S. C. Munro-Hay 1991. The Ona culture of Asmara and Hamasien. *Rassegna di Studi Etiopici* 35: 135-70.

S. Uhlig 1990. *Introduction to Ethiopian Paleography*. Stuttgart.

S. Uhlig 1993. Ethiopian manuscripts and paleography. Grierson 1993: 57-62.

E. Ullendorff 1951. The obelisk of Matara. *Journal of the Royal Asiatic Society* (1951): 26-32.

E. Ullendorff 1953a. James Bruce of Kinnaird. *Scottish Historical Review* 32: 128-43.

E. Ullendorff 1953b. The Ethiopic manuscripts in the Royal Library, Windsor Castle. *Rassegna di Studi Etiopici* 12: 71-9.

E. Ullendorff 1955. *The Semitic Languages of Ethiopia*. London: Taylor's Foreign Press.

E. Ullendorff 1956. Hebraic-Jewish elements in Abyssinian monophysite Christianity. *Journal of Semitic Studies* 1: 216-56.

E. Ullendorff 1960. *The Ethiopians*. London: Oxford University Press.

E. Ullendorff 1968. *Ethiopia and the Bible*. London: British Academy.

Valentia, Viscount (George Annesley) 1809. *Voyages and Travels to India, Ceylon, the Red Sea, Abyssinia and Egypt in the years 1802, 1803, 1804, 1805 and 1806*. London: Miller.

G. Van Beek 1969. *Hajar bin Humeid: investigations at a pre-Islamic site in South Arabia*. Baltimore: Johns Hopkins Press.

X. Van der Stappen (ed.) 1996. *Aethiopia*. Tervuren: Musée royal de l'Afrique centrale.

D. Van Endt 1977. Amino acid analysis of the content of a vial excavated at Aksum. *Journal of Archaeological Science* 4: 367-76.

D. Van Endt 1978. Was civet used as a perfume in Aksum? *Azania* 13: 186-8.

N. I. Vavilov 1931. The wheats of Abyssinia and their place in the general system of wheats. *Bulletin of Applied Biology, Genetics and Plant Breeding* Supplement 51.

A. J. de Voogt 1997. *Mancala in Africa and Asia*. London: British Museum Press.

G. Wainwright 1942. Cosmas and the gold trade of Fazoqli. *Man* 42: 52-8.

D. Welsby 1996. *The Kingdom of Kush: the Napatan and Meroitic empires*. London: British Museum Press.

B. West and B-X. Zhou 1988. Did chickens go north? New evidence for domestication. *Journal of Archaeological Science* 15: 515-33.

D. Whitcomb 1994. *Ayla: art and industry in the Islamic port of Aqaba*. Chicago: Oriental Institute.

A. R. Willcox 1984. *The Rock Art of Africa*. London: Croom Helm.

R. Wilding 1989. The pottery. Munro-Hay, 1989a: 325- 316.

R. T. Wilson 1977. The vegetation of central Tigre, Ethiopia, in relation to land use. *Webbia* 32: 235-70.

E. O. Winstedt 1909. *The Christian Topography of Cosmas Indicopleustes*. Cambridge: Cambridge University Press.

W. Wolska-Conus (ed.) 1968-73. *Cosmas Indicopleustes: Topographie Chrétienne (Sources Chrétiennes 141, 159 and 197)*. Paris: Editions du Cerf.

W. Wright 1877. *Catalogue of Ethiopic MSS in the British Museum acquired since the year 1847*. London: British Museum, Department of Oriental Printed Books and Manuscripts.

U. Zanetti 1996a. L'Ethiopie chrétienne. Van der Stappen 1996: 160-80.

U. Zanetti 1996b. Les langues de l'Ethiopie et de la Corne de l'Afrique. Van der Stappen 1996: 214-19.

B. Zurawski 1993. Nubia and Ethiopia in the Christian period – some affinities. Henze 1993: 33-41.

INDEX